The Crisis Manual

The Crisis Manual

A Guide for Teachers and Carers of Young Children

Karen Miller

Floris Books

First published in 1996 in the United States
by Gryphon House, Inc, Beltsville MD 20705.
This British version published in 1999 by Floris Books.

British Library CIP Data available

ISBN 0-86315-299-6

Printed in Great Britain
by Redwood Books, Trowbridge, Wilts.

Contents

Introduction

More and more teachers are reporting the increasing incidence of crises in children's lives. These crises interfere with children's ability to learn. However much we might like to shield children from unpleasant events and emotions, we cannot do so.

One frustrated early years teacher expressed the feelings of many: `I resent having to spend so much time nurturing these children and dealing with difficult behaviour. I got into this field to educate children, and I'm finding I can't do that because children are having so many problems in their lives.' Even though we can empathize with this teacher's feelings, we know that a developmentally appropriate curriculum should respond to the issues that interest and concern children at the present time. If a child is experiencing a crisis in their life, lessons that only 1relate to the teacher's agenda will not relate to the child's life. Indeed, children who are experiencing extreme stress and trauma are at risk of developing emotional and developmental learning difficulties, whether from community violence, the death of a loved one, a serious illness in the family, homelessness, living with substance abusers or any of the other crises discussed in this book.

A young child has not yet learned to keep certain topics at home and others at school. For them, life and school are more integrated than for older children. We know that we must deal with the whole child — both the intellectual and the emotional parts. The challenge is how. Few people working in the early childhood sector have specific training in addressing psychological traumas of young children.

Teachers are hesitant to get involved or talk about certain situations, fearing that they may do more harm than good.

However, early childhood teachers and carers can do a lot to help a child and the child's family to deal with a crisis. During difficult times, the child's teacher is often the one stable element in the child's life. The childcare centre, nursery, playgroup or child minder can be a haven for the child where they can express themselves, and where there are caring individuals who listen and help them sort out what is going on in their life. These adults have an important role to play in responding to the child in a helpful and supportive way, thus increasing the child's coping mechanisms. Early years staff can also help parents to see things from the child's perspective, or to recognize when further help might be needed and direct parents to other professionals.

In this book, I have included resources that might be helpful in dealing with various crisis situations. It is unlikely that you will sit down and read this book from cover to cover, but you may turn to various chapters as the need arises.

This is a source book, which I hope will give you many points to think about as you approach a problem — a little background information, things to try, helpful resources, numbers to call, and people to talk to.

Each chapter has a few insights about child development. These are general statements about how a young child might perceive a situation. Principles cited are summaries of information I found reflected in various resources.

As I compiled the *How to Respond* section of each chapter, I found that I was repeating myself. Almost all crisis situations call for curriculum practices that allow children to express themselves, and most importantly, to be heard by caring, sensitive adults. I therefore created Chapter 23, *Curriculum Ideas and Activities,* which goes into greater detail by listing more specific activities that can be used in numerous situations.

Each crisis chapter offers a list of children's books that relate to the topic. Books are a wonderful resource and may allow you to bring up a topic in a neutral, non-threatening way. Some books are appropriate to read to the whole group; others are better read one-on-one with a child. You will have to make that decision yourself, depending on what you know and feel about the situation. Examine several of the books listed before selecting the one you feel is most appropriate for the particular child and situation. You might be able to simplify vocabulary from time to time, but check to see that the child understands what the book is trying to convey. Do not assume that the situation has been handled adequately just because the child does not ask any questions when you have finished reading the book. Books should be used to open doors of communication and let children know that they are not alone in what they are experiencing.

Crises rarely happen in isolation. In addition, every child and every crisis is different. Ultimately, it is up to you to piece together the resources and the strategies that will work best for your situation.

Bear in mind that the best crisis management technique, no matter what the crisis, is to have a plan in place beforehand. Think about the eventuality. Do what you can to prevent it, but if a crisis occurs, act professionally and use the resources available to you in your community. Turn a crisis into an opportunity to sharpen your skills, and extend your professional network. I am very conscious of the fact that many early childhood professionals already feel overwhelmed. Progress only happens in the context of society and within the support systems that exist for you as a professional, as well as for the families you serve. Chapter 1, *The Carer's Role,* discusses ways to function effectively with others.

Everybody wishes there were some magic words to say to help a child through a crisis. Of course, there are no perfect phrases. All we can do is our best. When a crisis is occurring in a child's life, an early childhood programme can either add to the problem or help to alleviate it. The goal of this book is to increase the odds that a child will learn and grow, even in a crisis situation, because of the sensitive responses of caring adults. It is with abiding respect for the important work that you do that I offer you this book and hope that it is helpful to you.

Karen Miller

Part I: Crisis and the Carer

CHAPTER ONE

The Carer's Role

How can we be helpful? When do we step in? How much can we help? In our field, we talk about the fact that on any given day, an early childhood worker or manager must be a teacher, a caretaker, a plumber, a cook, a nurse, a psychologist, and an all-around fixer. More and more, we are finding that the job of social worker must be added to that list of assignments.

When does a situation become a crisis?

Early childhood staff are accustomed to interacting with children; planning their activities, observing their play and helping them sort out social problems with others. However, we are often hesitant to intervene when it comes to situations involving the children and their families. We ask, 'Is this my business? Should I be involved?' Sometimes it is difficult to decide if a situation has become a crisis and needs professional intervention. You might learn about a particular problem when the child is first enrolled or later, when the child or the child's parent says something to you about it. As a rule of thumb, when you feel the child's physical or emotional development is at risk, you have a responsibility to take further action.

Generally speaking, if it concerns the child, it is your business. Children cannot learn and benefit from the programme when distracted by traumatic events in their lives. When you help a child with a problem, you become closer to the child. You can also help a child be mentally and emotionally stable, while supporting and strengthening the family. You are the child's advocate.

Staff do not want to make the situation worse by saying or doing the wrong thing. It is natural to worry about this, but here are a couple of things to bear in mind:

Realize that you do not have to be perfect. If you sense that you did the wrong thing, try again. Children respect honesty. You can say, 'You know, I'd like to go back to what we said about.... I've had a few more thoughts about it.'

Remember that you are not alone. When faced with a difficult or sensitive issue, always work as part of a team with other concerned individuals in your organization and community.

Be part of a team

Synergism is an exciting concept. Basically, it is the idea that the whole is more than the sum of the parts. When people work together on a problem, exciting things can happen. With collaboration, you might accomplish things that no one could have accomplished working independently.

Work with your manager and supervisor

It is important to work with your manager and supervisor. There should be written procedures for you to follow, which outline your roles and responsibilities within the team, and which detail how concerns should be recorded and reported (to both managers and families). Your manager and supervisor needs to be kept informed as there may be legal implications, therefore keep them appraised of the situation as it progresses. Check how they would like you to keep them informed — with verbal reports, written reports, or using standardized forms.

You should go through the proper channels. Work first with your immediate supervisor. You will accomplish much more in the long run if you avoid stepping on toes.

Respected colleagues can provide a second opinion. You might say, 'I think I'm seeing this. What do you think?'

Your supervisor will support the team when planning to deal with the problem. They may have more information that sheds new light on the situation. This will give you the opportunity to suggest approaches or helpful resources, such as special books or encouraging the child to talk about the problem. It is important that everyone in the team is aware of special aims and plans for individual children, and that regular team reviews take place so that targets can be established, and up-to-date information shared. Where possible, parents need to be included and made aware of special plans for their child.

If you are a child minder, you probably work independently. Seek information and support from your childcare association or other groups you belong to in your community. Often local Social Services can provide advice or information.

Work with other professionals

Learn where your educational expertise ends and the specialized expertise of other professionals begins. As one early childhood teacher aptly stated, 'I know what the norm looks like and when something seems unusual, but I don't know how to pinpoint a problem.' Often parents will ask you for advice and referrals. In the *Who Can Help* section, there is a list of the types of professionals to seek out for further assistance. Also contact the organizations and hot lines listed at the end of each chapter. Many national organizations are aware of local resources.

Learn who's out there

The first step in making a referral is to know what each type of professional does and who is available in your community. Is this a problem for a paediatrician, a psychologist or a social worker?

Many families bring all their problems to their child's paediatrician or family practitioner. If the doctor knows the child and the family well, this may be a good place to start. However, sometimes paediatricians only look at the medical side of a situation and fail to take the social and emotional aspects of the problem into consideration.

The following professionals in your community may be helpful:

— HEALTH PROFESSIONALS: paediatricians, family doctors, health visitors, therapy services (speech, hearing, physio- and occupational therapists), and dentists.
— PUBLIC SAFETY PROFESSIONALS: police officers, fire officers.
— Mental health professionals: child psychologists, family therapists, counselling services.
— REGULATORY AGENCIES: Social Services, environmental health inspectors.
— EDUCATIONAL AND SPECIAL NEEDS SERVICES: including advisory services and school psychologists.

Compile a list of these professionals to have ready when needed.

Find out the following from community professionals:

— The scope of their services-who they serve and what problems they deal with.
— Proper procedures for contacting them. Must clients be referred by some other agency? In many cases the parent must make contact directly.
— How you can be helpful when working with them. What information do they need to know about the case? How can you be part of the follow-up or support team and carry out recommended activities or interventions?
— What kinds of strategies, resources and consultation services can they provide for parents and teachers?

Get to know them

While creating a list of professionals in your area is a good start, it is advisable to get to know some of these individuals. Talk to other parents or early childhood professionals who have worked with these individuals to gather opinions.

Try to develop a pleasant and mutually respectful relationship with these individuals. That will make future working relationships much easier. Speak to them as one professional to another, exploring ways to work together to assure the welfare of children and families in the community. Here are a few ways to get acquainted:

— Ask your manager to invite them to the centre or school to meet the children and staff.
— Invite them to talk about their work at a staff meeting, in-service training or parents evening.
— Invite them to attend professional meetings of local early childhood professional associations, possibly presenting a workshop.

Many centres or schools prefer to keep a list of professionals as a service for parents and do not necessarily recommend a particular individual. You might say, 'Many of our parents use this dentist,' or 'We have worked with this person before and found her to be very helpful,' but make it clear that the parents must choose the person they will feel most comfortable with.

Use good problem solving techniques

Whether you and other staff members choose to work on a problem within your own organization or to involve professionals outside your organization, it helps to be systematic in your actions as you proceed. Here are some general problem solving strategies that work in most situations.

Define the problem

What is really concerning you? Try to get it down on paper in a succinct description. As you become more informed and insightful, you can go back and rewrite the description.

Gather the team

The manager should gather together all those who work with the child, as well as the parents and possibly other family members, and other professionals already dealing with the child.

Gather information

From the child's record and from other team members who are acquainted with the family, gather as much factual information about the situation as possible.

Learn

Find out all you can about the topic or problem in general. Read and talk to other professionals. What does the research say? How do other children and families respond? What types of action have been successful for others?

Share insights and ideas

Make sure you are all seeing the same thing. Does someone have a different viewpoint? List possible things to try. As you plan for possible activities and interventions see Chapter 23 on curriculum and other chapters on specific crises. You will need to ask yourselves, 'How can we help both this child and the other children in the group?'

Develop a plan of action

From the list of options you developed while brainstorming, decide what you will try first, and who will do what and when.

Keep others informed

Decide how you will communicate any progress to the people involved.

Meet, evaluate and record

If all goes well and the plan achieved the desired results, congratulate each other. If it didn't work as well as you had hoped, go back to the drawing board and decide together what to try next. Document all of your meetings. Note the date and the people involved, decisions made, interventions tried and results obtained.

This can be useful if future intervention is necessary, or if you ever need to explain what you did.

Professional ethics

When you are involved in children's lives you are often forced to make judgements about how to act. Sometimes the answers are not clear. You have responsibilities to your employer, the child's family, other children's families, your funding sources, the child and to yourself. Sometimes there are conflicting interests.

It is a great help if you have colleagues whom you trust and respect and with whom you can discuss the issue. It also helps if you have developed guidelines for responsible behaviour ahead of time. The topic of ethics should be part of every early childhood worker's training, as well as part of their job specification.

Two major ethical considerations to bear in mind when you deal with children in crisis situations are:

— The well-being of the child should come first in all considerations. The law requires that you report abuse or suspicion of abuse in any form. If you feel that the agencies that handle abuse cases do not do so adequately, you and your colleagues have an ethical responsibility to take steps to bring this to your employer's attention so that the situation can be corrected.

— The privacy of the people involved should be guarded. Confidentiality is critical. Only those directly involved with the problem should know the details. When others — such as supply staff or placement students — are with the child, decide how much they need to know in order to interact appropriately. Do not pry into family affairs that do not pertain to the situation at hand. Only situations that affect the child directly or indirectly should be discussed. If other parents hear you gossiping, they are likely to conclude that you will also talk about them and might be hesitant to confide in you if they need help in the future.

There will be many times in your career when you will have to rely on your own personal and professional judgement to decide a course of action. For example, when you and a parent disagree about discipline, when you question the actions of a colleague, when a child reveals that something illegal is going on at home, or when a parent uses you to unload their own personal problems.

Work with the family

You cannot help the child during a crisis without working with the family. An important aspect of the teacher's role is to help strengthen the bond between the parent and the child. Childcare providers and teachers are only temporary influences in children's lives. The family is permanent. Making families more effective is the best way to help children. Each chapter has specific suggestions for working with the parents, but here are some general principles:

Develop a rapport with the parents

Parents need to feel your respect before they can hear your suggestions and advice, starting with the very first meeting you have with them. Take your time with the intake interview. Both the child's keyworker and the manager should be involved. Naturally, there will be forms to fill out and policies to go over, but take time to let parents tell you about themselves and their child. Every child is special. Ask them what is special about their child. Show an interest. Ask them what their hopes are for their child, and how they think their child will benefit by attending the centre or school. Use this opportunity to make them feel welcome in the facility. Discuss the ways you intend to communicate with them — daily notes, occasional phone calls, regularly scheduled parent meetings, and special meetings whenever you or the parents feel the need.

Inform them that you consider this to be a partnership. Many early childhood staff are surprised to learn that parents are often intimidated by them. Parents consider teachers to be experts on young children, and are in awe of their ability to get a whole group of children to co-operate when they can barely handle one child. Some parents may know that they have real problems parenting this little human being and suspect that you see right through them. Tell them that while you know about child development in general, and have training in handling groups of children, you feel they are the expert on this particular child. Together you can make positive things happen for this child.

In addition to the intake interview, it is worth the time and effort it takes to get to know parents in relaxed social settings, such as picnics and joint fund raising events. When adults have spent time together in friendly social surroundings it is easier to address problems when they arise.

Settling in

It is natural for parents and their children to have difficulty parting from each other, especially before they know and trust you. The adult can rationalize the separation and, knows that it is temporary, but the child is entering a strange and exciting (but also frightening) new arena. If there has been a trauma in the family separation can be particularly difficult, and the family will need sensitive support from you.

Encourage the parent to visit with the child and stay most of the morning. Some children eagerly join in, but other children need longer to adjust. Most staff are now eager to work with parents as long as necessary, encouraging the parents to stay with the child for part of the day and gradually lengthening the times of separation until the child feels totally comfortable. While concentrating on the distress of the child, do not forget to also offer empathy to the parent who may be better at masking emotions.

Helping the child to settle in

All of the following techniques have helped children through this adjustment process:

— A transitional object such as a favourite stuffed animal or a security blanket can help the child feel more secure in the new setting.

— An object that belongs to the parent such as a scarf or an old wallet can provide comfort by reassuring the child that the parent is really coming back.

— Take a photo of the parent, or have the parent bring one in. Place it on the wall at the child's eye level, where the child can go over to it, touch it, talk to it. Or laminate it and let the child carry it around all day. You could also punch a hole in it and pin it to the child's clothing.
— Allow the child to telephone the parent at work or elsewhere. At that time the parent can say, 'I still love you, and I will be back for you.'
— Let the child pretend to call the parent on a toy telephone. You play the part of the parent and answer from another toy telephone. This game of pretend will reassure the child that you, the teacher, know that she misses her parent and respect that feeling.
— Let the child dictate a note to the parent, telling the parent how he misses them and wants to be with them. Do not edit what the child wants to say. Give the note to the parent while the child is present. Again, this shows respect for the child's feelings.
— Take a photo of the child having fun. Give the picture to the parents. This will help the parents realize that the child was not miserable all day. The parents can use the picture to talk to the child about the fun they are having at the centre.
— Send home a picture of the child at play with some friends. By putting it on the refrigerator or in the child's room, parents can use it to talk to the child about the centre or nursery.

Home visits

Home visits prior to entry can help tremendously. Your purpose is to develop a rapport with the child on their home turf, where they feel safe, and to explain what happens in the centre or nursery. While there you can meet the other family members and pets. Parents often feel more comfortable talking about their child over a cup of tea in their own kitchen. You also have the opportunity to begin to build the partnership that will aid your work with the child and family.

Interpret for the child

Often this means helping parents learn to see things from the child's perspective. You can offer insights and observations about how the child is reacting to a situation, sharing your knowledge of child development. Sometimes children will reveal feelings to you that they are unable to express at home. If you have a good relationship with the parents and they believe that you have the child's interests at heart, you can easily share your insights with them. If a problem or crisis arises, you can call the parents, talk to them when they collect the child or set up a parent conference. Your manager or supervisor will need to approve the appropriate course of action.

Help parents address the root of the problem

Supporting parents might also mean putting them in touch with help and intervention. This is especially true in situations involving child abuse and substance abuse. In these cases, your manager most often initiates intervention, in conjunction with other community resources. You can help by bringing the situation to the attention of the supervisor and/or manager.

Remember that you cannot do much about a problem until the parent admits there is one. When the problem or crisis is beyond their control, such as the death of a family member or a natural disaster, parents often welcome help and support. When parents are responsible for the problem, as in instances of abuse or neglect, finding the most effective way to intervene is more difficult.

Try not to be judgmental

Sometimes this requires overcoming your own feelings of resentment or even outrage at the actions of the parent. Seek support and personal advice when dealing with these emotions. Many workplaces are developing staff support groups to help employees cope.

When working with families, always focus on the mutual circle of concern for the child. Assume that parents do love their children, and talk to parents from the point of view of the child.

Provide resources

Recognize the credibility of the written word. People often believe something if they see it in print, even though you are telling them the same thing. It is a good idea for childcare staff to have a resource library with a variety of books or pamphlets to lend to parents. Have a list of books to recommend. Remember that parents are less likely to use resources if they have to go to a library or book shop. The resource section of each chapter lists books that will be helpful to both parents and staff.

Be a good listener

Finally, do not feel that you always have to have advice or suggestions to offer the parent. Sometimes just listening to the parent talk is the most appropriate action.

Enjoy the rewards

While many early childhood staff list working with parents as one of the more difficult and frustrating aspects of their jobs, they also see it as one of the most rewarding. When you help families to function effectively, you have a positive influence on a whole circle of people, which lasts long after the child has left your care.

Focus on the children

Your main function is to support the child by answering questions and giving information in appropriate ways to increase the child's understanding and emotional well-being. The curriculum chapter (Chapter 23) contains many strategies and activities to allow children to express themselves and be heard. Here are a few principles to keep in mind.

Learn to observe

The better you know the children, the more you can help them. Take time during your busy day to observe what is happening with the children. Be systematic in the way you observe. One way is to observe a different child each day. While you are engaged in other activities, follow this child with your eyes, make notes about where the child chooses to play, with whom, for how long, the child's use of language, conflicts that arise, and any other events of the day. If you do this, each child in your group will have an in-depth observation about every two weeks. Over time, you will learn a lot about that child's personality, skills, interests and play preferences. This will give you a good basis for comparison if a crisis occurs.

Date all observations and keep them in a notebook with a divider for each child, or keep a file folder for each child in the group. Of course, you can add notes and anecdotes at any time when something interesting happens.

When a crisis occurs in a child's life, be conscious of the child's behaviour, not just their words. Also be aware of the content of play episodes, drawings, or stories, but be careful not to over-interpret. Is the child using red paint because they are angry or just because they like red? Are they loud and hyperactive as a response to tension, or are they just imitating the play of friends? When you overhear unusual play themes in the dramatic play area, make a note but try not to jump to conclusions.

Be accessible to the child

The most important thing you can do to help the child during a crisis is to encourage them to talk about their feelings or to act them out through play so that they can understand them better.

When you know the child has experienced some sort of crisis or trauma, learn as much as you can about what happened. Find out what the family has told the child, and what has already transpired between the child and adults who are close to them so you can be supportive.

Staff often wonder if they should bring up the topic if the child does not do so spontaneously. Generally it is best to follow the child's lead and respond to any questions the child has. Sometimes just letting the child know that you know about the situation is helpful. Offer to talk about it any time the child wants to. You might bring up the topic in a neutral, non-personal way. For example, read a book about a similar problem to a small group, or use a puppet to describe a similar situation.

Stop what you're doing if the child brings up a tender topic. If it is really not possible to interrupt what you are doing, make a date with the child. 'I can't stop and talk to you right now, but let me clean this up, and then I really want to hear what you have to say. We can go over and sit under the tree and talk.' Afterwards, thank the child for talking to you about what they had on their mind and tell the child that if they want to talk again to let you know.

Be conscious of non-verbal language. When a child says something, we sometimes involuntarily roll our eyes or send messages over their heads to other adults. Think about how this affects children — it can add to the pain and shame they feel. They learn quickly that some things should not be mentioned, and may even feel that their problem should be a family secret.

In conversation children remember good listening techniques:
— Give the child time to express themselves and do not interrupt.
— Paraphrase what the child said to make sure you understood them correctly.
— Let the child know that it is okay to have those feelings, that feelings should not be a cause of shame.
— Help the child feel that they are not alone, that other children have felt like that in similar circumstances.
— Avoid judgmental statements such as 'You shouldn't feel that way,' or 'I'm sure he didn't mean that.'
— Do not worry if you do not know the answer to a child's questions. It can be hard to know how to respond sometimes. Turning the question back to the child, 'What do you think?' is one way to see what the child needs. If you do not know the answer, say so. A good question to ask children to get them talking is, 'What do you think about?' Offer sympathy.
— Help put things in perspective. Be there. Be safe. Be accepting of the child's full range of emotions.

When to seek help

One important role of early childhood staff is to notice when something is not right with the child. When others in the child's life are distracted by traumatic events, they are less likely to notice subtle changes in the child's demeanour or behaviour. The early childhood worker who is often with the child most of his waking hours, can notice changes and help the parents and others respond appropriately.

Sometimes it is hard to differentiate between a behaviour that simply represents a normal phase of development or reaction of the child, and a behaviour that indicates a more serious problem that requires professional intervention.

The *When to Seek Help* sections in this book are sometimes repetitive because children have a limited repertoire of behaviour to indicate that something is wrong. Their behaviour may indicate there is some type of problem, but you will have to probe further to figure out the specific problem. Since young children often cannot verbally express what is bothering them, we have to be very astute in reading their behaviour.

Common stress indicators in children include:

REGRESSION. Children under stress often revert to more immature behaviour, as though they were going back to a time when life felt safer. This includes bed-wetting, loss of toilet habits, thumb sucking and baby talk. Bear in mind that regression in the face of stress is a normal reaction.

CHANGE IN BEHAVIOUR OR MOOD. A child might display unusual aggression, defiance, or conversely, become overly clingy and whining.

DEPRESSION. A depressed child might lose interest in what is going on around them and isolate themselves or be overly inhibited during activities or discussions.

LOW SELF-ESTEEM. If a normally confident child seems to suddenly lack confidence or show low self-esteem, you need to investigate. Children display low self-esteem by giving up or crying easily, becoming frustrated very quickly, having frequent tantrums or behaving aggressively.

Unreasonable and extreme fear. While almost all children develop some fears in the course of normal development, sometimes their fears are triggered by real events.

Problems with concentration. When a child is overly worried about what is going on at home, they can find it difficult to sit through circle time or a story, or to complete a chosen piece of work.

Physical symptoms. Stomach-aches, headaches, and inability to rest are all symptoms of stress.

Practically all of these symptoms could be present in any child, and may be perfectly normal. So it is very important not to jump to conclusions. The key is to know each child. The operative word may be change. Is there a change in the child's behaviour? Is the child displaying behaviour that is unusual for that child? You need to find all the pieces and fit them together. You should have access to the records for each child in your care so that you know about their background and family situation, and what the child might have experienced before entering your care. Talk to people who know the child. When signs persist over a period of time and disrupt family life or normal classroom activities with peers, further action may be necessary.

Keep a diary. Make specific notes about the child's behaviour that concern you. Note exactly what the child did, the date, the time of day it occurred, who else was involved, how you responded and how the child responded. Sometimes a pattern will emerge that will give you clues. At the very least, you will have more specifics to discuss with the parent and other professionals. If you keep regular written observations of all of the children in your care, you will see more quickly when a change in behaviour patterns occurs.

If you or the parent feel that the child is acting in extreme or unusual ways, seek help. The earlier you uncover problems, the sooner you can start to work effectively to resolve them with the child.

Concluding thoughts

Although many crises are the result of adult problems, children are deeply affected by them. Without sensitive adult intervention, clarification and talking, a child may suffer great psychological and cognitive damage as a result of the crisis. The early childhood worker has, therefore, a dual focus. You have to deal with the child in your care, with the situation of the moment, responding in a way that will give the child strength and comfort. But you also have to look at the cause of the problem to prevent an ongoing string of crisis situations for the child. Within the context of your organization, you must also try to help the parent work on the problem. You cannot do it all, of course. But you are likely to feel frustrated if you have no resources to offer the parent.

Remember that you are not trained as a therapist. Getting involved in people's problems, analysing their situation, offering advice can be seductive. It can make you feel competent and powerful, but it is not what you should be doing. Instead, educate yourself on the topic and realize that you are part of a team. In your community, there are resources that can be to help the families in crisis connect with the professional help that they need.

Early childhood education and care is really a series of judgement calls. Every situation is different. There are no perfect answers. The most important thing to get across to children is that people can survive hard times, and that you are there to help them.

Resources

Books

People under Three, Goldschmied, Elinor, and Jackson, Sonia, Routledge, 1993.

Special Issues in Childcare, O'Hagan, Maureen, and Smith, Maureen, Balliere-Tindall, 1999.

Managing to Change: Training materials for staff in day care centres for young children, Cowley, Liz (Ed.), National Children's Bureau, 1995 and 1997. A series of training modules on five topics: Child Protection; Equality of Opportunity; Management and Supervision; Partnership with Parents; Playing and Learning.

Videos

Baby it is You. A series of videos based on a Channel 4 series on child development. Available from Channel 4.
Child Studies I and Child Studies II, Video Productions, Child Development Series.
Infants at Work, Goldschmied, E., National Children's Bureau, 1986.
Heuristic Play with Objects, Golschmied, E., and Hughes, A., National Children's Bureau, 1992.

Useful Contacts

See Appendix for contact details

British Association for Early Childhood Education (BACE)
The Pre-School Learning Alliance
National Children's Bureau
Children in Scotland (Scottish partner of the National Children's Bureau)
The National Early Years Network
Kidscape

Chapter Two

Avoiding Burn-Out

Sometimes people choose to work with young children because they believe that childhood is a happy time of life and children are sweet, innocent, happy beings. These same people may be shocked when they realize this is not always so and may feel they must work all the harder to make everything right. When they discover they cannot do that, disillusionment sets in.

Adults who work with children and families suffering from trauma can experience vicarious trauma. If the symptoms are ignored, these adults can experience serious psychological consequences, and there can be a constant staff turnover, which has a serious impact on the quality of their services.

People working with children and families in crisis often feel that they are ineffective and wasting their time — that nothing they do makes a difference. They may feel unappreciated and unsupported. When people feel unprepared to deal with the situation, they also fear doing more harm than good and worry about being criticized. If many of the children in their care have severe problems, the staff can easily feel overwhelmed.

How managers can help

There are things that managers can do to support staff so that they can develop personal and professional skills and strategies to address these problems head on.

Pay attention to the needs of staff

When managers encounter the enormity of problems faced by children and families, they sometimes fail to focus on their agents for change — the people working directly with the children. If you are a staff member feeling the threat of burn-out, be your own advocate and talk to your supervisor. Tell your manager what you need. Make some practical suggestions.

Build staff cohesiveness

Staff should have regular, weekly staff support meetings to evaluate and discuss events of the past week. Discussion should go beyond the mechanics of housekeeping and curricular planning. Many managers with families in crisis have emphasized the importance of developing support groups among staff to discuss feelings and difficult situations that have developed.

When problems do arise among staff, inevitable in almost any early childhood setting, do not ignore them and hope they will go away. Address problems and conflicts in positive, respectful ways. *Nursery World* magazine (listed in the resource section at the end of the chapter) frequently has articles on supporting staff in their roles.

Clarify expectations

The cause of burn-out often stem from what motivates people to help and from the expectations people have for themselves. It is not uncommon for people in the early childhood profession to have a *save the world* complex. When expectations are too high, feelings of disappointment and disillusionment in the organizations and individuals around us can result.

Having a sense of mission helps. Does your school or centre have a mission statement to describe why the organization exists and what you hope to accomplish? Working together to develop a mission statement can be a powerful way to build staff cohesiveness and mutual respect. If you have a clear and realistic idea of what you expect to accomplish, you will be better able to measure your success.

Have a plan

Just as you would prepare for a possible fire or other disaster, work as a group to develop a plan for how you will handle any crisis that may come up for a family or child. Who will do what? What people in the community are available to you? What resources do you have? Being prepared can go a long way toward reducing the inherent stress in any situation.

Develop a crisis contact list of people and resources in the community for various crises addressed in this book. You could use this book as an outline to develop a *Just in Case* list.

How individuals can help

Remember, you are not alone

Firstly, you need the support of your manager and other staff members. Also, as mentioned in the chapter on the carer's role (see Chapter 1), when you work with children and families you should take advantage of the network of community professionals in related fields. Find out who else is working to support the needs of this family. Ask to be part of the team. Although this may take some extra time on your part, it may make you more effective and less frustrated.

If you are a child minder, be sure to take advantage of your local association to put you in contact with other providers and services available to you.

Pay attention to your emotions

Remember that people must start with themselves when they develop strategies to deal with a crisis. It is essential to deal with any unfinished business you may have on a personal level before you can be fully effective and professional in working with the children and families.

Working with children who are experiencing various crises or trauma in their lives sometimes reminds carers of painful experiences in their own childhood. Talking about them in a support group with other staff can be very helpful. As suggested in many of the chapters, inviting a professional to speak about the psychological dynamics of many of the issues can help you understand yourself. If the problem is very painful, perhaps now is the time to join or found a support group. Staff have to first come to terms with their own feelings about these issues before they can help children.

Sometimes the most difficult situations to deal with professionally are those we have dealt with successfully in our own lives. We may be impatient with people who stay mired in the situation rather than taking corrective action, as we have. These situations are also painful reminders of our own previous suffering.

While keeping confidentiality and professional ethics in mind, seek out a level-headed and trustworthy colleague to discuss your concerns. This might be your manager or supervisor. Talking things out can clarify the situation and give you greater understanding and insight into what is going on. You need to be able to test and measure your responses against someone else.

Knowledge is power

Educate yourself about the issues. The more you know, the more options you have. Remember that there are many ways to learn. The following are some of the possibilities:

— Take a course.
— Attend conferences and workshops.
— Bring consultants in to talk with staff.
— Read articles, pamphlets and books.
— Call local professionals and ask questions.
— Call helplines and local contacts for advice.
— Visit other settings.
— Observe others in action.

All you can do is your best!

Make all your decisions based on the best information you have at the time. Knowing you have given a situation your best effort allows you to rest easier.

Keeping a diary can be a very useful process, both in developing a systematic approach to a situation and giving yourself peace of mind. When you observe a child carefully, take notes on what activities you have tried and why. You will be able to look back and see how far the child has come.

If the situation does not improve, you will at least be able to see that you acted professionally. Your diary will help you to analyse what went wrong, and to determine if there is anything you would do differently if confronted with a similar situation in the future.

Do something

Be proactive. Combat the feeling of impotency by doing something that might contribute to correcting the situation, even if what you do is a small thing.

You cannot solve all the problems of poverty or racism in this country, but you can improve life for one child or one family. Together with other staff you might organize a clothing exchange or raise funds for outings for the families you serve.

Be an advocate

While you recognize that you cannot save the world, you can be part of a network of professionals and concerned adults that make up a larger voice. Join your local and national professional organizations such as the British Association of Childhood Education, The National Children's Bureau or Children in Scotland, and be supportive of their advocacy efforts both nationally and locally.

A sense of futility at not being able to alter society's course of direction can be a prime burn-out factor. It makes us angry, and we want to blame someone or some institution. Rather than criticizing others, it is better to focus on the search for solutions.

One powerful way to advocate for children is to tell real stories either about how children benefited from skilful intervention or about how the system failed a child. The public — taxpayers and legislators — tend to respond better when a human face is put on the problem.

Take care of yourself

There are many fine resources available on personal stress management. Proper diet, exercise and rest are all extremely important in maintaining physical and mental stamina. If you start to feel guilty about the time it takes to guard your own health, remember — if you are worn out you're not doing anyone any good.

If you suffer from some of the physical symptoms of stress such as stomach-aches, headaches, heart palpitations and shortness of breath, your body is trying to tell you something important. Pay attention to these symptoms and see if you can find ways to deal constructively with them.

The most important way to develop more power is to acquire more knowledge. It helps you assert yourself and act decisively.

Include positive sharing time for staff

Share the funny and heart-warming things that happen every day. Some managers start each weekly staff meeting with staff sharing a positive experience from the past week, as well as a not so positive experience. Some excellent strategies for circle time self-esteem building are outlined *in Turn your School around* by Jenny Moseley (see Resource section at end of chapter).

Strive for some balance

It can be difficult, but it is important not to let your work take over your whole life.

As a fun exercise, make a list of things you enjoy doing and that help you relax. The more the better. A good massage can do wonders! A long walk, a bubble bath, reading a novel, playing with the dog, playing a vigorous game of badminton, painting a picture, playing the piano — all are examples of things people came up with that they find both enjoyable and relaxing.

While you are at it, develop your own support network. Personal relationships outside of work can be very nurturing and healing, helping you keep everything in perspective.

Analyse what went right

When we work with stressed children and families in crisis, we ask ourselves many questions: 'Did I handle this well?' 'Was this activity really helpful?' 'Why did that parent say that?' 'What was going on with this child this morning?' 'Did I really make a positive difference for this family?'

We very rarely sit down and systematically analyse what went right. But you should identify strategies that seemed to work and give yourself the well-deserved pat on the back.

Conclusion

Do not accept burn-out as a fact of professional life. Instead, pay attention to the things that wear you down and address them individually and with your colleagues. Notice and value all the things that keep you going and keep you excited about your work.

Resources

Books

Moseley, Jenny, *Turn your School around,* LDA, Duke Street, Wisbech, Cambridgeshire.

Covey, Stephen R., Merrill, Roger A., and Merrill, Rebecca R., *To live, to love, to learn to leave a legacy,* Simon and Schuster, 1996.

Hillman, Carolynn, *Recovery of Your Self-Esteem: A Guide for Women. New Techniques and Understanding for Women who want to feel better about themselves more of the Time.* Simon and Schuster, 1992.

Kirsta, Alix, *The Book of Stress Survival: Identifying and Reducing the Stress in your Life.* Simon and Schuster, 1987.
Schaef, Anne Wilson, *Meditations for Women who do too much.* Harper San Francisco, 1990.

Magazines

Nursery World and Nursery World Scotland, Scholastic Publications.
Child Education Nursery, Scholastic Publications.
Early Years (Quarterly magazine). Trentham Books.

Useful contacts

See Appendix for contact details

British Association for Early Childhood Education (BACE)
The Pre-School Learning Alliance
National Children's Bureau
Children in Scotland (Scottish partner of the National Children's Bureau)
The National Early Years Network
Childcare Helpline

Part II: Crisis by Crisis

CHAPTER THREE

Child Illness and Hospitalization

Example 1

Mark was first diagnosed with brain cancer as a four-year-old. Four years later, he is still alive, but has been in and out of the hospital numerous times and has also had a life-threatening bout of meningitis. When his hearing became impaired, his mother had to fight to keep him in the same school as his friends, rather than have him transported to another town where there was a special facility for hearing-impaired children. She was successful. Throughout his illness, the support of his teachers and friends has made life worthwhile for him. The teachers and children benefited from seeing a video from the Cancer Society to help them understand what was happening to Mark. The cassette tapes and large packages of cards and drawings they sent him while he was in hospital made him feel like a valued part of the gang. Mark has learning problems and some behaviour problems, however, he has a strong social network, many friends and feels valued and loved.

The Issue

Any time a child is hospitalized is a stressful time for the family. The child will undoubtedly be anxious and may come face to face with some real fears. The parents' anxiety about their child's well-being will also affect the hospitalized child and the other children in the family. The family routine is disrupted. One or both parents may have to take time off from work. If there are other children at home,

Example 2

Another centre manager tells this story: The eight-year-old son of the school cook kept vomiting for no apparent reason. Finally after much medical investigation they did a CAT scan and found that he had a brain tumour. The surgeon took out as much as they could, but some of it was inoperable. Radiation caused him to lose his hair and he became huge and puffy. He was in a wheelchair for a while. He attended the centre after school and in the summer when he felt well enough. The other children kept asking questions that were hard to answer: Why is he in a wheelchair? Why is he all puffy? Why did he lose his hair? Why does he have those stitches? The doctors gave him six months to live. When he told the other children he was going to die, the questions really started coming: Will I die too if I get sick? When I have chicken pox does that mean I will die? Will I catch this from him and die? So I called the local number for the Cancer Society and they came to the centre and talked to the children about good cells and bad cells and what cancer cells are. They were a really good resource for us. We also found that the local hospital runs a similar service through their hospice unit. They have discovered that it is not only adults who need help in dealing with the reality of death and serious illness.

they will miss their parents and have worries of their own. If the child is hospitalized over a long period of time because of a serious illness, the impact on the family will be even greater.

There has been much improvement in how hospitals consider the emotional well-being of both children and parents. Depending on the circumstances, parents are often allowed to stay with the child for comfort, even until the child is anaesthetized in the operating room. Many hospitals allow a parent to sleep in the room with the child. Hospitals often offer pre-admission visits to familiarize the child with his surroundings and explain all of the procedures he can expect. Hospital play workers may be available to work with children ahead of time involving dramatic play with stuffed animals or other techniques to allow the child to play out fears and gain some sense of control. These measures are not universal, however.

During severe illnesses such as cancer, where there are prolonged hospitalizations and repeated painful procedures, the child may suffer from Post-Traumatic Stress Disorder (PTSD). The child, even when cured of the disease, may still suffer an emotional handicap, and the family may experience the lingering effects of anxiety, overprotectiveness and general stress.

Whether you are working with the child who is anticipating, or who has recently had, a hospital stay, or for whom visits to the hospital are a regular part of their existence, or if you are working with other children in the family, there are things that you can do to help the child and support the family.

Insights from Child Development

Children feel helpless and vulnerable in a hospital. They are truly in a situation over which they have no control or power. So they may play to show that they have power. Regression to younger behaviour is also a common and expected behaviour.

Dramatic play is important. Children typically re-enact scenes from the doctor's office or hospital in their dramatic play. This should be encouraged.

The child might think they are ill because they were bad. Even if the child does not express this, it should be made clear to the child that they are not ill because of anything they did.

Children may ask the same questions over and over again.

Children understand little about how the body works. Children's ideas of what is inside their bodies are far from reality. Most of them think it is like an empty sack filled with blood, food and waste products. One common fear is that if there is a cut or an incision, everything inside of them will spill out.

Children who have been chronically ill for a long time and are now back with a peer group may need help with social relationships. They have suffered social isolation from peers and have not had the practice in play and give-and-take with other children.

Social development might also be impeded because other children think that they might catch the condition from the child.

The child's family may need help. The way parents cope with the child's illness has a great impact on how the child learns to handle the experience.

When to seek Help

It is common for a child to want more attention and comfort after a hospital stay. For instance, they might become very particular about what they eat or what they will wear. A parent may think that the child is manipulative, but generally it is good to give the extra attention. However, if the parent feels that the child is not moving beyond the experience, and if, for that child it is unusual for the following things to occur, some professional counselling might be necessary.

The child's demands for attention and fear of separation seem excessive, or continues longer than the situation seems to warrant.

The child exhibits fear or continuing sleep disturbances.

Normal regression — bed-wetting, loss of toilet habits, thumb-sucking, baby talk – continues longer than the situation seems to warrant.

Who can help

Hospital play workers and family therapy services
Child psychologists
The family's paediatrician
Social work services may be able to help with other family needs, or counselling services.

How to respond

While it is certainly the parents' primary responsibility to prepare the child for the hospital stay, you also have a role helping prepare the child if the child is with you before the anticipated experience. Afterwards the child may be working through many of her recent experiences.

With the staff

Try to learn something about the child's condition so you have a better understanding yourself.

Communicate with the parents. Find out from the parents what the child is going to experience so that you will be able to answer the child's questions honestly and sensitively.

With the child

If the hospital stay is more than a day or two, a visit can be a wonderful way to say to the child and to the parents, 'We care about you. You are important and cherished by all of us.' You might bring pictures or home-made cards from the children.

Be honest with the child. If the child asks you, do not tell the child that it will not hurt when it probably will hurt. It is better to say that it may hurt for a little while but the doctors and nurses will do everything they can to make the hurt go away as quickly as possible.

Do not discount the child's fears by telling them that there is nothing to worry about. Instead, let them talk about what worries them. Offer empathy, acknowledge their feelings and offer support.

Read a book to the child or to the group about going to the hospital so the child knows they are not alone in what they are going through or in the feelings they are having.

Use a puppet, doll or stuffed animal to tell the children that he has to go to the hospital and he is frightened. See if the children know how to comfort the puppet. Let the puppet ask some of the questions and express some of the fears you suspect the child might have. If the child can put themselves in the role of comforting the puppet, they might remember some of their own strategies later on. Perhaps the puppet could go to the hospital with them, or return to the group at the same time the child does. The puppet and the child can compare experiences.

Include appropriate accessories for dramatic play. Small dolls and accessories depicting doctors, nurses, examining room equipment, ambulances and even wheelchairs are available. If you do not have or cannot purchase a set of these, perhaps you can improvise props and costumes for other small dolls. When children play with these small figures, the child becomes a giant, manipulating people and events in their imaginative play. This position of power can be of great benefit to a child.

Encourage dramatic play about hospitals and doctor visits. Include such things as play doctor's kits (either purchased or that you make up yourself), first aid kit supplies, examining tables, doctor's coats, surgical masks, stuffed animals and dolls to be patients. Use this opportunity to incorporate literacy props into the children's play. Include magazines in the waiting room, clip boards, pamphlets from the doctor's office, prescription slips for the doctor to fill out.

Children need to learn basic facts about their illness, in ways they can understand, to reduce fears and imaginings.

Ask the child to list all the people who care about them and help take care of them. Some will be family members, others will be health workers, neighbours, friends and community people. Talk about relationships, how people help each other in many different ways.

If a child has had a protracted illness, they may act more dependently than is appropriate for their age. Work on building independence skills — doing things for themselves, helping with classroom chores, and feeling satisfied at a job well done.

Support children's social interactions by encouraging parallel playing, giving them ideas for how to enter play, and generally coaching them in social skills.

With the other children

The children in the class could send their greetings to the hospitalized child by making a cassette tape recording of themselves. It might include a few of their circle time songs and poems.

A book made up of individual photos of their friends with dictated greetings from each child could cheer up an ill friend.

Make cards and drawings. Encourage the children to make cards and drawings for their ill friend.

Take a trip to the hospital or local clinic. It can be interesting and beneficial for all children, even if no child in the group is anticipating a hospital stay. Many medical facilities now offer such tours. Meet with the people ahead of time to find out exactly what the tour entails. Talk about how children's questions might be handled. Ahead of time, make an experience chart letting children dictate to you what they already know about hospitals. This will let you know any misconceptions they have. You might read a book about the hospital or show them some pictures as well. Take a camera along on the trip. Afterwards, let children help you make a display of the photos you took and dictate what the captions should be. Focus on the helping and caring nature of the people they encounter. The more they know about what to expect, the less anxiety they will have.

Teach children about how their bodies work, then they can better understand when something goes wrong and needs to be fixed.

Discuss the child's condition. In discussions with the other children in the group, stress that the child's condition is not catching and they cannot be harmed by playing with the child. Help them to understand some basic facts about the illness, if appropriate. You might involve the parents and the child themselves to help explain to the other children what happened to them. Often they have the words worked out since they may have had to explain it many times before.

With the parents

Be supportive. Let the parents know that you are there to help, and tell them some of the things you might do in the classroom to prepare the child for the experience, or as follow-up activities.

You may be able to let parents know about useful resources in helping to explain what lies ahead for the child.

Ask parents to keep you informed about the child's condition.

Further Information

Resources for children

Your local library should have a comprehensive list of appropriate children's titles.

Books

Bradman T. and Brown, E., *Through my Window,* Mammoth, 1989.
Nicoll, H, and Pienkowski, J., *Mog's Mumps,* Heinemann Young Books, 1977.
Bruna, D., *Miffy in the Hospital,* World International, 1997.
Mercer, G. and Dennis, P. *A Visit to the Hospital,* Kingfisher Books, 1992.Brown, Marc, *Arthur's Chicken Pox,* Red Fox, 1998.
Civardi, A. and Cartwright, S., *Going into Hospital,* Usborne Publishing Ltd., 1992.
Strong, Jeremy, *Dinosaur Pox* (Illustrated by Nick Sharratt), Puffin, 1999.
Adamson, Jean and Gareth, *Topsy and Tim visit the Dentist,* Ladybird Books Ltd., 1998
Adamson, Jean and Gareth, *Topsy and Tim visit the Doctor,* Ladybird Books Ltd., 1998
Carlstrom, Nancy White, *Barney Is Best,* HarperCollins, 1994.
Krisher, Trudy, Illustrated by Nadine Bernard Westcott, *Kathy's Hats: A Story of Hope,* Albert Whitman Publishers, 1992.
Lansky, Vicki, *Koko Bear's Earache: Preparing Your Child For Ear Tube Surgery,* The Book Peddlers, 1990.
Pirner, Connie White, Illustrated by Nadine Bernard Westcott. *Even Little Kids Get Diabetes,* Albert Whitman Publishers, 1994.
Rogers, Fred, Illustrated by Jim Judkis, *Going to the Hospital,* PaperStar Books, 1988.
Sanford, Doris, Illustrated by Graci Evans. *No Longer Afraid: Living With Cancer.* Multomah Publishers, 1992.

Resources for adults

Organizations and helplines

Most major illnesses have national offices and phone numbers to call *(See Appendix for details*). Many have specific resources for children and families. The child's doctor, local libraries, *Yellow Pages,* telephone directories and charitable and voluntary organizations may also have information about these sources.

NHS Direct (NHS 24 hour helpline) Tel. 0845- 4647
CancerLink. Cancer Information Service. Tel. 0800-132 905
Macmillan Cancer Relief. Information Line. Tel. 0845-601 6161

Cancer BACUP. Tel. 0808-800 1234
British Diabetic Association.
Tel 020-323 1531
AIDs Helpline. Tel. 0800-567 123
Alzheimer's Helpline.
Tel. 0845-300 0336
Asthma Helpline. Tel. 0345-010 203
Epilepsy. Tel. 0800-309 0030
National Association for Mental Health (MIND). Tel. 0345-660 163
Terrence Higgins Trust Helpline.
Tel. 020-242 1010
SANELINE Tel. 0345-67 80000
Health Information Service.
Tel. 0800-665 544
The Samaritans, Tel. 0345-909 090
Carers National Association. CarersLine.
Tel. 0345-573 369
ParentLine. Tel 01702-559 900
CareLine. Tel. 020-514 1177
NSPCC. Tel. 0800-800 500
ChildLine. Tel. 0800-1111

CHAPTER FOUR

Illness in the Family

Example

Six-year-old Mary has an older brother with cancer. He has had cancer for five years. She is his best friend. Often when he is feeling bad, only Mary can make him feel better. When he will not eat, she can sometimes get him to take a few bites. Mary is also the only one who will punch him when she's mad at him. The family is very proud of how she is *there* for her brother. However, Mary has started playing up with her friends and being disruptive in class. It is as though she's saying, 'What about me? When do I get to be the centre of attention?' At home she has started to express resentment towards her brother. 'Why is everyone always asking about Larry? Why does he always get all the attention and presents?' When people ask, 'How's the family? How's Larry doing?' the mother reminds them that the family includes Mary and she's doing really well too. Mary's caring, understanding parents are doing what they can to help her feel valued and important just for being herself. They try to include her teachers in this thinking so that Mary can feel important at school. She knows that she matters to her brother and her family, and she is also learning that she is important just because she is who she is.

The Issue

When someone in the family has a serious illness, physical or mental, the whole family can be thrown off balance. The person with the illness often becomes the centre of attention, and younger children in the family tend to feel left out or even abandoned. Parents under stress may deny the seriousness of the situation. The demands of caring for a sick person at home can also take its toll on family members. There may be economic as well as emotional hardships. The family may become socially isolated. All of this can have a profound effect on young children.

When one parent is mentally ill, the children may have only the other parent to count on during times of need, and as a result might have to take on more responsibility than they are ready for. The social stigma connected with mental illness may further isolate the family.

It is a certainly a challenge for families to meet the needs of the ill person while keeping the healthy child's life as stable and normal as possible. This is an area where the childcare provider or teacher can play a major role.

Insights from Child Development

Understanding illness. Young children have a hard time understanding illness and disease. Since they can only really understand what they can perceive with their senses, it is difficult for them to understand micro-organisms or internal organs. Four- and five-year-old children can begin to learn more about how the body works and what causes illness.

The child may feel responsible for the family member's illness.

Fear of developing an illness. Older children may be preoccupied with causality and experiment with cause and effect. They may question what caused the person to become ill and whether they, too, will become ill.

When a parent or grandparent is ill

The child may feel resentment or anger and then shame for having those feelings.

The child may feel abandoned, invisible, unimportant. Self-esteem suffers.

Feeling helpless. The child knows there is nothing they can do to make the situation better.

When a sibling is seriously ill

Loss of security. A sibling of the ill child may feel insecure. Because the parent is away a lot (if the child is hospitalized) and because the parent's attention is focused on the ill child, the healthy child may feel unimportant, left out, even unloved.

When a child in a family becomes seriously ill, especially with a life-threatening disease, family members may over-compensate out of grief, showering the ill child with presents. The healthy sibling may feel resentful or jealous of the ill child. The child may even say, 'That's not fair.'

Retaliation. The sibling may even be mean to the child who is ill, to show their resentment.

To regain their fair share of attention, the healthy child might get into trouble at school, in the neighbourhood, or with carers.

The healthy child may develop psychosomatic symptoms or exaggerate minor physical complaints in order to get more parental attention.

The healthy sibling may feel vulnerable and fearful that they too might become ill and have to go to the hospital.

Self-blame. Because of egocentric thinking, the sibling may think that they caused the illness by wishing that something bad would happen to that person. Or they may think the ill person is trying to get even with them for something they did.

Mental illness

Mental illness can be especially confusing and difficult for young children to understand. There is often inconsistency in the way a mentally ill person responds to the child.

Since mental illness does not have visible symptoms other than the person's demeanour, it can be even more difficult to explain to a child. The adult could say, 'Some illnesses show outside the body, some do not.' One worker described mental illness to children as when someone is 'sick in their feelings.'

Feeling invisible. The child may feel unnoticed and uncared for when the parent is unable to focus on them.

When to seek Help

Child develops aches and pains. Stress may cause the child to develop aches, pains or stomach problems. These psychosomatic symptoms can accompany real physical effects.

The child may play up in extreme ways as a cry for attention: behaving in an aggressive and angry manner; hurting other children; crying too easily in frustration — all may be signs that the child is not coping well and needs more help.

In some cases, especially in the presence of mental illness, a child takes on more responsibility than is appropriate or typical for their age, such as caring for younger siblings and preparing food.

Who can help

Social workers
Counselling services
Child psychologists
Hospital play therapists
Community mental health services, family doctor, health visitor

How to respond

With the staff

Ask the family to keep you informed about what is going on with the child. In case the child asks you for information about the illness, find out what the family has told them and be consistent in your explanations.

With the child

Reassure the child that they did nothing to make the person ill. Perhaps a puppet could voice this concern, feeling sad because someone in his family is unwell and he feels responsible. Then you and the children can explain to the puppet that other people do not cause that type of illness.

Since the child may feel forgotten or unimportant at home, do all you can to make the child feel special and important in your environment. Make them your special helper, play with them or ask their opinion.

The child could draw pictures or dictate stories for the ill person. You can suggest this to the child and provide materials and offer to take dictation. This helps the child feel important, and that they are doing something. It is a useful way to help the child communicate with the ill person.

Talk about how all living things change. Point out changes in trees, flowers and growing plants. Cut out and paste pictures of changes in nature. Collect pictures of how people change as they grow and develop. Discuss people's feelings about change. Some changes we have control over, some we do not.

Plan activities about feelings (see Chapter 23). Invite the child to talk about what they are feeling and be accepting and uncritical of what you hear. Offer outlets for anger such as clay, messy art, and outdoor play.

Encourage dramatic play. It is one way children *talk it out* and come to terms with difficult situations. Make sure the child has plenty of opportunities to engage in socio-dramatic play. Do not dictate themes of play, but do provide props such as doctor's outfits and dressing-up clothes worn by hospital workers.

Offer puppets of doctors, nurses and other community helpers to help the child recreate scenes from life and imagination.

Provide children with doll's house-size people and furniture that depict hospital equipment. Encourage children to express their feelings as they play.

Encourage the family to give the child as much factual information as the child can understand. You might be able to help them with this. Without factual information, children can imagine things are much worse than they are.

If the ill person is being cared for at home, the child could be involved in appropriate ways in caring for the person. Perhaps the child could help bring the person food or add a pillow to make the person comfortable. The child will feel less helpless and more valued.

If a family member is seriously ill and might die, the family should prepare the child and let you know they have done so. You might be able to help them find words which the child can understand (see Chapter 6). Sometimes people hesitate to prepare the child, in case the person gets better. But the child can sense that something is terribly wrong by the tension in the household, visitors and phone calls. If they are not told the facts in ways they can understand, children are likely to feel even greater anxiety. Children need to know that they will be told when important things are happening.

The family should prepare the child for the experience of visiting a seriously ill person in the hospital. It is best not to force a visit. In the classroom you could show the child books about hospitals.

Help the child be noticed in positive ways. Send the parents upbeat reports, notes and artwork. This may help the whole family feel more positively about things in general.

With the other children

Do what you can to promote friendships with peers and strengthen the child's social ties outside of the family. Let the child feel important in their own social realm. You might encourage other parents to invite the child to their home to play or to spend the night.

Mental illness

As the child's home life may be very unsettled at this time, the child needs a sense of security and predictability in your environment.

Play and have fun. The child should be encouraged to enjoy themselves as much as possible.

The child needs to know of your acceptance so they do not feel ashamed or embarrassed. The parent may be temporarily unable to nurture the child. Although you cannot substitute for the parent, you can help make the child feel valued.

Further Information

Resources for children

Books

Your local library should have a comprehensive list of appropriate children's titles.

DenBoer, Helen, Illustrated by Janice Galanter Goldstein. *Please Don't Cry, Mom.* Learner Publications Co., 1994.

Kohlenberg, Sherry, Illustrated by Lauri Crow. *Sammy's Mommy Has Cancer.* Magination Press, 1993.

Sherkin-Langer, Ferne, Illustrated by Kay Life. *When Mommy Is Sick.* Albert Whitman Publishers, 1995.

Bruna, D., *Miffy in the Hospital,* World International, 1997.

Mercer, G. and Dennis, P. *A Visit to the Hospital,* Kingfisher Books, 1992.

Civardi, A. and Cartwright, S., *Going into Hospital,* Usborne Publishing Ltd., 1992.

Rogers, Fred, Illustrated by Jim Judkis, *Going to the Hospital,* PaperStar Books, 1988.

Resources for adults

Books

Fitzgerald, Helen, *The Grieving Child: A Parent's Guide.* Simon and Schuster Trade, 1992. Contains useful discussions on dealing with illness in the family, preparing a child to visit someone who is seriously ill, giving the ill person a gift, and debriefing after the visit.

Curriculum materials

Small doll figures and puppets representing community helpers, including hospital and emergency medical personnel, firemen and police officers.

Dressing-up clothes depicting nurses, doctors, police officers, and firemen as well as play doctor's kits.

Organizations and helplines

Many major illnesses have national support organizations which provide resource materials *(See Appendix for further details).* For additional listings of organizations, contact a doctor or check with the local hospital library.

NHS Direct (NHS 24 hour helpline) Tel. 0845-4647

CancerLink. Cancer Information Service. Tel. 0800-132 905

Macmillan Cancer Relief. Information Line. Tel. 0845-601 6161

Cancer BACUP. Tel. 0808-800 1234

British Diabetic Association. Tel. 020-323 1531

AIDs Helpline. Tel 0800 567 123

Alzheimer's Helpline. Tel. 0845-300 0336

Asthma Helpline. Tel. 0345-010 203

Epilepsy. Tel. 0800-309 0030

National Association for Mental Health (MIND). Tel. 0345-660 163

Terrence Higgins Trust Helpline. Tel. 020-242 1010

SANELINE Tel. 0345-678 0000

Health Information Service. Tel. 0800-665 544

The Samaritans, Tel. 0345-909 090

Carers National Association CarersLine. Tel. 0345-573 369

CHAPTER FIVE

Child or Family Member with HIV or AIDS

Example

The mother of three-year-old Jonathan has AIDS. She did not know that she had the HIV virus until long after she had given birth to Jonathan and she had already enrolled him in a local childcare centre. Jonathan has tested positive for the HIV virus, but as yet is showing no symptoms of AIDS. Realizing that the HIV virus is not spread by casual contact, his mother decided not to say anything to the director or staff of the childcare centre because she is afraid they would not allow him to continue to attend. She needs childcare while she is still able to work, and she also wants Jonathan to continue to enjoy his friends and the benefits of the centre as long as possible.

The Issue

All people who have the HIV virus will eventually develop AIDS, is eventually fatal. Finding that there is a child who is HIV positive in your nursery or centre can cause staff members and parents to react in fear and panic.

It is possible that you might have a child who is HIV positive in your centre and be unaware of it. The child may be a-symptomatic and the condition could even be undiagnosed. Many parents of children who are HIV positive choose to keep it a secret because of the general fear and prejudice of uninformed neighbours, friends and employers. They fear becoming social outcasts, losing their jobs, or being the subjects of violence. Also, parents may feel guilty and ashamed and are, therefore, reluctant to reveal the condition.

If you have a child who is HIV positive or has AIDS in your care, you may also have a parent with AIDS. Working with the family may be difficult. AIDS can cause grief, guilt, and depression. The parent may be too ill to fulfil normal parental duties. You may be dealing with foster parents, grandparents or other relatives instead of the biological parents, indicating that the child has already experienced separation. You can be sure there is stress in the family.

Being well informed about paediatric AIDS, and practising excellent hygiene can go a long way to diffusing the initial fear that people express. However, even when staff members are informed and well educated about caring for children who are HIV positive and the child is showing no symptoms, there may be added stress on the carer. Extra vigilance in hand-washing and general hygiene procedures should not cause undue stress, because it should be general policy for all staff under all circumstances. However, there may be an underlying sadness or anger at the parents (even if inappropriate) that must be handled. Since the keyworker, the health visitor and the manager may, because of confidentiality policies, be the only ones to know about the child's special condition, the carer may feel isolated to an extent, needing someone to talk to. It is wise to be conscious of this and create avenues for the staff member to discuss and work through his or her feelings.

Basic Information about HIV and AIDS

HIV stands for **Human Immuno-deficiency Virus.** Someone having antibodies for that virus is said to be HIV positive, which means their system has been exposed to that virus. A person who is HIV positive may appear perfectly healthy. Eventually a person's immune system will wear down and will no longer be able to fend off infection. That is when AIDS begins.

A person who is HIV positive but not yet showing symptoms of AIDS may still pass on the virus to someone else.

AIDS stands for **Acquired Immune Deficiency Syndrome.** A person's immune system is no longer able to fend off germs that cause infection, which eventually results in the person's death.

The four ways someone can acquire HIV/AIDS are:

— By prenatal or perinatal exposure. The virus crosses through the placenta from the blood of an HIV positive mother to the unborn infant, or the infant is exposed to the contaminated blood during birth.
— By being exposed to contaminated blood, either from a contaminated blood transfusion (very rare today), or by blood from the HIV positive person mixing with blood from an infected person through a wound or abrasion.
— Exposure to HIV contaminated blood from sharing unsterilized needles in intravenous drug use.
— Through sexual contact with a person who is HIV positive.

HIV/AIDS are NOT spread in these ways:

— Saliva
— Mosquito bites
— Sharing eating utensils
— Sneezing or coughing
— Any casual, non-sexual contact such as hugging, dancing or playing

When a child has a family member with AIDS

When one person in a family has AIDS, the whole family suffers stress. The knowledge that AIDS is a long, painful and eventually fatal disease causes grief and stress, no matter what the other circumstances of the family are. A child may reflect this stress through angry, frightened, withdrawn, or confused behaviour. Unfortunately, because many people choose to keep the existence of AIDS in the family a secret, you may not know what is causing the child's behaviour.

In addition to the stress of the illness, in a large percentage of families where a family member has AIDS, there are other behaviours that create a chaotic life style. Often one or more family members has been involved in intravenous drug use. With substance abuse there is an increased likelihood of domestic violence, child abuse, neglect or depression, all of which contribute to dysfunctional parenting. Shame, guilt, anger, frustration, and feeling hopeless and powerless are also likely to be present in the adults. Needless to say, all of this can make the family very difficult to work with. Be sure to connect with other support services working with the family as you interact with them.

For information on responding appropriately to other issues that may become part of the child's life see Chapters 4 and 6.

When a member of staff is HIV-positive

Many people who are HIV positive or have AIDS choose to work as long as they are able. Adults who are HIV positive or have AIDS and work in a childcare setting, can continue in their jobs as long as they meet regular performance standards. Since HIV is not spread through casual contact and everyday activities, there is no reason a person cannot continue to work, provided he or she feels up to it.

Inform and educate the rest of the staff and the parents to overcome fears and misconceptions, and provide social support for the individual. However, the individual's right to confidentiality should be maintained if they wish. Often people choose not to share the fact that they are HIV positive for fear of ostracism and prejudice.

When they become ill with AIDS, staff should check with their physicians about the advisability of continuing to work in a childcare setting or school where they may be exposed to more infectious germs than in other settings, thus putting themselves at heightened risk of infection.

Basic Facts about Paediatric AIDS

The great majority of children who have HIV/AIDS contracted it prenatally or at birth. Only about one-third of children born to HIV positive mothers will themselves develop AIDS.

Almost all new babies born to HIV positive mothers will initially have the HIV antibodies in their blood which they have received from their mothers, and will test positive for HIV.

With tests currently available, it is impossible to tell for sure if a baby has AIDS before the child is 15 to 24 months of age because it takes time before the baby's own immune system takes over.People who are HIV positive do not always have symptoms. It is impossible to tell whether or not an individual, child or adult, is HIV positive without a laboratory test.

The individual is not said to have AIDS until specific symptoms of the disease emerge.

Although in adults it can take ten years or more for HIV to turn into symptomatic AIDS, children with HIV become ill much sooner.

While 82 per cent of children with HIV are diagnosed with AIDS by the age of three, some children do not develop symptoms until three or four years of age or older.

The spread of the HIV virus is easy to prevent

There is no evidence that a child has ever contracted HIV/AIDS through casual contact with other children.

Even biting is not considered a major risk. Toddler bites rarely draw blood. The contaminated blood of the HIV positive child must contact the blood of the other child for the second child to be at risk of infection.

Children may alternate periods of being well and feeling good, with bouts of infection.

A child who is HIV positive should not attend a regular childcare setting if there is an outbreak of chicken pox or measles.

It is possible to prevent the spread of HIV/AIDS

The most important staff training issue is practising excellent infection control procedures in the childcare setting. These measures, of course, are important to reduce the spread of illness in general in your setting. So everyone benefits if training, and especially policies and practices, are tightened up.

Keep informed

Since new information about HIV/AIDS is constantly being generated, childcare providers should make every effort to be informed about the latest findings. It is a good idea to assign one individual the responsibility for keeping up to date.

Insights from Child Development

All children benefit. Children who are HIV positive or have AIDS and whose symptoms do not require exclusion under ordinary circumstances will benefit, like any other child with special needs, from developmentally appropriate early childhood education, social interaction and playing with other children.

Vulnerable to illness. Because of the extent of their illness and their vulnerability to infection, children who have AIDS may be best cared for in specialized facilities that care only for children with AIDS. This decision must be made on an individual basis.

Behaviour problems may also occur as a result of the neurological damage. Stress in the family. Because there may have been a death or another ill person in the household, or because the child may have been removed from the family, the child may display anger, fear, sadness, anxiety, confusion and behavioural problems, all the general signs of stress within the family.

Child may lose developmental milestones. Because of the virus' effect on the nervous system, the HIV-infected child may lose developmental milestones previously attained.

Children have a hard time understanding anything they cannot perceive with their senses. Therefore germs and viruses are difficult concepts, as well as trying to understand what goes on inside their bodies or how diseases are spread.

Children who have a family member with HIV/AIDS

Children may have picked up from adults that AIDS is a terrible thing, and there may be an aura of fear around the discussion.

Children are concerned about themselves first. They might ask, 'Am I going to get AIDS?'

Any child who is aware that a loved one has AIDS or is HIV positive, and also understands its seriousness, will suffer emotional reactions. The fear of abandonment and loss, and the confusion resulting from the emotional turmoil in the household will affect the child's behaviour.

When to seek help

When you know that a child in your care is HIV positive, be aware of signs of possible health deterioration. The family should be encouraged to seek medical intervention when any of these conditions appear:

— Loss of developmental milestones previously attained
— Fever
— Chronic weight loss
— Frequent infections
— Thrush (white patches in the mouth that appear in children six months of age or older). Thrush is usually not seen in healthy children after three months of age.
— Skin rashes
— Signs of stress. Also, be sensitive to signs of stress in the child — sadness, isolation, anger, anxiety — and work closely with the family to comfort and reassure the child.

Who can help

It is advisable to have a multidisciplinary team available for the consultation on each HIV/AIDS child.

In addition to the parent or foster parent, include some of the following professionals on the team:

— The child's paediatrician
— The family's social worker
— The health visitor
— Play therapists

See also the organizations listed in the resource section of this chapter

How to respond

With the staff

All staff members need to realize that it is possible to work positively with children with HIV/AIDS so that they receive the benefits of early childhood education and social contact, and at the same time not jeopardize the health of other children or staff who come in contact with the child.

All staff, volunteers and parents should be made aware of the playgroup's, nursery's, centre's or school's written policies about working with children who are HIV positive, and about employing staff who are HIV positive. Implement all appropriate HIV related policies, and revise them as needed.

Since any early childhood facility in the country might, with or without their knowledge, be caring for a child who is HIV positive, this is an essential issue for staff training and parent awareness.

Require staff to honour confidentiality. They should not discuss any child's or staff member's HIV status.

Consider bringing in a resource person for staff and parent meetings occasionally so that all questions can be answered fully.

Develop a staff training outline and system to make sure that every individual who works or volunteers has accurate information about the disease and knows precautionary measures to prevent its spread.

Staff training topics should include:

— Information about infectious diseases in general and how they are spread
— The centre's policies for exclusion of ill children for all illnesses, in compliance with your local childcare regulations and health service guidance.
— Current information about HIV/AIDS
— The differences between someone who is HIV positive and someone who has multiple symptoms of AIDS
— How the disease progresses in adults and in children
— How HIV/AIDS can be contracted
— How HIV/AIDS is not spread

— Precautionary hygiene measures to prevent the spread of the virus (practices that are required)
— The stress on the family caused by illness and how best to be supportive of parents and carers in their roles
— Community organizations and resources

Carers need an outlet to discuss their feelings about this topic in general, as well as specific feelings about infected children and parents in their care. Create opportunities for both informal and structured discussions at staff meetings.

Review frequently hand-washing and nappy changing and other hygiene measures. Guidance is available from Health Education Boards. Local Authorities and Pre-School Play Associations also provide guidance for those facilities registered or managed by them.

Consider keeping a pair of latex disposable gloves in your pocket so that you have them handy and can respond immediately if a child is injured and bleeds.

It is not enough to have excellent hygiene policies in place. It takes frequent monitoring and thorough training of all childcare staff, new staff, supply staff and volunteers. It is easy for people to become careless. Place copies of proper procedures at the changing areas and sinks, and in the staff room. Develop a system for checking and monitoring each other to make sure the procedures are followed consistently by all people.

With the HIV-positive child

Separation is a big issue with children who have AIDS. They may already have been separated from their mother or their family. They may have been hospitalized, and they will certainly face major separations in the future. The mother may die before the child. So take great care in introducing the child and the parents or foster parents to the centre.

Bear in mind that children who have AIDS may experience neurological damage that creates learning disabilities. Revise your expectations of the child accordingly. Individualize your work through assessing the child's various skills and devise appropriate activities that challenge their current capabilities without frustrating the child. Let the child practise success.

Since ill people, especially children, often feel helpless, create situations where the child feels less helpless. Offer the child choices and allow them to make decisions when appropriate.

Ask the child's opinion and preferences, when appropriate. 'Where do you think I should hang this picture?' 'Shall we have snack inside or outside today?' 'Do you think I should put out playdough or finger paint to play with today?'

Allow time and opportunity for dramatic play when the child can dictate the action and be the powerful star of their own dramas (see Chapter 23). Any child who has been ill a lot with many visits to the doctor or hospital will probably enjoy playing doctor's office or hospital. Provide dramatic play props, uniforms, doctor's kits, examining tables and doctor's office settings. Take on a role yourself, if it seems necessary, to facilitate the play, but allow the child to direct the action. Children will also enjoy playing with doll's house hospital furniture and people.

Puppets. Doctor, nurse and ambulance staff puppets can encourage children to express themselves about illness.

Be sure to set the same limits and expectations for behaviour with this child as with the other children.

Make special efforts to reduce the risk of biting, reducing frustration, crowding, fighting and aggression (see Chapter 24).

Make sure that children do not feel guilty when they become ill. Let them know they did nothing to cause their illness.

Make sure that the child is welcomed back warmly after having been ill and away from the centre for a period of time. Help to ease the child's social re-entry into the group.

With the other children

How they can play together. If it is openly acknowledged that a child has AIDS, focus on how the other children will not catch the disease rather than how it is contracted. With the children, make a list, or even an illustrated poster, of ways AIDS is not spread, including:

— Playing
— Hugging
— Sharing food
— Sharing eating utensils, dishes
— Sitting in the same chair
— Drinking out of a water fountain
— Mosquito bites
— Dancing with someone
— Using the same telephone
— Using the same toilet

Stress that other germs that can make you unwell in different ways might be spread in some of these ways, but not HIV.

Ask what they already know about AIDS. Talk about it with the other children.

Teach all children not to touch

someone else's blood. Review with them what to do if someone gets hurt and is bleeding; call a staff member.

Talk about being sick and being healthy. Talk about, act out and illustrate things people do to stay healthy such as eating properly, exercising, sleeping and washing hands. However, do stress that children who are sick with AIDS did nothing to cause their illness.

With the children, rehearse basic hygiene routines such as using a tissue, and washing hands after blowing their nose, going to the bathroom and before eating. Praise them for appropriate actions they do on their own as well as with prompting from you. Make posters and illustrations.

When a classmate is ill and not attending, the other children could make cards and pictures for the ill child.

With the parents of the child who is HIV-positive

The child may be in a foster family or with the biological parent. In either case, the illness will certainly be a cause of added stress.

Look at the whole family situation. Some children who are HIV positive or have AIDS may come from a chaotic family setting with dysfunctional parents who, because of substance abuse or other problems have been unable to be responsive and caring toward the child. They may abuse or neglect the child. All of this adds to the child's behaviour problems. Be sure to rely on and work closely with the family's social worker and other professionals involved with the family.

Being supportive to the family to help them learn how to be positive parents is more important than usual if they have a child with HIV/AIDS. If you accept the parents and respect their difficulties and pain, you will be a valued social contact.

It is important to remember that these parents did not purposely infect their children, nor did they purposely become addicted to drugs.

If a parent is a substance abuser, the addiction must be treated effectively, with all the necessary social supports, before the parent can put the child first.

The biological mother and possible other family members may be ill with AIDS or at least be anticipating the illness, facing their own deaths while trying to cope with the difficulties of caring for an unwell child. Be aware of resources in your community which support people with AIDS and refer parents to them if they are not aware of them.

Foster parents, grandparents or carers other than the biological parent, who may have custody of the child, will also need community support and understanding of their difficulties.

It is essential to respect the confidentiality of the family. Many people choose not to reveal the child's condition for fear of stigma and retaliation by society. If you are in their circle of confidence it can be valuable for them to feel that they can talk to you without worry.

With the parents of the other children

All parents should be informed of your policy to accept children who are HIV positive.

Parents need to know that a child who is HIV positive may be in your care without your knowledge, and that this is possible in any childcare setting.

Give parents a copy of your written policies. Also inform them about your policies for exclusion of any child who shows certain symptoms of illness.

Have a parent meeting at least once a year to discuss the topic, how HIV/AIDS is not spread and what you do to prevent the spread of infection in your centre or school.

Discuss the topic with parents thoroughly and to their satisfaction during your intake interview. Offer to be available to answer any further questions they may have.

Talk openly and honestly with parents. When parents threaten to withdraw their child because of your policies or knowledge that a child who is HIV positive is in your centre, remind them that service might have such a child present with or without the knowledge of the administration. Because you are open about it and conscientious about staff training and hygiene practices, their child may actually be safer with you.

Honour confidentiality. Do not comply with parents' requests or demands to know the identity of children or staff in your setting who are HIV positive. Their knowledge of this may only lead to prejudicial action against the affected individual. At the same time, respectfully reassure them of your conscientious policies.

Further Information

Resources for children

Your local library should have a comprehensive list of appropriate children's titles.

Books

Giard, Linda Walvoord, Illustrated by Blanche Sims. *Alex, The Kid With AIDS.* Albert Whitman Publishers, 1994.
Newman L. and Stock C., *Too far away to touch,* Clarion Books, 1995.
Verniero, Joan C. (1995). Illustrated by Verdon Flory. *You Can Call Me Willy: A Story for Children About AIDS.* Magination Press, 1995.
Arnold, Lynda, *My Mommy has AIDS.* Dream Publishing, 1998.
Jordan, M. and Friedman, J., *Losing Uncle Tim,* Albert Whitman and Co., 1989.
Merrifield M. and Collins, H., *Morning Light,* Mountain Press Publishing Co., 1996.
Alexander, E., Rudin, S., Sejikora, P. and Shipman R.W., *My Dad has HIV,* Fairview Press, 1996.
Katz, I., Schwartz, S.A. and Wilson, T, *Uncle Jimmy,* Cimino Publishing Group, 1993.
Merrifield, Margaret, Illustrated by Heather Collins. *Come Sit by Me.* Stoddart, 1998.

Resources for adults

Books

Schwartz, L. and Clemmensen, D., *AIDS: First Facts for Kids,* Learning Works, 1997.Jewett, Claudia, *Helping Children cope with Separation and Loss,* Free Association Books, 1994.
Hogg, Christine, *Living Positively: A guide for parents and carers.* National Children's Bureau, 1996. A guide for parents or carers who look after children with HIV, or who themselves have HIV. It provides information about what support is available.
Orr, Neil (Ed), *Children's Rights and HIV: A framework for Action.* National Children's Bureau, 1995. An overview of children's rights for those working with children and families affected by HIV. It also acts as an introduction to the relevance of children's rights in the context of HIV infection.
Anderson, Gary R. (Ed.), *Courage to Care: Responding to the Crisis of Children with Aids.* Child Welfare League of America (CWLA) Inc., 1991.

Organizations and helplines

See Appendix for further contact details.

The Health Information Service. Provides up-to-date information on National Health Service services, and on illnesses and treatments. Also provides information about relevant support groups and helplines.
Tel. 0800-665 544

National AIDS Helpline.
Tel. 0800-567 123

The Terrence Higgins Trust Helpline.
Tel. 020-242 1010

NHS Direct. Tel. 0845-4647

The Samaritans. Confidential, emotional support for anyone experiencing a crisis. Tel. 0345-909 090

Local hospitals, AIDS clinics and hospices. See your local *Yellow Pages* for details.

CHAPTER SIX

Death of a Family Member or Friend

The Issue

As much as we would like to shelter innocent young children from the concept of death and grief, we cannot. Death is a natural fact of life and in all cultures children will be exposed to it. In most cases the child will encounter death first by seeing dead insects or small animals on the road, or by experiencing the death of a classroom or family pet. In other cases, the child first experiences the loss of a friend, family member or even a parent. In all these situations, the sensitive presence of a trusted adult and thoughtful discussion that addresses the child's questions, confusions and fears can go a long way toward helping the child deal with the situation in a healthy way. Because unresolved grief can be the cause of serious psychological problems at any age, it is important for the child to have help in dealing with feelings related to death.

One reason it is difficult to discuss death with children is because we often worry about how much of the topic to discuss. It is always good to follow a child's lead and respond to the child's questions and worries. Generally, children can be told facts about the death and what dead means. However, simply telling children the facts does not mean they will understand death.

Insights from Child Development

Young children acquire an understanding of death in progressive stages. Children, ages five and younger, see death as neither final nor inevitable, and cannot understand the causes of death. They expect that people and animals can come back to life again. Usually between five and nine years of age,

Example 1: Death of a parent

Five-year-old David's mother had cancer. She was often in the hospital for longer and longer periods of time. Finally she died, but for weeks, overcome with grief, the father could not bring himself to tell David and went on with the funeral without his son. He wanted to wait until he could tell his child sensitively, discussing calmly what had happened. In the meantime, David sensed that something was terribly wrong, but nobody was telling him anything. At the childcare centre, the staff were aware of what happened, but felt it was not their place to break the news to the child, so they tried to carry on as though all was fine. All was not fine. David, who had been a mild mannered little boy, became angry and aggressive and was hurting other children.

Finally, with encouragement and support from the childcare staff, David's father gathered his courage and took the time to tell his son what had happened. David was confused and angry. For a while, feeling betrayed, his behaviour at the centre became even more aggressive. He began seeing a counsellor who also helped David's father and the childcare staff find ways to answer David's questions and address his fears.

In the process, a bond of support was formed. The father often lingered at the centre at pick up time, enjoying the feeling of friendship with the staff and playing with his child and the other children. David's behaviour improved with the love and attention from the staff and his dad. However, much confusion, resentment and anger might have been avoided had his father openly acknowledged his grief to his son and allowed David to share in the initial grief and participate in the mourning process.

children can accept the idea that a person has died, but not accept that death ultimately happens to everyone, especially themselves. Children may ask over and over again what dead is. Do not be surprised if children repeat questions you thought they understood. Repeat the information you gave the child earlier, perhaps in a dif-

Example 2: Death of a pet

Squeaky, was a guinea pig who for years greeted children in the lobby of a childcare centre, and was a frequent visitor to classrooms. He even joined them on the grassy area of the playground from time to time. The children were very fond of him and would bring him snacks from home now and then. One morning the supervisor discovered that Squeaky had died during the night. She quickly consulted with each staff person as they came in and plans were made. In each classroom they read *The Tenth Good Thing About Barney* and then listed the things they liked best about Squeaky. A shoe box was filled with soft cotton and each classroom added special decorations. Just before lunch all the children assembled under a tree in the playground, sang songs and told the things they liked best about Squeaky. They helped dig a hole and placed Squeaky, inside his shoe box coffin, in the hole and buried him. Notes were sent home to the parents to let them know the proceedings of the day. The next day the staff were dismayed when several children dug up Squeaky's body.

ferent way. In explaining what dead means, include the following: not moving, not breathing, not feeling, not hurting, not being afraid.

INDIVIDUAL DIFFERENCES. There are no simple ways to help a child cope with death. Children as well as adults differ widely in their reactions to death. There are no timetables for grieving, adjusting to, or understanding death.

CHILDREN MAY WORRY ABOUT BEING ABANDONED. 'Are you going to die?' is a typical question of children, even when a pet dies. Sensing how dependent they are, children worry about who will take care of them if their parents die. Separation anxiety can become extreme. 'I don't expect to die for a long, long time,' is a good response.

GUILT AND RESPONSIBILITY. Adults are often surprised that after a long illness of someone close to the child, the child still feels responsible for the death. 'If I had behaved better, Grandma wouldn't have died.' Young children also engage in magical thinking. They sometimes believe that wishing something would happen or thinking bad thoughts can cause things to happen. Or if they wished a sibling would disappear and the sibling dies, the child can feel responsible.

Curiosity about death. It is not uncommon for a child to dig up the body of a pet buried in the yard. They are curious about what happens to the body. Even after the child has participated in burying a pet or attending a funeral, the child might ask when the dead pet or person will return. Especially in pre-school years children show a matter-of-fact interest in dead things-what they look like and feel like. Young children are also curious about how someone can breathe or eat or go to the bathroom after they are buried, or whether they will be cold or miss their friends.

Accurate information. The child should be told about the death as sensitively but as factually as possible, in response to their questions or concerns.

Need to feel included. Times of family crisis can actually be an opportunity for enhanced feelings of closeness and connection. In most cases it is best for the child to be included with talk, active remembering and shared feelings of sadness, as well as possible attendance at the funeral or memorial service.

Understanding cremation may be very difficult to explain to children. Be sure to emphasize that the dead body can feel nothing, no pain.

Use plain and simple language. Young children have a very concrete understanding of language. Be careful not to use the common euphemisms surrounding death: 'we lost him' or 'gone to heaven.' These phrases are confusing for children. It might also be a good idea to tell children that they might hear these phrases from other people and what the phrases mean.

It is typical for children to reenact in their dramatic play the part of the death that they witnessed, whether it is an accident or hospital play, or most typically, the funeral or memorial service. This is healthy and good. Just as adults talk about the death over and over in processing their grief, re-enacting the death in play is a child's way of gaining greater understanding and acceptance of death.

Young children respond to death and grieve differently from adults. Children process their grief intermittently, pausing to be sad or to think about it and ask questions from time to time and then give their thoughts a rest as they return to play.

When to seek help

All of the following characteristics could be normal reactions. The difference is in the length of time these symptoms persist and in their intensity. The most important thing is to know the child well. If any behaviour seems too extreme or seems to continue longer than the situation seems to warrant, encourage parents to seek the help of a trained therapist or grief counsellor. A parent's denial can get in the way of a child wanting to talk about the death. So look at how the parent seems to be handling it as well.

Encourage parents to get professional help for the child if:

— the child seems intent on denying the death
— the child leaves the room every time the dead person's name is mentioned and cannot talk about their feelings
— sleep disturbances continue for a long time
— separation anxiety becomes extreme
— the child shows heightened anxiety, clings more, whines more, cries more for long periods of time or if other fears become more intense, such as fear of the dark
— the child's anger does not dissipate and is affecting someone else, such as a sibling or a pet
— the child seems depressed or withdrawn for a long time
— regressive behaviour is excessive or prolonged.

Common signs of regression are normal. The child may retreat to a time when the world felt safer. Pay attention if the following behaviour seems to continue for a long time:

— Toilet skills diminish
— Bed-wetting begins or re-emerges
— Thumb sucking becomes excessive or re-emerges
— The child starts using baby talk
— The child crawls after having walked

Who can help

In many communities there are grief counselling services. Seek out someone who is not only familiar with the processes of grieving but also knows child development and can work effectively with very young children.

Social services may be able to provide, or give advice on, grief counselling.

Psychological services may have someone specially trained in grief counselling

The church, mosque, synagogue

or other religious organization have traditionally been where religious families turn for help. Like any other profession, some are better than others at explaining abstract concepts to young children.

How to respond

With the staff

Become acquainted with children's books dealing with death and life cycles in nature (see the resource section at the end of this chapter).

Talk about death. Many adults, including those who work with young children, have not themselves come to terms with the concept of death. In order to help children sift through their conflicting and confusing feelings about death, the adults guiding them must understand their own feelings. Discuss your feelings about death with your supervisor or trusted colleagues, or include this topic in staff training.

Meet someone from a grief counselling service. In some situations, it can be helpful for a grief counsellor to come in and have a meeting, or a series of meetings, with the staff.

With the child

HELP THE CHILD FEEL SECURE. Give the child reminders that they are loved and will be cared for. Name the people who are there for them.

Give the child a special comforter It might help to give the child a special comforter — a special stuffed toy just for themselves — to carry around and keep them company. This may help the child feel special and cared for.

Maintain stability for the child. When a child has experienced a death, try to keep as many things in their life the same. This gives them security and reassurance.

GIVE THE CHILD EXTRA ATTENTION. Grieving children, no matter how they are acting, need extra attention. All adults in the child's life should make an effort to spend time with the child and be there to talk, answer questions, and give reassurance and love. Give the child a special job they can do with you, like watering the plants or going with you on an errand.

ALLOW THE CHILD TO EXPRESS THEIR EMOTIONS. The child may have felt helpless during the events that have been going on around the death. By encouraging the expression of emotions and involving the child in activities, you will help move them from this passive, helpless state to one of actively coping.

TALK ABOUT DEATH IN AN APPROPRIATE CONTEXT, for example, when discussing life cycles in nature.

Point out that every living thing has a beginning, a time in between — for some things, like people, this is a long time, for others, like butterflies, this is a short time — and an ending, which is death.

Answer only what is asked, or turn the question around first, 'What do you think?,' to see what the child is really asking.

Ask the child questions. Are there words the child does not understand? Or ask the child, 'What are you thinking about?' This might help open up discussion when a child is hesitant to bring up the topic.

Answer the child's questions as often as asked. Do not be surprised when questions are repeated.

Read carefully selected children's books about death. Read to the whole group and to the child individually.

Help the child address feelings of guilt. Explain that the child did nothing to cause the death if the child seems to be expressing guilt. Adults must point out, repeatedly sometimes, that the child did nothing to cause the death. Then explain as factually as possible why the person or pet died. The child should hear that death is not a punishment. Children need to hear from you that just thinking something does not make things happen, that everybody has *bad* thoughts sometimes, but that doesn't make them *bad.* Children should also be told that nothing they can do or wish will cause the person or pet to come back to life.

Let the child know what to expect. If the child is to attend the funeral, it is important that someone close to the child prepares the child ahead of time by explaining the things that will happen, what the child will see, what people will say and how people will act. (Check with the child's family to see if they want you to help with this.)

Be available as an adult friend to take the child out of the family home for a break from time to time, or to visit the child and then take the child home for the rest of the wake, depending on your relationship with the family.

Focus on feelings. Let the child experience their sorrow. Adults are often intensely uncomfortable with children's grief. We want children to be happy. Be careful that you do not deny children's feelings of sorrow. Let them express it in different ways. Only then can they move through the sorrow to accepting the death. Instead of trying to get a child to stop crying, by distracting the child or telling the child to stop crying, simply comfort the child.

Do not try to hide your own feelings of sadness. It is important for children to see that real people express real feelings.

Empathize with the child. Let the child know you understand their feelings and accept them as natural. Invite the child to express themselves in many different ways such as talking, artwork, play or stories.

Acknowledge the anger part of grief. Offer the child the opportunity to express anger of this type by doing such things as scribbling, painting, making a mess, pounding clay or play dough, making loud noises or hitting pillows or a punching bag. Talk with the child about the anger they are feeling so that the child is not ashamed of the feeling.

Use puppets. Have puppets on hand so the children can talk through them. Sometimes it is easier for a puppet to express angry feelings than for the child to say it themselves. The child might be more willing to talk openly to a puppet than to an adult. Children can use puppets to talk to the deceased and say things they wish they had said when the person was alive.

Tell children that although they feel sad now, they won't always feel so bad.

Focus on happy memories. Remember together the enjoyable things the child did with the deceased.

Write a letter to the deceased. Offer to help the child write a letter to the deceased. If necessary, take dictation.

Help the child make a book or scrapbook about the deceased. The child could illustrate it, if they are able to make representational drawings, or find pictures in magazines of what the person or pet liked to do.

It can be comforting for a child to have an object that belonged to the person who died, as a token to help the child remember the person.

Death of a parent, sibling or grandparent

The death of a parent is the most devastating loss a child can experience. The whole family will need your empathy and support. The death of a sibling can cause profound or subtle changes in the way a child's parents relate within the family. For some children the death of a grandparent may be the first loss of a family member. Find out how close the child was to the grandparent. The child's grief will depend on how close the child was to the grandparent.

If a family member is dying,

maintain close communication with the family members so that you know what the family is telling the child and can help them understand the child's point of view.

Attend the funeral. This shows visible support to the family and the child, and may let the child know that you know about what happened.

Talk to the child about his or her concerns. The child's first fear is that they might be left alone, that the other parent might die. Adults should tell the child again and again that they are loved and cared for. The child may also feel anger at being abandoned.

Watch for feelings of guilt. The child may have wished the parent, sibling or grandparent dead at one time and now feels responsible. Or the child may feel guilty for being unkind to the person. It is even possible that the child will feel they caused the death in some way. The child may also feel guilty for having felt jealous of the attention received by the deceased.

Respond to the child's needs for reassurance. When a sibling dies it can be very frightening for a child, because of their closeness in age. The child may feel that they will die soon as well. They may need frequent reassurance.

A child may need to work on establishing their own separate identity. Sometimes a child may feel they must replace the dead sibling in order to console grieving adults.

Answer questions about age. How old is old? Avoid saying, 'Grandma was old and that is why she died.' To a young child, a teenager is old! The child may ask the parent or you, 'Are you old?' Try to reassure the child that you expect to live for a long time.

Death of a pet

Treat the grief seriously and respectfully. Grief at the death of a family pet can be just as intense as the loss of any loved one and should be taken seriously. Very often, the death of a pet is the child's first exposure to death of someone they love. Regard this very painful experience as a learning opportunity.

Provide dramatic play opportunities of a veterinarian's office, including a doctor's kit, stuffed animals, cages, and an examining table.

Talk about the death with the child. Perhaps share a similar experience that happened to you.

Do something symbolic, such as plant a tree or some special flowers in memory of the pet.

With the other children

Select one or more of the books listed in the resource section. Reading a book about death, when children have not experienced a death directly can be a good way to bring the concept into the child's awareness, before intense emotions are involved.

Talk about death before it happens. As a routine part of your curriculum, include discussions of what being dead means. It is important to talk about death before children actually encounter death on a personal level.

Take nature walks. They can provide ideal opportunities to routinely point out things in nature that are dead. Talk about the difference between dead insects and living insects. If you encounter a dead bird or small wild animal, let the children look at it (from a distance of a few feet). Point out how it is not moving or breathing or afraid because it doesn't feel or think anymore. Rather than aversion, try to show sadness and respect.

Take advantage of the death of a classroom pet. It can be a good educational experience. Have a funeral for a classroom pet that dies. Let the children decorate a box, dig a hole, bury the box, sing a song and tell stories or recount memories about the pet. Ritual is important. The children may reenact this in their play.

Find out how things decay. To help children understand what happens to a body of a buried pet after death, you might let them see something else decay, such as a pumpkin or a piece of fruit. You could put this in a heavy, zip-close plastic bag or a sealable plastic container and examine it every few days. Try not to express revulsion, but help children see it as a process of nature. Think about what would happen if things did not decay when they died.

Death of a classmate or friend

Answer the children's questions. When a classmate or a child's friend dies, they may fear that the same things might happen to them.

Explain sensitively and factually why the child died, and that this is unlikely to happen to them.

The class could make a group scrapbook about their friend and their memories and give it to the family.

Help children think of ways to respond. The children might like to do something symbolic like plant a tree or some flowers to help them remember their friend.

With the parents

Ask the family to tell you as much as they can about the circumstances surrounding the death and what the child experienced and what was told to individual children so that you can respond appropriately.

Show your support of the family by attending the funeral, if you knew the individual. Perhaps you can be the one to help with the child during the service.

Notify the other parents in the centre about the child's death. Also tell the other parents the follow-up activities you plan to do with the children and how they might answer some of the questions.

What not to do:

— Do not avoid acknowledging or talking about death with children.
— Do not assume that children will understand death if they are told 'the facts.'
— Do not tell the child how they should be feeling or reacting.
— Do not seem surprised if a child does not appear sad or unhappy.
— Do not impose your religious beliefs on the child.
— Do not use the word 'sleep' when explaining death. 'Grandma has gone to sleep,' might make the child afraid to go to sleep.
— Do not tell a child someone died 'because they were ill.' The child may fear that whenever they or someone else becomes ill, that person will die. Let the child know that most of the time when people are ill they get better again.
— Do not tell the child someone died because they were old. To a very young child, a teenager is old.
— Do not use euphemisms. Saying 'We have lost Grandpa,' is very upsetting to a child. Children's literal interpretation of language makes words like *departed* confusing and distressing to children. Saying something like, 'Your sister was so good, God decided to take her to heaven to be with Him,' might make the child determined to be very bad so that God doesn't come after them too! In fact, saying that God took someone to be with Him in heaven might make the child very resentful of God.
— Do not tell a child to 'be a big help' to their parent(s) at this special time.

Further Information

Resources for children

Your local library should have a comprehensive list of appropriate children's titles.

Books

Connolly, M. and Manahan, R., *It isn't easy,* Oxford University Press, 1999.
Joslin, M., *The Goodbye Boat,* Lion Publishing, 1998.
Perkins, G. and Morris, L., *Remembering my Brother,* A & C Black, 1996.
Burningham, John, *Granpa.* Puffin Books, 1988.
Dale, Elizabeth, *Scrumpy.* Andersen Press, 1994.
Gould, Deborah. *Grandpa's Slide Show.* William Morrow Books.
Isherwood, Sheila, *My Grandad.* Oxford University Press, 1996.
Limb, Sue, *Come back, Grandma.* Red Fox, 1995.
Madenski, Melissa, *Some of the Pieces.* Little, Brown and Co., 1991.
Perkins, Ginny, *Remembering Mum.* A & C Black, 1996.
Varley, Susan, *Badger's Parting Gifts.* Picture Lions, 1992.

Resources for adults

Books

Turner, M., *Talking with Children and Young People about Death and Dying: A Workbook.* Jessica Kingsley Publishers, 1998.
Smith, S, and Pennells, M., *The Forgotten Mourners: Guidelines for working with bereaved Children,* Jessica Kingsley Publishers, 1994.
Geldard, K. and D., *Counselling Children: A Practical Introduction,* Sage Publications Ltd., 1997.
Ward, Barbara, *Good Grief 1.* Teacher's Pack exploring Feelings: Loss and Death with under 11s. 1995. Available from Cruse Bereavement Care.
Jewett, Claudia, *Helping Children cope with Separation and Loss,* Free Association Books, 1994.
Smith S. and Pennells, M., *Interventions with Bereaved Children,* Jessica Kingsley Publishers, 1997.
Sargoni, M. and Consultant: Dr Dora Black, *Supporting Bereaved Children and Families.* A training manual from Cruse Bereavement Care, 1993.
Heegaard, Marge, *The Drawing out Feelings* series. Workbooks for children. available from Cruse Bereavement Care.

Journals

Bereavement Care. Published by Cruse Bereavement Care.

Organizations and helplines

See Appendix for further details.

Cruse Bereavement Line. Helpline for bereaved people and those caring for bereaved people. Tel. 0345-585 565
Child Death Helpline. Helpline for anyone affected by the death of a child. Tel. 0800-282 986.
Cot Death Helpline. Tel. 020-235 1721
The Compassionate Friends. Support for bereaved parents by bereaved parents. Tel. 0117-953 9639.
The Samaritans. Tel.0345-909 090
ChildLine. Tel. 0800-1111

CHAPTER SEVEN

Separation and Divorce

Example 1

Five-year-old James was driving the teachers crazy with his generally obnoxious behaviour. He was hungry for attention, whether positive or negative. He always wanted to be first, and the centre of everything that was going on. He frequently argued with other children. If any new adult — parent, teacher or visitor — entered the classroom, James would try to get their total attention. James was especially demanding of one father who frequently volunteered in his daughter's classroom. James was always clinging to him and climbing all over him. This father handled the situation appropriately, becoming a friend to James without allowing himself to be distracted from the other children. Then suddenly James calmed down and became much easier to get along with. The change was so remarkable that the teacher mentioned it to the mother one day when she came to pick James up. 'Well, it is probably because his dad and I have got back together again,' she responded. They had been separated for six months, and nobody had mentioned anything to the childcare staff! The staff were quite frustrated and felt that they might have handled situations with the child differently if they had known, offering him more of the emotional support he needed.

The Issue

Other than the death of a parent, divorce may be the most devastating thing that can happen to children. So many things in their lives change. Usually one parent is physically absent from the home. Depending on circumstances, they may have to move. Money may become a problem, and a previously non-working parent may have to go to work outside the home, causing changes in childcare arrangements.

Divorce is not a one-time problem or event. It goes on and on, starting with family stress and arguing, and progressing to separation, custody battles, family adjustments, difficult feelings at visitation time, difficulties with other family members, parents dating other people, remarriage and stepfamilies. Conflict between parents sometimes increases after the divorce has taken place, with negative consequences for the children. Families going through divorce usually feel some degree of pain and tension.

Joint custody is becoming a common practice. Parents with joint legal custody share in the decision making process on issues relating to the child, such as religious training, schooling and medical care. Parents with joint physical custody share in the actual physical care of the child, with the child spending part of their time in both residences. The best way parents can help their children adjust positively to the divorce is often very difficult for the parents themselves: they must try to get along, be civil to each other in the child's presence and not criticize each other.

Whether a childcare arrangement is new or the child has already been in the centre, the childcare setting may be the most stable element in the child's life and the carer can be influential in the child's positive adjustment. The childcare setting or school, because it is neutral ground, often becomes the place where children are transferred from one parent to the other and where messages can be left. Remember that it can be helpful to parents to have you there in a supportive stance. But both parents, and above all, the child, must feel respected and supported. Avoid taking sides or representing one parent to the other.

Insights from Child Development

Seeing parents as a unit. Parents are a package deal to their children, who tend not to think of their

Example 2

When parents do not get along, they sometimes find it hard not to make negative remarks about each other to the staff. The staff may even be the target of their rude or angry remarks, simply because they are the ones who are handy when the parent is feeling frustrated.

One father frequently made snide remarks about his ex-wife in front of his four-year-old son, often on the subject of money or how the child was dressed. Little Matthew whined a lot, cried easily and had difficulty making friends, reflecting low self-esteem and a feeling of powerlessness. The father was also rude to the manager when he learned that his ex-wife had been informed of a change in the child's classroom situation but he had not. This caused the manager to sharpen her policies of communicating with both parents in cases when there was joint custody of the child. However, she also took the father aside and informed him that she and her staff would prefer it if he did not speak negatively about his ex-spouse in front of the child. The manager doubts that her admonitions will have much effect, and wishes she had been able to be proactive rather than reactive in this situation.

parents as separate beings with their own interests and needs.

Children may fear that if their parents stopped loving each other, they can stop loving them too. They do not understand that a husband and wife's love for each other is different from the love that parents feel for their children.

It is common for the child to deny the problem initially, as though they do not understand the information. The parent might need to repeat the message numerous times.

Guilt and responsibility. Young children, because they are egocentric and believe that everything happens for or because of them, often feel that they caused the parent to leave or that they are responsible for their parents fighting. The guilt they carry erodes their self-esteem.

If they are very, very good, then... When children feel that they caused the divorce, they sometimes think they can *reverse* the divorce by being very good and loveable, by getting ill, by becoming a problem at school or by doing other things to demand the attention of both parents.

Feeling powerless. A child's self-esteem often suffers when they fail to reunite their parents. They may feel unimportant because they are not their parents' primary concern.

Insecure children often demand extra attention from the newly single parent, who frequently has much less time and mental energy to devote to the child. As the parent struggles to develop independence and self-esteem, the child is sometimes left behind.

Parents often have diminished parenting skills during and immediately after a divorce. They are preoccupied and children may receive less supervision and less attention.

Children might feel abandoned by the absent parent and fear that the other parent will leave as well. To make matters worse, parents sometimes offer their young child no explanation when they hire a babysitter and go out for the evening, thinking that the child is too young to need an explanation. This heightens the child's feeling of abandonment and can make the child more fearful and insecure.

In situations of joint physical custody, the change-over day, when the child changes from one residence to the other, can be difficult as the child gets their bearings in the new environment and tests limits. This is especially true for younger children.

Aggression and anger. When it comes to dealing with conflict, children often imitate the actions of those around them. Children who have witnessed domestic violence are more likely to be physically aggressive.

When to seek help

All of the following behaviour could simply indicate normal, healthy reactions of a child to a difficult situation. To determine when this behaviour indicates a need for special intervention and professional help, consider the individual child. If the behaviour continues for a prolonged time or is unusual for that particular child, consult with others and consider recommending that the child get help.

Regression. Children under stress sometimes want to return to a time when they felt safer or more loved. They may act out this longing with behaviour such as thumb-sucking, using immature speech patterns, bed-wetting and increased clinging.

Lowered self-esteem. Some children with low self-esteem engage in antisocial behaviour — bickering with friends, withdrawal, aggression, or temper tantrums.

Depression. Extreme sadness, withdrawal, listlessness, lack of concentration and involvement in activities, are all symptoms of depression in children. If such symptoms last for a prolonged time, they are signs that the child needs special help.

Playing up. The child may behave aggressively and get into frequent trouble at school, perhaps hoping to divert the parents' attention back to themselves.

The child may feign illness, develop a real illness or injure themselves to get the parents to focus on them rather than their conflict.

Who can help

Psychological services
A family counselling service
Family therapists or social worker
Clergy members

How to respond

Offering stability, friendship and support to both the child and the parents can help during the stress of a divorce.

With the staff

Discuss positive terminology. Encourage people not to use the term *broken home.*

Examine unrelated issues. Do not assume that all the child's difficulties are solely the result of a divorce. Some issues might be totally unrelated.

With the child

Be available to the child. Let them know that you are aware of the situation and that you are available to talk and listen, but do not intrude or pressure the child to open up.

Encourage expression. Do a lot of activities about feelings to let children know that everyone has a range of feelings and emotions and to help them talk about them. They should feel free to express their emotions (see Chapter 24).

Work on accepting change. Talk about change and do activities to reinforce the idea that change is part of life.

Discourage self-blame. Children need to be reminded that they are not to blame for their parents' divorce or separation. Parents are the best people to get this message across, but the teacher or childcare provider can help too. Children also need to hear that they cannot do anything to bring their parents back together.

Reinforce parental love. Parents never stop loving their children. Emphasize to the child that although people can stop being a husband or a wife, they never stop being a daddy or a mummy.

Stress love and safety. The child must be told by parents, with the message possibly reinforced by you, that they will be taken care of and protected and loved, no matter what the adults decide to do about their living arrangements.

Draw pictures of loved ones. Point out to children all the different people who love them and take care of them (including yourself). Perhaps encourage children to draw pictures of all the people in their lives who love them.

Provide consistency. It may be best if the child does not change classes or staff at this time. The younger the child, the more true this is.

With the other children

Teach family words. Discuss words related to family: newly-weds, mother, father, sister, brother, grandparent, aunt, uncle, cousin, nuclear families, single-parent families, stepfamilies. Build vocabulary. Talk with the children about all kinds of families.

Display children's books. Select ones that represent all different kinds of families.

With infants and toddlers

Notice infant stress. Infants and toddlers cannot understand what is going on, but they definitely feel the stress. They may exhibit more anxiety at separation and may need extra physical contact and comforting.

Do not change carers for the child while the family is in this transition period. Stability of care with a familiar, loving carer is very important.

With the parents

Keep informed. Get the message across to parents that the manager and staff should be informed of any major changes at home that might affect the child's behaviour at school. This message might be included in the written policies of the school or centre and restated from time to time in newsletters, school handbooks or other material that is sent home.

Support parents. Parents feel vulnerable during this time. They may even fear your criticism. They need your support, respect and acceptance as people and as parents.

Stay neutral. Do your best not to get in the middle or take sides. If a parent needs to vent anger, discourage him or her from doing so in the presence of the child. Often parents think children do not understand or are not paying attention because they have heard it all anyway. However, children are not served well by hearing negative things about either parent. Point out to the parent that the child really needs to have positive feelings about both parents. If appropriate, suggest that the parent talk to you in private, or suggest another professional, such as a family counsellor, whom the parent might talk to.

Your role is to present the child's perspective to the parent and make the parent aware of how to avoid possible damage to the child. Share insights about what the child might be thinking if the child reveals something to you.

OFFER RESOURCE BOOKS. If appropriate, recommend helpful reading materials for adults and children and refer parents to other community resources.

The childcare setting is often the transfer point for children who are in the care of both parents, with one parent dropping off the child and their things in the morning, and the other picking the child up in the afternoon. Try to develop systems for this so that there is less likelihood for missed messages or lost possessions. Keep it as smooth and as comfortable as possible, for the child's sake.

Note changes of address. Keep track of which days the child resides with the mother and which days with the father. You may need to call home in case of illness or emergencies, or to send written messages concerning the daily routine or plan.

Keep records of legal custody arrangements.

COMMUNICATE WITH BOTH PARTIES. Make sure both parents receive all written communications, such as written policies, notices of meetings, invitations to special events and changes in the child's staff or classrooms.

Further Information

Resources for children

Your local library should have a comprehensive list of appropriate children's titles.

Books

Baum, Louis, *Are we nearly there?,* Bodley Head Children's Books, 1986.

Hoffman, Mary, *Grace and Family,* Frances Lincoln, 1997.

Osman, T. and Carey, J., *Where has Daddy gone?* Mammoth, 1994.

Stones, Rosemary, *Children don't divorce,* Happy Cat Books, 1998.

Brown, Marc and Lawrence, *Dinosaurs Divorce: a guide for changing Families,* Little, Brown and Co. 1988.

Goff, Beth, Illustrated by Susan Perl. *Where is Daddy? The Story of a Divorce.* Beacon Press, 1985.

Ives, Sally Blakeslee, et. al., *The Divorce Workbook: A Guide for Kids and Families.* Free Spirit Publishers, 1985.

Lindsay, Jeanne Warren, Illustrated by Cheryl Boeller. *Do I Have A Daddy? A Story about a single-parent Child.* Morning Glory Press, 1991.

Resources for adults

Books

Bienenfeld, Florence, *Helping your Child through your Divorce,* Hunter House Inc., 1995.

Grollman Earl A., *Talking about Divorce and Separation: A Dialogue Between Parent and Child,* Beacon Press, 1975.

Jewett, Claudia, *Helping Children cope with Loss and Separation,* Free Association Press, 1994.

Lansky, Vicki, *Vicki Lansky's Divorce Book for Parents: Helping your Children cope with Divorce and its Aftermath,* Book Peddlers, 1996.

Ricci, Isolina, *Mom's House, Dad's House: Making Shared Custody Work,* MacMillan Publishing Company Inc., 1982.

Teyber, Edward, *Helping Children cope with Divorce,* Free Press, 1992.

Organizations and helplines

The Samaritans. Tel. 0345-909 090

The National Council for One Parent Families. Tel. 020-267 1361

Gingerbread. Provides lone parents with support and advice. Tel. 020-336 8184

Parent Network. Tel. 020-735 1214

Family Mediation Service. See your local *Yellow Pages.*

ChildLine. Tel. 0800-1111

Barnardo's. See your local *Yellow Pages.*

NSPCC. Tel. 0800-800 500

Relate. Tel. 01788-573 241

ParentLine Tel. 01702-559 900

Careline. Counselling for children, young people and adults. Tel. 020-514 1177

Save the Children. See your local *Yellow Pages.*

National Children's Bureau. Tel. 020-843 6000

British Association of Early Childhood Education. Tel. 020-7539 5400

CHAPTER EIGHT

After the Divorce

Example

Martin, a successful businessman, was married for twelve years to Yvonne, an alcoholic. They had four children, all boys, aged 10, 7, 4 and 18 months when Yvonne left, leaving Martin to raise them. The divorce was finalized and Martin received sole custody of the boys. Visits to their mother turned out to be extremely difficult for the boys. After several years, visits became infrequent and then stopped altogether.

In the meantime, Martin had difficulty developing relationships with another women. Although he had no difficulty finding women to date, relationships with them never lasted. When they encountered his troop of rowdy and by now hostile sons, they would disappear, some after just a few dates. Because his demanding job required long and sometimes unpredictable hours, he hired live-in carers to drive the boys to and from school and childcare centre, and to provide evening and weekend supervision. However, the boys were such a handful that the carers never lasted very long. Martin felt that the boys almost made a sport out of getting rid of any woman who entered their lives, be it a girlfriend or a carer.

Staff members at the childcare centre where the two younger boys were enrolled were concerned that the children did not have positive female role models in their lives and went out of their way to give them a lot of attention. The boys adjusted well. The manager also gave Martin the names of several family therapists, which Martin gratefully accepted. They continue to lend support and care to this family.

The Issue

When divorced parents get on with their lives and develop new relationships, their children — who may still be struggling with their grief, anger and fears about divorce — have a new and complicated adjustment to make.

Young children often find it easy to get attached to a parent's new partner. However, when a parent has a series of new relationships, the child may feel confused and anxious. The child may re-experience grief and feelings of guilt and rejection with each break-up, and may even learn to distrust people.

A parent's dating may cause feelings of jealousy and resentment in the ex-spouse. Sometimes the ex-spouse uses the child as a spy to gain information and even coaches the child in ways to sabotage the new relationship. This is always damaging to the child, placing the child in the middle, increasing the child's feelings of guilt and potentially destroying the child's relationship with the other parent. Also, while the dating parent is caught up in the joy of a new relationship, they may not be as emotionally available to the child and may not notice that the child is uncomfortable with the situation.

As a general rule, the younger the child at the time of the remarriage, the easier the child adjusts to the new parent. Each blended family develops its own dynamics and experiences problems common to all families, such as sibling rivalry, as well as those common to blended families. For example, the child may have had a special, close relationship with the divorced parent, and now resents the new adult partner. The new parent as well as the biological parent may hesitate to discipline the child consistently, fearing the child's disapproval. The child may become angry and demanding.

There are no easy answers. Once again, it is best for the child if both biological parents treat each other with respect in their child's presence.

Insights from Child Development

WISHFUL THINKING. A child may harbour a fantasy that their parents will get back together again. A new partner and new marriage makes this impossible. The child sometimes resists and feels angry and betrayed.

A child may want to like the step parent, but their loyalty to the biological parent may cause feelings of guilt and confusion.

FITTING IN TO THE NEW FAMILY. The child may feel displaced by new siblings.

It helps if parents can manage to spend special one-on-one time with their biological child, to reassure them that they are still special and to reduce problems of rivalry.

It is also good for step parents to spend time alone with stepchildren, doing something fun together, to build a relationship.

Stepfamilies should create their own traditions and celebrations to develop feelings of camaraderie.

The step parent should avoid speaking critically of a child's biological parent.

When to seek help

All of the following behaviour could simply indicate normal, healthy reactions of a child to a difficult situation. To determine when this behaviour indicates a need for special intervention and professional help, consider the individual child. If the behaviour continues for longer than the situation seems to warrant or is unusual for that particular child, consult with others and consider recommending that the child get help.

REGRESSION. Children under stress sometimes want to return to a time when they felt safer or more loved. They may act out this longing with such behaviours as thumb-sucking, using immature speech patterns, bed-wetting and increased clinging.

LOWERED SELF-ESTEEM. Some children with low self-esteem engage in antisocial behaviours — bickering with friends, withdrawal, aggression, or temper tantrums.

DEPRESSION. Extreme sadness, withdrawal, listlessness, lack of concentration and involvement in activities are all symptoms of depression in children. If such symptoms last for a long time, they are signs that the child needs special help.

PLAYING UP. The child may behave aggressively and get into frequent trouble at school — perhaps hoping to divert the parents' attention back to themselves.

The child may feign illness, develop a real illness or injure themselves to get the parents to focus on them rather than their conflict.

Who can help

Psychological services
Family therapists
Family counselling services

How to respond

With the staff

Describe family background. Staff should be aware of the living arrangements of the child, and other details of the family situation.

Stress confidentiality. Re-emphasize to staff the importance of confidentiality. When encouraging parents to reveal situations in their lives that might affect children's behaviour, reassure them of their privacy.

Urge staff not to become sounding boards for parents' complaints about each other. While some of this is inevitable, encourage staff to set limits and suggest to parents the name of local counselling services instead. Encourage staff to role play with words they might use with the parent.

With the child

Offer security. While the child struggles to find their place in the new family or relationship, your classroom is one place they can feel. Plan group-building activities, helping children to value each other.

Encourage doll's house play. A doll's house with miniature people might have real appeal. The child can then create a perfect world where they feel more in control of the situation. Have extra dolls to represent new grandparents, siblings and parent figures.

Do puppet shows. A couple of puppets could talk about their feelings of rejection or jealousy when someone new comes into their parent's life and ask the audience for advice.

Be accepting of all the feelings expressed by the child. Resist countering. These judgmental sounding phrases will only make the child feel guilty, angry and ashamed. Instead, give the child many ways to express feelings. Use creative art, sensory materials and play. You can talk about how people have all different kinds of feelings, and that this is okay. The child might learn she is not alone in having these feelings. Read a story that illustrates that it is possible to have different feelings about the same person.

Destroy the myth of the wicked stepmother. Avoid reading fairy tales that reinforce these myths. If a child is exposed to these stories, counter them immediately.

With infants and toddlers

Offer security. Infants and toddlers need the security of a stable carer. Consider having the keyworker move with the children as they mature and move into the next group. The added security of someone who knows and loves them can provide a young child with security.

With the other children

Stop children from taunting. If you hear a taunt explain to the children that there are all kinds of families.

Make a family book. Create your own *All Kinds of Families* book with the children. Let them look through old catalogues and magazines and cut out pictures of people to represent their families. Then page by page, describe each child's family.

With the parents

Encourage parents to let the staff know when something emotionally taxing may be going on in the child's life. Emphasize to parents that you do not wish to be intrusive, but that staff need to know about such things in order to respond to the child appropriately and supportively.

Find out what each child's family situation is. Who do they live with? Is there a step parent? Does the child have regular contact with the non-custodial parent? As you would for other children, try to get to know or at least recognize any relative who might collect the child.

Be sensitive about family events. Make it clear in your invitations that any significant adults in the child's life are welcome at centre events.

Reinforce relationships. If the step parent drops off and picks up the child, try to make them feel at ease. If the child appears happy to see the step parent at the end of the day, reinforce the relationship by commenting on the child's positive response.

Set limits. Stop parents immediately if they start complaining about an ex-spouse in the child's presence.

Further Information

Resources for children

Your local library should have a comprehensive list of appropriate children's titles.

Books

Hoffman, Mary, *Grace and Family,* Frances Lincoln, 1997.

Adoff, Arnold, Illustrated by Arnold McCully. *Black is Brown is Tan* HarperCollins Publishers, 1992.

Kroll, Virginia, Illustrated by Stacey Schuett. *Beginnings: How Families Come to Be.* Albert Whitman Publishers. 1994.

Simon, Norma, Illustrated by Joe Lasker. *All Kinds of Families,* Albert Whitman Publishers, 1976.

Simon, Norma, Illustrated by Dora Leder. *Why Am I Different?* Albert Whitman Publishers, 1993.
Baum, Louis, *Are we nearly there?,* Bodley Head Children's Books, 1986.
Osman, T. and Carey, J., *Where has Daddy gone?* Mammoth, 1994.
Stones, Rosemary, *Children don't divorce,* Happy Cat Books, 1998.
Brown, Marc and Lawrence, *Dinosaurs Divorce: a guide for changing Families,* Little, Brown and Co. 1988.
Goff, Beth, Illustrated by Susan Perl. *Where is Daddy? The Story of a Divorce.* Beacon Press, 1985.
Ives, Sally Blakeslee, et. al., *The Divorce Workbook: A Guide for Kids and Families.* Free Spirit Publishers, 1985.
Lindsay, Jeanne Warren, Illustrated by Cheryl Boeller. *Do I Have A Daddy? A Story about a single-parent Child.* Morning Glory Press, 1991.

Resources for adults

Books

Burns, Cherie, *Stepmotherhood: How to survive without feeling frustrated, left out or wicked.* First Perennial Library, 1986.
Teyber, Edward, *Helping Children cope with Divorce.* Jossey-Bass Publishers, 1994.
Jewett, Claudia, *Helping Children cope with Loss and Separation,* Free Association Press, 1994.
Bienenfeld, Florence, *Helping your Child through your Divorce,* Hunter House Inc., 1995.
Grollman Earl A., *Talking about Divorce and Separation: A Dialogue Between Parent and Child,* Beacon Press, 1975.
Lansky, Vicki, *Vicki Lansky's Divorce Book for Parents: Helping your Children cope with Divorce and its Aftermath,* Book Peddlers, 1996.
Ricci, Isolina, *Mom's House, Dad's House: Making Shared Custody Work,* MacMillan Publishing Company Inc., 1982.
Teyber, Edward, *Helping Children cope with Divorce,* Free Press, 1992.

Organizations and helplines

The Samaritans. Tel. 0345-909 090
The National Council for One Parent Families. Tel. 020-267 1361
Gingerbread. Provides lone parents with support and advice. Tel. 020-336 8184
Parent Network. Tel. 020-735 1214
Family Mediation Service. See your local *Yellow Pages.*
ChildLine. Tel. 0800-1111
Barnardo's. See your local *Yellow Pages.*
NSPCC. Tel. 0800-800 500
Relate. Tel. 01788-573 241
ParentLine Tel. 01702-559 900
Careline. Counselling for children, young people and adults. Tel. 020-514 1177
Save the Children. See your local *Yellow Pages.*
National Children's Bureau. Tel 020-843 6000
British Association of Early Childhood Education. Tel. 020-7539 5400

Chapter Nine

Natural Disasters and Emergencies

The Issue

Fires, floods, landslides, storms and other severe weather phenomena are experienced by people everywhere. The randomness of these occurrences makes them all the more frightening and devastating to victims. Unlike many personal disasters, which develop over a long period of time, natural disasters are sudden and unexpected.

Children are greatly influenced by the behaviour of the adults around them in times of emergency. This type of trauma, though frightening for everyone, is not usually as psychologically devastating to children as community or domestic violence, for instance, because the child's trust in his family and neighbours is not affected.

Like other types of personal trauma, being the victim of a disaster involves loss and separation. There is an economic impact. There are long-term repercussions. A natural disaster is a 'life marker,' and people sometimes organize their memories in terms of 'before the fire, after the fire.'

Whatever the situation, stress will be felt by the adults, and that stress is likely to continue as people struggle to put their lives together; dealing with transportation problems and financial difficulties. When adults are distracted, they often have less emotional energy left over for the children. Children may feel angry or emotionally abandoned when important adults in their lives are so focused on other things.

If there is a positive side to emergencies, it is that people often come together to deal with the resulting problems. Children will observe people helping people, and community helpers doing their jobs. Disasters often bring out the best in people. They sometimes bring families closer, because when people lose possessions and are grateful just to be alive, they think again about what is really important in life.

'Be prepared!' is the consistent advice for families, childcare centres and schools. All local authority licensing regulations require that schools, centres and childcare homes have emergency plans and escape routes for fire and other disasters. However, having it in the regulations and posting a chart on the wall is not enough. True preparation requires a well thought-out plan for your particular location, assignments of who will do what, systems for contacting parents and frequent rehearsals with the children.

Insights from Child Development

Natural disasters that terrify adults are even more frightening for children who really have no understanding of what causes these events.

How children respond depends on how family members and other adults respond. Adults need to address their own fears as best they can.

Though frightening, natural disasters may not be as emotionally traumatic as community or domestic violence.

Children need reassurance. Adults experiencing a natural disaster are understandably upset and may act in a way that children are not accustomed to seeing. Children may need to be reminded that they did not cause the adult's anxious or irritable behaviour.

Children's self-esteem can suffer as a result of feeling powerless and helpless.

When to seek help

After a disaster **WATCH FOR SIGNS OF EXTREME STRESS** in children. While all children who have experienced a natural disaster or emergency situation will show some of the following behaviour, the child may need professional help if it persists.

LONG-LASTING SLEEP DISTURBANCES. It is common for children to want to sleep with parents after a terribly frightening event, and often parents prefer this as well.

FEARFULNESS.

EXTREME SEPARATION ANXIETY.

HEIGHTENED AGGRESSION.

EXAGGERATED REGRESSION. The child may turn to thumb sucking, bed-wetting or baby talk, in an attempt to feel safer. In allowing regression you can reassure them, 'Sometime you will feel comfortable again. But now we'll help you get through this.'

Who can help

Local professional contacts such as your local fire station, police station, early childhood professional organization, local childcare resource and referral agency will probably have guidelines for emergency plans and know where specific training is offered.

Your local Red Cross group or ambulance association will also have information on emergency plans.

How to respond

With the staff

PRACTISE FIRE AND OTHER EMERGENCY DRILLS so that children and staff members know what to do.

DESIGN A BROAD DISASTER PLAN to accommodate staff needs where an entire community may be vulnerable. Recognize that staff may experience inner conflict, knowing that, in the event of a major catastrophe, they should remain with children at the centre but will also want to be at home with their families. Talk about this ahead of time. One centre's plan is that staff members who have young children at home may leave. Discuss if you can cover for one another while a few staff members go to find out about their own children. It is an ethical concern.

Encourage staff to create their own family plan, knowing that they may have to remain at work. Suggest they plan for other family members to be with their children.

With the children

Some people wonder if they should encourage children to talk about the event or act it out in play, fearing that they will intensify or prolong the children's fears. Generally, this is not the case. The children are already thinking about it. Talking about it may relieve some of their anxieties and show them that they are not alone in their feelings. You may also be able to clear up any misconceptions they have about the event.

PRACTISE DRILLS. Knowing what to do in the event of an emergency makes children feel safer and more in control. Talk about what you will all do if a particular event happens again.

It is important to **MAKE CHILDREN FEEL SAFE** and create stability and routine in their lives as quickly as possible after the disaster.

Let children re-enact the event in their dramatic play. This is the way many children work it through and gain a sense of power and control over the situation.

Encourage miniature play. Offer children small dolls, cars, blocks and doll's house furniture to recreate in miniature the scene or event that they experienced in real life. This makes children feel less helpless.

Arrange group time or circle time. Encourage children to talk about the disaster while others are listening. They can discover that they aren't the only ones who were scared or whose parents were distressed by the event.

Encourage the children to use creative movement to express feelings about the event.

Share your own feelings about the event. Be truthful. Talk about how you coped.

It might help children to draw or paint pictures of their experience. Very young children might just scribble. If so, you might ask the child to tell you about the scribbles and take dictation, if you think it is appropriate.

Write diaries. Older children could make an illustrated diary about the event. They could dictate their story for you to record, draw pictures and put in small souvenirs.

Read books about the event. If you cannot find any, make your own book about it. Let the child help.

Point out all the people in the community who helped out-police officers, firemen, counsellors, neighbours, teachers and hospital workers. Talk about how people come together in times of crisis to help each other.

Talk about helping others. Ask the children how they might help others during different types of disasters.

Do lots of activities about feelings to allow the children to express how they felt in the situation.

Include clay, sand or water play. Children can use these materials to recreate a natural disaster in their play.

Talk about the good part. Children need to know they are survivors. If you concentrate on something good that happened, the children will focus less on the negative.

With the other children

If not all children were involved, talk to the others about what happened to their friends. Exaggeration, even among four-year-olds, can make the situation much worse than it really was.

Encourage altruism. You may have an opportunity to involve the children in altruistic, empathetic activities. Encourage them to think of ways they can help their friends who were affected.

With infants and toddlers

Infants and toddlers show heightened separation anxiety after experiencing a disaster.

Sleep disturbances, fearfulness, regression in toileting are all common reactions. Urge parents to show extra patience.

With the parents

Explain your emergency plan. Parents should provide the centre with current information such as phone numbers and emergency contacts.

Encourage them to be good role models. Let parents know that children usually do as well as the adults around them when a disaster happens. If the parents fall apart and show great fear and anxiety, so will the children. If the parents are able to put the event behind them, the children are also likely to recover faster.

Remind them to keep their children's needs in mind. During a disaster, they may forget the importance of comforting their child.

You need to learn about every family's situation so that you can respond to the children appropriately.

Further Information

Resources for children

Your local library should have a comprehensive list of appropriate children's titles.

Books

Harshman, Marc, illustrated by Mark Mohr. *The Storm.* Cobblehill Books, 1995.

Polacco, Patricia, *Tikvah Means Hope.* Dell Publications Co., 1996.

Resources for adults

Books

Yule, William and Gold, Anne, *Wise before the Event,* Calouste Gulbenkian Foundation, 1993.

Organizations and helplines

Emergency Services: Fire, Police, Ambulance, Mountain and Cave Rescue, and Coastguard. In an emergency Tel. 999. For information and advice about emergency plans see your local *Yellow Pages* for general contact numbers.

Social Services. See your local Yellow Pages.

St John's Ambulance and St Andrew's Ambulance Associations. See your local *Yellow Pages.*

Samaritans. Tel. 0345-909 090

Shelter. Tel. 0800-446 441

Cruse Bereavement Trust. Tel. 020-332 7227

Citizens Advice Bureaux. See your local *Yellow Pages.*

ChildLine. Tel. 0800-1111

ParentLine. Tel. 01702-559 900

CareLine. Tel. 020-514 1177

CHAPTER TEN

Child Abuse

Example

When four-year-old Sarah came into the childcare centre one Monday morning, the manager noticed that the left side of her chin was bruised and purple. When asked what had happened, Sarah said, 'My mum pushed me down on the carpet.' The manager looked at the mother and asked, 'Is this true?' The mother said, 'Oh yeah, it is just a carpet burn.' It was obvious to the manager that it was more than a carpet burn, as the bruise went all the way up into her cheek area. The director called Child Protection Services (CPS) and found out that they had an open abuse case on this family. When CPS came to the centre, they asked the seven-year-old brother what had happened. He said that he was not there and did not know what had happened. When the CPS worker telephoned from the manager's office, she was heard to say, 'Well, we have another complaint of abuse about Sarah.' The manager thought, 'Another complaint of abuse? Why aren't we doing something about this, and why didn't they let us know?'

The Issue

Child abuse is a complex problem which cannot be addressed or solved by a single individual or agency. It is a community problem which requires a community response to support families so they will stop their abusive ways of handling stress and solving problems. As an early childhood professional, you have an important role to play on the team of professionals that addresses the problem.

The manager in the example expressed the frustration of many workers and administrators. Sometimes the intervention is inadequate, and the centre loses the child. Social services are trying hard to address the rising tide of abuse in communities. Work with Social Services to improve the situation, but the fact remains that no matter what, you are required to report any form of child abuse, or suspicion of abuse.

Your role includes identifying and reporting suspected abuse, providing a safe haven for the child while in your care, and providing case managers with pertinent information about the child and what you know about the abuse. Ideally, your role will also include working with other professionals, continuing to lend support to the child and the family, and giving feedback to case managers about the child's and the family's progress.

As the manager in the example indicated, it can be very difficult to work respectfully with parents when you are outraged at their actions. It is no easy matter breaking the cycle of abuse. For instance, simply teaching parenting skills or stress management techniques is usually not enough. Child abuse is often connected with or compounded by substance abuse. Poverty and family stress can also be complicating factors. Often these parents were never parented themselves, and they have no positive role model to call to mind. In addition, the great majority of people who physically or emotionally abuse their children were themselves abused as children, and it is apparent that intervention needs to come from a team of trained professionals with different areas of expertise.

From a proactive, or prevention point of view, childcare settings can support families and parents, relieving stress, confirming their role as parents, and ultimately preventing situations that lead to abuse such as low parental self-esteem, isolation and lack of good parenting strategies. This is accomplished by providing a warm, welcoming, fun and respectful atmosphere. Reach out to parents. Share positive things about their child. Let them know they are important. Develop an atmosphere of empathy, support and friendship.

If there is a bright side to discovering child abuse it is that once discovered or uncovered, help can be given. It is ideal when the early childhood education setting can be positioned as a support to parents, helping to relieve their stress and understand their child's behaviour and needs, and to learn positive techniques for discipline.

Types of abuse

Child abuse is often broken down into three broad categories: physical abuse, sexual abuse and neglect. (Sexual abuse is discussed in Chapter 11.)

Physical abuse

This usually manifests itself as personal injury (for example, bruises and fractures) resulting from punching, beating, kicking, biting, burning, or otherwise harming a child. Although the injury is not an accident, the parent or carer may not have intended to hurt the child. The injury may have resulted from harsh discipline or physical punishment that is inappropriate to the child's age or condition.

The injury may be the result of a single episode or repeated episodes and can range in severity from minor bruising to death. A single bruise may be inflicted inadvertently; however, old and new bruises in combination, bruises on several areas of the face, or bruising on an infant suggests abuse. In addition, any punishment that involves hitting with a closed fist or an instrument, kicking, inflicting burns or throwing the child is considered to be child abuse regardless of the severity of the injury sustained.

Neglect

Definition: Omissions by the parents or other responsible persons that could cause serious behavioural, cognitive, emotional or mental disorders.

In cases of neglect, the most successful examples of intervention work intensively with the whole family and endeavour to build a positive, secure attachment between the parent and the child. Since the abusers often have low self-esteem and associate intimacy with pain, the intervention programmes work to support the parent in having successful relationships with their children. As the parent learns to read their child's cues, play interactively and elicit positive responses from their child, the parent's self-esteem and confidence gradually increase. When the parent feels nurtured and respected by the staff they can then begin to listen and learn. This involves a lot of sensitivity and empathy as well as specific training.

Child abuse may occur in a home where other grave problems are also present. Very often when there is domestic violence there is also child abuse. Substance abuse is often involved. They are adults who, for one reason or another, are beyond their limits of stress. In most cases, adults do not get out of bed in the morning with the intent to abuse their children during the coming day. It is the accumulation of intolerable stress factors and a lack of coping skills, that lead to their harmful actions. They need help. The children need help. But first, the abuse must be stopped.

Insights from Child Development

Infants and toddlers

When an infant is abused by a parent or trusted carer, basic trust is betrayed.

Infants may become limp and **NON-RESPONSIVE**, as though they have shut down and stopped trying.

Infants may have **SLEEP DISTURBANCES** and increased crying, which in turn, adds stress to the family and increases the potential for more abuse.

DEVELOPMENTAL DELAYS are created both by possible physical damage to the child and by the destruction of the child's curiosity and initiative. They are less likely to explore, play with objects, experiment with cause and effect because of severe punishment, and lose the cognitive benefits of these activities.

LANGUAGE DELAYS emerge in physically abused, ignored babies.

Young children

Physical abuse

Physically abused children sometimes become aggressive and hostile towards other children. They identify with the powerful aggressor in their lives.

Other children may become withdrawn and fearful.

Children may act out abuse which they have experienced in their dramatic play, to help them feel a sense of power and control over the situation.

Children's social skills are often inadequate because they have not had the example of problem solving and empathy at home.

If you are dealing with a child who has been removed from the home, you have some added, complex problems. Although the child may be safe from physical harm, the child is likely to be suffering emotionally from separation, loss of trust and the daily awareness that they could be removed from their present home. This can affect the child's ability to develop trusting relationships with teachers, carers or friends.

Neglect

Erosion of self-esteem. Neglect results in the erosion of a child's self-esteem. The child feels worthless, like they are a burden.

Antisocial, hostile, angry, aggressive behaviour can also result from neglect.

When to seek help

Signs of physical abuse:

- **On the Body.** Physical signs on the child's body including welts, bruises, marks, bites, or burns on any part of the child's body such as the face, lips, mouth, back and buttocks. Be especially suspicious if there are both new and old bruises on the child, or if there are marks in the shapes of objects such as extension cords which have been used for beatings.
- **Unexplained or vague injury.** The child becomes confused or flustered and is not able to explain the mark, or is inconsistent in what they say about it.
- **Covering up marks.** The child wears a lot of clothing in warm weather, possibly covering up marks.
- **Ignoring a problem** that requires medical attention. The parent continues to ignore an obvious physical problem that needs medical attention.
- **Injuries more common after weekends** or holidays. The child comes back from holiday or a weekend with an injury. Are symptoms of abuse worse after the child has been home for a while?
- The parents frequently keep the child at home.

Signs of neglect:

There are few, clear indicators of neglect.

- The child may be aggressive or passive and withdrawn.
- The child usually exhibits low self-esteem and poor social skills.
- The child may be overly compliant, listless, apathetic or depressed.
- The child may have poor expressive language skills.

Listen to how the parents talk to the child. Often the most obvious clue is hearing inappropriate, humiliating remarks to the child coming from the parent such as name-calling and frightening threats.

Listen to the child's pretend play. Sometimes the child will reflect these remarks in their pretend play when they are playing the role of a parent. Be careful not to jump to conclusions based on this alone.

Who can help

Social Services is the agency in your area that deals with child protection. Check the telephone directory under the name of your town or county for your local office.

How to respond

With the staff

REGULAR IN-SERVICE TRAINING. All staff must be aware of how to recognize all types of suspected child abuse. Regular in-service training on this topic should be provided.

Find out the **PROPER PROCEDURES FOR REPORTING** suspected child abuse in your area. It would be a good idea to obtain a copy of procedures from the local department of social services. You need to know who should report abuse, who to call, what needs to be reported, what type of information they need and what will happen.

TRAINING SESSIONS. Invite a representative Social Services to an in-service training session to describe what happens when a report is filed. What happens next?

Give Social Services as much information as possible about why you suspect the abuse and where the victim is, as well as where you think the perpetrator is at the time.

Remember, your report is not an accusation. It is a required attempt to find out if abuse is taking place, so that if it is true, efforts can be made to intervene on behalf of the child and start the helping process.

If abuse is substantiated you can express an interest in working with other professionals on a multidisciplinary team to benefit the child and support the family. Since childcare professionals are often forgotten when a team is formed, it is good for you to take the initiative and express interest. You may have direct opportunities to help the child and family, and you may learn strategies for dealing with the situation from the advice of the other members of the team. Your input and feedback can give them valuable information in addressing and resolving the problem.

If you or any of your staff were yourselves abused or neglected as children, talk about it to try to come to terms with it, and if needed, seek professional counselling. This is necessary before one can deal with it in children.

Barriers to reporting abuse:

FEAR THAT THE CHILD MAY BE REMOVED FROM THE CENTRE. This is a legitimate concern for childcare centres in circumstances where parents have other options for care. If parents are told with sensitivity of the report, the centre might eventually be seen as an ally rather than an enemy, communicating to parents the desire to support the parent in the difficult task of looking after young children.

FEAR FOR PERSONAL SAFETY. Sometimes the reporter is afraid that violent parents may come after them. It is true that parents who have been accused of abuse will usually feel anger. In actuality, although some parents will shout and accuse, they rarely take action against the reporter, even when they know the reporter.

FEAR OF CAUSING TROUBLE AND STRESS FOR THE FAMILY. Staff hesitate to report if they are not absolutely certain abuse is taking place because they do not want to cause trouble and stress for the family. If parents know that you are required by law to report even suspicions of abuse, they may even express appreciation, if they are innocent, appreciating your vigilance.

Teachers may **WORRY ABOUT CONTRADICTING CULTURAL NORMS.** One teacher described a family who had recently come to this country. 'In their country hitting the children severely is accepted practice,' she said. 'What right do I have to tell them to change their cultural values?' The fact is that in this country hitting children in such a way is illegal.

People who have had a bad experience when reporting suspected child abuse may be reluctant to become involved a second time. There may be distrust of the agency investigating and treating the abuse, feeling that the previous case was not handled well. These concerns are real and often valid. In any case, early childhood staff must report abuse, regardless of their concerns or previous experience. In addition, while reporting does not guarantee that the situation will improve, not reporting it guarantees that the child will continue to be at risk if the abuse or neglect does exist.

FRUSTRATION AT THE SEEMING LACK OF FOLLOW-UP. Confidentiality laws and policies often make follow-up impossible for the staff. However, staff may offer to keep in touch with the agency and can request information about the disposition of the case, emphasizing their concern for the child.

With the child

First and foremost, **A CHILD NEEDS TO FEEL SAFE** in your setting. They need to know that the adult will protect them from outside dangers and from aggression of other children. A consistent routine with few surprises is also recommended.

The child needs to feel safe in relationships as well. They should have the same carer every day, who knows them well and on whom they can depend. A small group of children is best, so the child can learn slowly to build social relationships and the give-and-take of problem solving without being overwhelmed by too much competition.

When a child reveals something to you, do not express shock or disgust. The child will assume it is because of them that you are responding in this way.

respond to the child in a supportive way:

Tell the child it is not their fault.

You cannot promise not to tell.

Tell the child you will get them help so that the hurting stops.

Try not to be critical of the parent to the child. While you can say, 'It is not okay for adults to hurt children,' avoid saying, 'Your daddy was bad.'

Give the child ways to express themselves. It might help to draw or paint about it. Very young children might just scribble. Or you can ask the child to tell you about the scribbles and take dictation, if you think it is appropriate.

Have many activities and discussions about feelings to teach children that the whole range of feelings is acceptable and there are appropriate ways to express themselves (see Chapter 24).

Allow for a lot of dramatic play and try not to edit or intervene too much.

Work on building friendship skills and teaching children to compromise and resolve conflicts in peaceful ways (see Chapter 24).

In all situations, and especially when you are disciplining the child, treat the child with kindness, respect and empathy. Do set limits, but by your example, show that a person does not have to use violence or humiliation to solve problems.

With the parents

Include information about Child Protection and procedures in handbooks, newsletters, and other communications with parents. Explain during enrolment that you are obliged to pass on concerns, should they arise, to Social services.

Make parents aware of other community support services such as Alcoholics Anonymous, women's refuge services, health care and respite care that may reduce some of the stress they are experiencing, before problems develop.

Consider finding a facilitator and offering parent support, if that is practical in your situation.

When you tell the parent that you made the report you can say, 'We made the report because we are required by law to do so, even if we merely suspect abuse.'

Parenting the parent is often the most needed response. Often the parents were themselves abused as children. They may even feel jealous or resentful of their own children who are getting kind attention from professionals when they themselves still feel needy. This huge issue is out of the direct responsibility of the teacher or carer, but you might be a valuable resource on the team as you help that person understand and respond to the child, and empathize.

Further Information

Resources for children

Your local library should have a comprehensive list of appropriate children's titles.

Books

Pithers, D., and Green, S. *We can say No,* Red Fox, 1986.

Freeman, Lory, illustrated by Carol Deach. *It's my Body.* Parenting Press Inc., 1983.

Freeman, Lory, illustrated by Carol Deach. *Loving Touches.* Parenting Press Inc., 1986.

Girard, Linda Walvoord, illustrated by Helen Cogancherry. *Who is a Stranger and what should I do?* Albert Whitman Publishers, 1993.

Kehoe, Patricia, illustrated by Carol Deach. *Something Happened and I'm Scared To Tell: A Book for Young Victims of Abuse.* Parenting Press Inc., 1987.

Stanek, Muriel, *Don't Hurt Me, Mama.* Albert Whitman Publishers, 1983.

Resources for adults

Books

Child protection organizations often have their own publications and pamphlets. *See Appendix for further contact details.*

Armstrong, Helen, *Taking Care,* National Children's Bureau, 1998.

Pugh, G. and Hollows, A. (Eds.), *Child Protection in Early Childhood Services,* National Children's Bureau, 1994.

Wonnacott, Jane, *Protecting Children in School,* National Children's Bureau, 1995.

Under-Fives Programme for planning and teaching good Self-Defence for Children. Available from Kidscape Ltd., 152 Buckingham Palace Road, London, SW1W 9TR.

DePanfilis, Diane and Salus, Marsha K., *A Coordinated Response to Child Abuse and Neglect: A Basic Manual.* Diane Publishing Company, 1994.

Koralek, Derry, *Carers of Young Children: Preventing and Responding to Child Maltreatment.* Diane Publishing Company, 1995.

Magid, Ken and McKelvey, Carole A., *High Risk, Children without a Conscience.* Bantam Books, Inc., 1989.

Tower, Cynthia C.,*Understanding Child Abuse and Neglect.* Allyn and Bacon, 1995.

Organizations and helplines

Check your telephone directory for any local child abuse helplines or resource agencies not listed here.

ChildLine. Tel. 0800-1111
NSPCC. Tel. 0800-800 500
Kidscape. Tel. 020-730 330
Social Services. See your local *Yellow Pages.*
Rape Crisis Centre. Tel. 020-446 441
CareLine. Tel. 020-514 1177
ParentLine. Tel. 01702-559 900
The Samaritans. Tel. 0345-909 090
Save the Children. See your local *Yellow Pages.*

CHAPTER ELEVEN

Sexual Child Abuse

The Issue

In our example, the major mistake of the manager and carer was to attempt to talk to the parent first. The law states that staff must report any suspicion of sexual child abuse. It is not the responsibility of the staff to conduct an investigation.

Sexual abuse has undoubtedly been around since the beginning of time. Within the last decade and a half, the problem of child sexual abuse has received more recognition than ever before. This problem is not limited to a particular social class or group of people.

Child sexual abuse is defined as contact or interaction between a child and an adult where the child is being used in a sexual manner by the adult. Sexual abuse includes a wide range of sexual activity ranging from non-violent, non-physical offences such as exposure to offences involving physical (and sometimes violent) contact. Examples include fondling, oral or genital contact, vaginal and anal stimulation and penetration, and exploitation of children through pornography and prostitution.

In a great majority of child sexual abuse cases, the perpetrator is known to the victim. Many times the abuse takes place within the family. Both boys and girls are victimized by men and women. Sexual abuse occurs most often in the perpetrator's or the victim's home. Usually the abuse is followed by threats or bribes to coerce the child to keep it secret. A typical pattern of sexual abuse begins with the perpetrator befriending the victim, unless a relationship is already established, such as with a relative or babysitter. The friendship is solidified as the perpetrator gives extra attention to the child. After a period of time, the perpetrator sexually assaults the

Example

Four-year-old Kathleen had attended the centre for over a year. In the last month or so her teacher, Trudy, discovered Kathleen engaged in sexual play with other children. At first, Trudy considered this to be the normal exploratory play of four-year-olds. Several times other children came to Trudy and complained that Kathleen pulled their pants down and touched them. Trudy responded by telling the children that their private parts were their own and that they did not have to let other children touch them. She also told Kathleen to stop this type of play immediately. However, the problem only seemed to increase. In fact, Trudy noticed that other children now seemed to enjoy sneaking off with Kathleen to engage in sexual play. Trudy felt the situation had gone beyond the level of curiosity play. She decided to talk about the situation to her manager.

Trudy and the manager arranged a conference with the mother. The mother, a professional woman, became irate and hysterical when they described what was going on. When the manager asked the mother if she thought there might be any sexual abuse occurring in the child's life, the mother turned around and accused the centre, and Trudy in particular, of perpetrating the abuse.

Kathleen's mother called her solicitor and the Social services. The manager called the centre's solicitor and the same authority. Trudy went on paid leave while an investigation ensued. This investigation showed that there was indeed child sexual abuse, but the perpetrator was the father and not a staff member. The parents withdrew Kathleen from the centre. In the meantime, Trudy, back on the job, reports that the play of the other children has returned to normal.

child. This assault is usually followed by a bribe or threat

Insights from Child Development

A certain amount of sexual play or exploration is normal in young children. It becomes a matter for concern when it seems excessive and indicates sexual knowledge beyond what is typical of young children. This behaviour may indicate that the child has witnessed sexual activity rather than experienced it directly, but there is still cause for concern.

Because children are egocentric in their thinking, they often assume blame for sexual abuse. If people react with disgust or anger when children tell them about it, the child may assume that the adult is angry at them rather than at the situation.

The child might feel guilty or frightened for telling. The child may have been threatened.

Fear of reporting the incident. Young children rarely report sexual abuse to an adult. They may fear that they will not be believed or that they will be blamed.

Reporting the incident is also difficult because children usually cannot tell a sequential story until about the age of five. Even then, sequencing of events is still difficult. They will often start out by describing what is most important to them.

Young children may remember fewer details, but what they recall is just as accurate as children of older ages.

Child victims of sexual abuse often suffer from **lowered self-esteem and depression**. They may withdraw and participate less in the activities around them.

The sexually abused child may express anger toward others around them — including other caring adults in their life who are in no way involved in the abuse. In the child's mind, these adults are all-powerful and he may feel that they should know about and fix the problem.

It is not uncommon for a sexually abused child to become overly preoccupied with sex, and seductive with other children and adults. One child can draw a whole group of children into repeated sex play, so the situation must be dealt with, not ignored.

All young children need touching, nurturing and physical closeness with their carers. A place where little children cannot be hugged, rocked and held is not a good place for them. Staff should talk about what is appropriate touching and what is not. Let the child take the lead. Hug the child when the child wants a hug, not when the adult needs a hug.

When to seek help

Any or all of the following may be signs that sexual abuse is occurring in the child's life:

— **Genital or rectal problems:** itching or pain in the genital or rectal areas; soreness when sitting or walking; blood on underwear; bruising in genital area, or problems going to the bathroom. A young child might simply say, 'It hurts' while pointing to the genital area. Evidence of physical trauma to the genitals, anus or the mouth is another sign.

— **Sleep problems** such as nightmares, bed-wetting or being afraid to go to bed. Nap time may be difficult.

— **Noticeable, continuous regression** of any kind in developmental milestones such as speech patterns or toilet training.

— **Precocious sexual knowledge.** The child's vocabulary might include words not normally used by young children. Unusual interest in sexual matters.

— **Sexualized behaviour.** The child might be inappropriately affectionate, seductive or even sexually aggressive.

— Children often re-enact in play situations that they are unable to express verbally. So pay special attention to the child's role playing and dramatic play with dolls. You might notice a child acting out sexual acts which are beyond the normal experience of a young child.

— **Unusual or bizarre sexual themes** in art or stories generated by the child.

— **Restlessness or withdrawal.** There is often a lot of sadness in children who have been abused.

— **Fear** of a particular person or gender.

— **Reluctance to undress.**

— **Poor social relationships** with other children. Low self-esteem.

— **Indirect hints**; allusions to problems at home.

— **Revelation**. The child might actually come out and tell an adult about the abusive situation. More common statements are, 'My brother wouldn't let me sleep last night.' 'My babysitter keeps bothering me.' 'I know somebody who is being touched in a bad way.' 'I have a problem, but if I tell you about it, you have to promise not to tell anyone else.'

— **Unusual absences**. An abusive

parent might keep the child home a lot and may discourage peer relationships.

Some children show no signs, physical or behavioural, while being abused. It is not uncommon for abused children to do well in school, the one place where they feel safe.

Remember that with the exception of the child's reporting of the incident, all of this behaviours may indicate other problems not related to sexual abuse. While you must not jump to conclusions, you must take some action to verify your concerns.

Who can help

Your local Social Services department deals with child abuse reports. Look in the telephone directory under the name of your town or county for the listings, or ask the telephone information operator who to call in your area.

How to respond

With the staff

HAVE A STAFF MEETING WITH A PROFESSIONAL. It is possible that some staff members were themselves victims of sexual child abuse, so it is advisable on a routine basis to have a staff meeting about the topic under the guidance of a trained professional. The topic should be thoroughly discussed, and people who were victims should be encouraged to work privately with a trained counsellor.

STAFF ARE REQUIRED BY LAW TO REPORT CASES OF CHILD ABUSE. Social Services are the authority to whom you should report sexual. Have the name of the agency and if possible the name of a particular person within that agency on file, as well as the telephone number. Your supervisor or manager will take action. There will be clear procedures for reporting incidents within your centre.

Remember, it is not your role to conduct an investigation. However, **BE FULLY CO-OPERATIVE** with any investigation conducted by the proper authorities.

DEAL WITH YOUR OWN ANGER by talking in confidence to someone you trust.

DO NOT TALK ABOUT THE SITUATION to others not directly involved with the child. Respect the child's privacy.

Preventing sexual abuse in the childcare setting

Although the vast majority of sexual abuse happens in the home of the perpetrator or of the child, it is possible for it to occur in any setting. There are things you can do to reduce the possibility of sexual abuse in your setting.

Hire staff carefully. The law requires that those who work with children have a criminal record check carried out prior to employment. Conduct thorough reference checks on all applicants, including those who work in the building but are not carers.

Provide induction training for all new employees, supply staff and volunteers. State specifically that you will not tolerate any form of abuse. Describe the professional behaviour you expect. Emphasize discipline policies and ways to treat children with kindness and respect. These policies should be in writing and employees should sign a form when they have read them.

Encourage parents to train their child in personal care, especially wiping after going to the bathroom. Although you will occasionally have to help the child, you should also encourage them to do it themselves.

Include the topic of sexual abuse in staff training.

Assign a supervisor or staff buddy to all new employees. Avoid having a new staff person work alone with any group of children.

Do not allow people who are not regular employees, such as students, volunteers, or visitors to be alone with a group of children without a trained member of staff present.

Supervise all staff. Supervisors should visit classrooms without notice at all different times of the day, especially at nap time. Find errands that will take you into rooms for legitimate reasons at unexpected times.

Create an atmosphere that supports open communication. The supervisor should be ready to talk with people in private at any time.

Children's needs come first. Even though it may feel uncomfortable for one staff person to be reporting a suspicion of abuse by another staff person, help the total staff to realize that everyone is responsible for ensuring that children have a good experience in the centre or school. The rights and needs of children must come before staff loyalty to each other.

Make sure children are supervised at all times. Remember, the perpetrator of sexual abuse does not have to be an adult. Sometimes older children force younger children to engage in sexual acts when an adult is not present. Do not leave children alone while napping. Do not allow children to go into the building alone to use the bathroom while everyone else is outside. Pay special attention to transition times when children are moving from one place to another or using the bathroom.

Make sure children can be seen at all times. Take a look at your environment to make sure there are not places where children can sneak off together out of view of adults. While children in childcare need space alone, it is possible to arrange these so that the child feels separate from the group while adults can still see the child and supervise.

Do not allow field trips to staff homes unless there is a legitimate reason (such as the staff person lives on a farm) and other staff and parents accompany the group.

Field trips should be planned well in advance and have a specific educational focus. Parents should be informed about all the particulars of the field trip-times, destinations and purpose. Stick to your planned schedule as closely as possible and do not allow spontaneous side trips. Always make sure all children are accounted for.

Make sure your centre or childminding home is secure and no *unscreened* adult can enter the building or play area unnoticed.

Provide general educational programmes for parents and staff on child abuse. Both parents and staff could be included in the same training sessions. Make sure that sexual abuse is included in the topics covered.

Stop any abuse you see. If you actually discover a situation where an adult or older child is sexually abusing a child, tell the abuser to stop immediately. Take the child with you. Report the abuse to your supervisor. If you retreat, you may be considered part of the abuse.

If you are a supervisor and there is an allegation of child sexual abuse by one of your staff:

— You must notify your manager, or in his/her absence notify Social Services.
— The employee may be suspended with pay while an investigation takes place, providing the individual is totally co-operative in all matters pertaining to the investigation.
— Co-operate fully with the agency conducting the investigation.
— Do not be defensive. Let the authorities know you are genuinely concerned and will work to correct any problems they find. Maintain your professional demeanour.
— Ask what the investigative process

will be. If parents are to be interviewed, ask if you can inform the parents that an investigation is in progress so that they know you are aware and concerned.

— If an individual child or children have been named as victims, be sure to be supportive of the families and children involved. Maintain their privacy as much as possible.

— Notify the rest of the staff that allegations have been made. It is not necessary to give all the details. Ask other staff members individually and privately if they have any information that may assist in the investigation. Refer any witnesses to the investigating authority. In order to limit rumours and exaggerations, give the staff periodic status reports.

—If the allegations turn out to be true, the staff member will be dismissed. Be honest with your parents and describe what steps you have taken to correct the problem. They will probably appreciate your candour and realize that you are not trying to hide anything.

With the child

A child's long-term recovery from the trauma of sexual abuse depends very much on the sensitive and open responses of parents and carers.

If a child tells you about abuse:

— **Believe the child.** Young children rarely lie about sexual abuse.

— **Do not promise you won't tell.** You can promise the child that they will be protected. Tell the child that you and others will do everything you can to prevent this from happening again. Praise the child for telling you and emphasize that it is not their fault and that they are not *bad.*

— **Do not react with horror or disgust.** The child will assume your response is directed at them, not the perpetrator. Guard your facial expression as well as body language. React calmly and respond with empathy. Comfort the child and say you are sorry that this happened to them. Be a good listener. Make yourself accessible to the child to talk one-on-one if they need to in the future.

— **Avoid criticizing the adult.** Concentrate on the child.

If you have a child in your centre who has been sexually abused:

— **Let the child know that you know.** After the case has been investigated, or if the child is new in your centre, do not pretend that nothing has happened. Let the child know you are aware of what happened and that you are there to listen if they want to talk about it. The child must know they are not alone.

— **Be part of the team of professionals.** As the child's keyworker, you are in a circle of adults close to the child. Work with the other professionals to gain insights about the child and the situation and how to respond in a supportive way.

— **Document everything.** Write down and date what the child said and did. Do this *diary style.* Note as many details as you can, including the time of day and the circumstances surrounding any incident. This will help you avoid conjecture and jumping to conclusions.

— **Stop sexual play immediately.** If you discover the child in sexually explicit play, you have to stop the play. Find an activity that the children seem particularly interested in and help them get involved. When they are engaged in appropriate play, you can withdraw but try to maintain an observing eye.

With the parents

Have a parent meeting on the issue of child abuse (including sexual abuse) as part of routine parent educational events. Have brochures and hot line phone numbers available in the centre and include information on child abuse and sexual abuse in your handbook. Let parents know that you are on top of this issue.

Be honest with parents. Where centres and schools are supervised by the local authority there will be clear procedures for managers that will clarify how communication with parents should be conducted. Pre-School Play Associations may also have similar guidance. Managers should have procedures for communication with parents, including what they will do if there is an allegation of child sexual abuse against a staff member. As you would do with the press, give them only pertinent facts and information that relate to their children, and do not speculate or share hunches. A parent meeting with a local expert on the issue of child abuse can clear up a lot of confusion and give parents important information.

Parental denial is a strong tendency in families where sexual child abuse may be going on, as in our example when the non-perpetrating parent is unable to acknowledge and accept the reality of the situation. In other cases, a parent may have been aware of the situation but unable or unwilling to accept and deal with it.

Many perpetrators of sexual abuse were themselves victims of abuse.

WORK CLOSELY WITH OTHER PROFESSIONALS to develop helpful guidelines on how to interact effectively with families in the midst of this trauma.

Further Information

Resources for children

Your local library should have a comprehensive list of appropriate children's titles.

Books

Dayee, Frances S., *Private Zone*. C. Franklin Publishers, 1987.

Girard, Linda Walvoord, illustrated by Rodney Pate, *My Body Is Private.* Albert Whitman Publishers, 1992.

Porett, Jane, illustrated by S. Dmitri Lipczenko, *When I Was Little Like You.* Child Welfare League of America, 1993.

Sanford, Doris, illustrated by Graci Evans and Ruth Gregory. *I Can't Talk About It.* Multnomah Press, 1986.

Sanford, Doris, illustrated by Graci Evans. *Something Must Be Wrong With Me: A Boy's Book about Sexual Abuse.* Multomah Press, 1993.

Pithers, D., and Green, S. *We can say No,* Red Fox, 1986.

Freeman, Lory, illustrated by Carol Deach. *It's my Body.* Parenting Press Inc., 1983.

Freeman, Lory, illustrated by Carol Deach. *Loving Touches.* Parenting Press Inc., 1986.

Girard, Linda Walvoord, illustrated by Helen Cogancherry. *Who is a Stranger and what should I do?* Albert Whitman Publishers, 1993.

Kehoe, Patricia, illustrated by Carol Deach. *Something Happened and I'm Scared To Tell: A Book for Young Victims of Abuse.* Parenting Press Inc., 1987.

Stanek, Muriel, *Don't Hurt Me, Mama.* Albert Whitman Publishers, 1983.

Resources for adults

Books

Adams, C., Fay, J., and Fawkes, A.G., *Helping your Child recover from Sexual Abuse.* University of Washington Press, 1992.

Black, Claudia, *It Will Never Happen to Me.* Ballantine Books, 1987.

DePanfilis, Diane and Salus, Marsha K., *A Co-ordinated Response to Child Abuse and Neglect: A Basic Manual.* Diane Publishing Company, 1994.

Koralek, Derry, *Carers of Young Children: Preventing and Responding to Child Maltreatment.* Diane Publishing Company, 1995.

Tower, Cynthia C., *Understanding Child Abuse and Neglect.* Allyn and Bacon, 1995.

Protecting Children: a Guide for Social Workers undertaking a comprehensive Assessment. Her Majesty's Stationery Office (HMSO).

Protection of Children from above: the Role of Education Authorities, Schools and Teachers, Her Majesty's Stationery Office (HMSO).

The Abuse of Children in Daycare Settings. A conference report. Available from the NSPCC Training Centre, 3 Gilmour Close, Beaumont Leys, Leicester.

Under-Fives Programme for planning and teaching good Self-Defence for Children. Available from Kidscape Ltd., 152 Buckingham Palace Road, London, SW1W 9TR.

Armstrong, Helen, *Taking Care,* National Children's Bureau, 1998.

Pugh, G. and Hollows, A. (Eds.), *Child Protection in Early Childhood Services,* National Children's Bureau, 1994.

Wonnacott, Jane, *Protecting Children in School,* National Children's Bureau, 1995.

DePanfilis, Diane and Salus, Marsha K., *A Coordinated Response to Child Abuse and Neglect: A Basic Manual.* Diane Publishing Company, 1994.

Koralek, Derry, *Carers of Young Children: Preventing and Responding to Child Maltreatment.* Diane Publishing Company, 1995.

Magid, Ken and McKelvey, Carole A., *High Risk, Children without a Conscience.* Bantam Books, Inc., 1989.

Tower, Cynthia C.,*Understanding Child Abuse and Neglect.* Allyn and Bacon, 1995.

Organizations and helplines

Check your telephone directory for any local helplines or other resource agencies not listed here.

ChildLine. Tel. 0800-1111

NSPCC. Tel. 0800-800 500

Kidscape. Tel. 020-730 330

Social Services. See your local *Yellow Pages.*

Rape Crisis Centre. Tel. 020-446 441

CareLine. Tel. 020-514 1177

ParentLine. Tel. 01702-559 900

The Samaritans. Tel. 0345-909 090

Save the Children. See your local *Yellow Pages.*

CHAPTER TWELVE

Domestic Violence

Example

Monica, a quiet, fearful four-year-old, was being particularly nervous one morning. During their morning circle time when all the children sit down together to plan the day she blurted out, 'I just wish my daddy would stop hitting my mummy.' Her teacher, Diane, was taken aback and did not know how to respond. All the children became quiet and looked at her. Diane said to Monica, 'I'm really sorry that happened, Monica. I wish he wouldn't hit her too.' After the children left, Diane called the local social worker in the small rural community where they live. The social worker was already aware of the domestic violence and substance abuse in this family. There had been numerous previous incidents. Nobody had given this information to the teachers. As far as Diane could tell, nothing had happened. Monica mentioned this type of thing several times in later months, so the abuse seemed to be continuing. Each time, Diane reported it. Finally Monica and her sister were withdrawn from the centre and the family moved away.

The Issue

The greatest percentage of violence witnessed by children is domestic violence. It is also the single major cause of injury to women. Nearly half of the men who abuse their wives also abuse their children. Whether or not they are personally the target of abuse, watching their mothers being beaten by their fathers is extremely traumatic for children.

The causes of domestic violence are complex and interrelated. Often, substance abuse, or addiction to alcohol or drugs, is an accompanying factor. Domestic violence is always associated with low self-esteem and intense feelings of rejection on the part of the perpetrator. It is about power and control. It is usually, but not always, the man (the husband or boyfriend) who beats the woman.

It is often a repeated cycle. The child who witnesses domestic violence may see this as an acceptable way of life. Children growing up in such homes do not know what a healthy relationship is. Boys often become abusers themselves, identifying with their fathers. Girls often become victims in their own adult relationships, seeing violence as a normal fact of life that women must simply put up with, or even see it as a proof of affection.

Since the effects of witnessing domestic violence are so profound on children it has been described as emotional child abuse. If it is classified as child abuse, it means that as mandated reporters, if a child reports witnessing such an event to a staff member, the carer must report it to their supervisor or manager, who will seek advice from Social Services.

Often domestic violence is guarded as an ugly family secret. Children learn early on not to talk about it. However, young children are not very good at keeping secrets, and the teachers of young children are more likely than primary school teachers to hear reports of battering. While a teacher may say to themselves, 'I don't want to be hearing about this,' there is a need to break the silence around this issue. Finding the support for this family in crisis can be the beginning of their recovery. You can make a difference.

Insights from Child Development

This kind of violence is very damaging. It robs the child of the feeling of personal safety, since it is perpetrated by someone the child knows. **Fear and vulnerability** replace the basic trust they need to thrive and develop. The child has no solid base, nobody they can truly depend on to make their world stable.

A child loses the sense that the world is a safe place. A child's emotional development occurs within the context of the family. It is there that the child learns to interpret the emotions of others and identify their own responses, all within an environment of nurturing and support. When this disappears, the child loses the sense that the world is a safe place and that there is sense in people's actions. The family plays a crucial role in supporting the child in recovery from trauma. In cases of spouse abuse, this support becomes unavailable.

Children have the psychological choice of remaining helpless or identifying with the aggressor. It is not surprising that some children find it safer to identify with the powerful one. The outcome is that these children (frequently boys) become more violent and aggressive in interactions with others.

Aggression has been their only example in problem solving and they adopt this method themselves to get what they want. This mode of interaction gets in the way of developing solid friendships and good peer relationships, an important factor in resiliency against stress.

Children may become fearful and withdrawn. Some children, usually but not exclusively girls, become fearful and withdrawn. They try very hard to blend in and not make waves, not get noticed. They see the world as a hostile place.

Young children often blame themselves for causing a parent's anger. They do not have the skill to see situations from someone else's point of view and assess incidents that led up to the violence. Their self-esteem suffers.

Older children may blame themselves for not intervening or preventing the attack. They feel helpless and ashamed.

Children may *block it out*. They learn not to feel, not to empathize.

Children often have **difficulty concentrating at school**, thinking instead about what might be going on at home. This has a major impact on the child's ability to learn.

Children who accompany their mothers to take refuge in shelters continue to have problems, even in a safe environment. They suffer from the trauma of moving and losing their familiar surroundings, their points of reference, their favourite objects and toys and their friends. School-aged children especially miss the social supports of peers they knew in the neighbourhood and at school.

Children may suffer from post-traumatic stress, resulting from feelings of being overwhelmed and helpless.

The adults may unable to help their children. It is not surprising that when adults are traumatized by violence they may be less sensitive to their children. They fail to act as moderators for the child, helping the child make sense of it, as they might in other frightening situations.

Young children may accept family violence as a normal way of life. However, when they go to school, make friends, visit other homes, they learn that this is not the way it is in all families. Then children may feel embarrassed and angry. It is not uncommon, however, for these families to feel isolated. Children are sometimes not encouraged to have friendships or participate in school activities.

There may be severe problems in these families. Families where there is spouse abuse are deeply troubled families where there is often loud verbal fighting, and separation and divorce (see Chapter 7 on separation and divorce).

When to seek help

The young child might tell you of the incident. Or, you might see re-enactments in the child's dramatic play.

The child tries not to make waves. Tries not to be noticed.

The child becomes aggressive.

The child becomes excessively fearful. They might have more difficulty separating from the parent.

Children develop sleep disorders, wake up frequently or have nightmares.

School-aged children have trouble concentrating and school work suffers.

Sad demeanour.

Who can help

Local Police forces
Local social services (in some places called Child Protective Services)
Refuges for battered women (Social Services should be able to put victims in touch with these.)
Citizen Advice Bureau
Rape crisis centres.
Health workers: family doctors, health visitors
Child psychologists
Women's Aid National Helpline.

How to respond

With the staff

Offer support for the staff to work through the overwhelming nature of these stories and to support each other. Some staff may have experienced similar scenes as a child and need to deal with that in order to be effective and professional with the child.

Offer staff training about the

dynamics of domestic violence. People often need help in understanding why a woman (or man) could allow such abuse to go on, especially in the presence of a child.. They must learn not to blame the victim and explore how to be most supportive.

Be sure you know the **PROCEDURES FOR REPORTING** when you encounter an incident of a child reporting domestic violence.

WORK WITH OTHER PROFESSIONALS. Working in collaboration with other community support agencies, can be a helpful agent in supporting this family. You can encourage them to seek help, let the parents know how it impacts the child, and help parents with parenting skills.

With the child

Be an empathetic, listening carer. Establish a good relationship with the child. This is vital. The child can learn to use a secure and trusting relationship with an adult. You can become one stable place for the child.

AVOID EMBARRASSING THE CHILD. Children learn early not to say anything and to pretend that all is fine. Avoid embarrassing the child in front of other children when this topic is discussed. Remain available to the child, and encourage the child to talk to you about the subject.

Let the child know you are available. While you do not want to pry, if you learn of it from someone else let the child know that you know what went on and that you are available to talk if they want to. Make yourself accessible to the child.

BE OPEN AND EMPATHETIC. If the child reveals it to you, be open and empathetic to what the child is feeling. Be careful not to show shock or disgust when the child talks about it because the child may interpret that as criticism of themselves rather than your reaction to the situation, and may be embarrassed to share anything more.

VALIDATE THE CHILD'S FEELINGS. Let the child know that their fear, pain and anger are normal and understandable in such situations. Let them know that it is okay to have those feelings.

You cannot promise not to tell.

LET THE CHILD KNOW THAT THEY DID NOT CAUSE THE VIOLENCE. Be sure to communicate to the child that they did not cause one parent to attack the other. This can be difficult when it was an argument about the child that started the violence, as it sometimes is. Let the child know that there are many ways to express anger and that they did not cause the violence.

Help the child think about what they can do if it happens again, and ways to cope with traumatic situations. Help them plan a strategy. Which adults can they talk to? How can he maximize their own personal safety? Is there a safe place the child can go? To their room? To a neighbour's house?

Give children many constructive opportunities to express their feelings, by drawing about it or just using materials to express emotions as in creative movement and playing with clay. Children may also feel some relief when they act it out in their dramatic play.

If a child becomes more aggressive, work to help the child learn ways to channel aggression and anger (see Chapter 24).

If the child is withdrawn, consciously include the child in fun activities and give the child encouragement to express feelings. Also facilitate that child's friendship with at least one other child.

Reinforce the child's feelings of competence and self-esteem, since witnessing domestic violence often makes them feel guilty, vulnerable and helpless.

Help the child feel powerful. Give the child lots of ways to have power in the classroom environment. Ask the child's opinion about where to put things. Involve the children if you change the room arrangement. Have materials available which make them feel powerful — big blocks, clay, art or riding toys.

With the other children

Teach all children about using 999.

Talk a lot about different ways to deal with anger.

Set clear boundaries of safety and interactions, so the child will not have to test them so often. Set basic ground rules.

Build a sense of community in the classroom. Caring for each other, helping each other, talking things over, problem solving together.

Provide time, space and equipment for lots of dramatic play. Do not edit their play. If you are uncomfortable about the play, discuss it with your supervisor. However, stop children's play if it becomes sexual.

Offer to write down their stories on a routine basis, without judgement or editing. Then, if traumatic events occur, this will be an easy, everyday avenue of expression.

With the parents

Have information and pamphlets available for all parents about domestic violence and safe houses in your area as well as general family counselling services. You could place pamphlets in a display rack in your lobby, include them routinely in enrolment information.

TALK WITH THE PARENT. If you know that one parent has been the victim of spouse abuse that the child has witnessed, talk to that parent about how such scenes affect children. Perhaps the parent is unaware that the child is also traumatized. Sometimes this is the push that is needed to get that parent to seek help or to leave for safe shelter.

Know about available resources in your community, such as counselling services and refuges.

Work to build the self-esteem of the victim parent. If you sense that this person tries hard to be a good parent, mention that. Offer warmth and friendship and a feeling of respect.

FOCUS ON THE MUTUAL CONCERN ABOUT THE CHILD. In dealing with the parent, focus on the mutual circle of concern about the child. Assume that parents do love their children. Talk to them from the point of view of the child. Become an advocate for the child.

TRY TO UNDERSTAND THE PARENT'S POSITION. Working with the parents, try to eliminate the question, 'How could they...?' from your mind. It is unproductive. Be available for the parent. Make them feel comfortable in your setting. Talk. Share. Try to understand the parent and his or her situation. Being able to talk to a trusted person about it helps.

With infants and toddlers

For children under the age of two, working directly with the parents is the most helpful strategy.

Even very young children are aware of the situation. Parents may think a young infant is oblivious to fighting and is therefore unaffected. This is not true. The child is aware of tension and becomes more tense themselves. They may cry more, and have sleep and feeding problems, which in turn increase tension in the parents, which may lead to more abuse. Therefore, counsel the parents that fighting and tension in the child's presence does affect the child, and encourage them to get help in working out their problems.

Parents may have less emotional energy left for the child. When a parent is stressed because of the threat or actuality of abuse from a spouse, there is less emotional energy to be responsive to an infant. Depending on the severity, this can interfere with bonding and can lead to attachment disorders and neglect. Therefore, be a consistent loving carer to the child.

Further Information

Resources for children

Your local library should have a comprehensive list of appropriate children's titles.

Books

Burningham, John, *Avocado Baby*, Red Fox, 1999.

Hughes, David, *Bully*, Walker Books, 1995.

Wells, Rosemary, *Hazel's amazing Mother*, Dial Books, 1992.

Davis, Diane, illustrated by Marina Megale. *Something Is Wrong at My House.* Parenting Press Inc., 1985.

Otto, Maryleah, illustrated by Clover Clarke. *Never, No Matter What.* Women's Press, 1988.

Resources for adults

Books

Jaffe, Peter G., Wolfe, David A. and Wilson, Susan K. (Eds.), *Children of Battered Women.* Sage Publications Ltd., 1990.

Black, Claudia, *It Will Never Happen to Me.* Ballantine Books Inc., 1987.

Eth, Spencer and Pynoos, Robert S., *Post-Traumatic Stress Disorder in Children.* American Psychiatric Press Inc. 1985. Chapter Two deals with children traumatized by witnessing acts of personal violence.

Organizations and helplines

See your local telephone directories for information about other locally based organizations.

Refuge. 24 hour crisis line providing advice and support for women experiencing domestic violence. Tel. 020-995 4430

Shelter. Tel. 0800-446 441

Women's Aid National Helpline. Tel. 0131-221 0401

Zero Tolerance Charitable Trust runs campaigns which are excellent for staff training and parent evenings. They also have a wide range of publications and information. Tel. 0131-221 9505

ChildLine. Tel. 0800-1111

NSPCC. Tel. 0800-800 500

The Forum on Children and Violence. Tel. 020-843 6309

The Samaritans. Tel. 0345-909 090

Rape Crisis Centre. Tel. 020-837 1600

Social Services. See your local *Yellow Pages.*

Citizens Advice Bureaux. See your local *Yellow Pages.*

CHAPTER THIRTEEN

Substance Abuse in the Family

The Issue

It is a myth that people who abuse drugs or alcohol only hurt themselves. No group is more aware of this fallacy than the people who work with the children of substance abusers, and see the damage done to their self-esteem and general development.

The problem of alcohol and drug abuse in our society is so pervasive that at any given time, virtually every teacher will have children from homes where substance abuse is a way of life. We are all too aware of the subversive damage this does to children's self-esteem, emotional development and sometimes physical well-being.

Should staff be doing anything in classrooms to address the issue directly? Can a teacher in any way influence what goes on in a child's home, or the child's attitude and ability to resist alcohol and drugs later in life? Substance abuse is a family issue and the only way to intervene effectively is to deal with issues of the whole family, supporting a parent's difficult recovery in the context of their social survival.

The staff role is to provide the child with a safe place, supporting the child's emotional well-being and intellectual growth while others in the professional team see that the family receives assistance. The carer might be the person to serve as a supportive and sensitive example to help the parent learn how to interact effectively with the child and to give suggestions for pleasurable things to do at home with the child, building a positive relationship between parent and child.

When people are addicted to alcohol or other drugs, the addiction is the most important thing in their lives. All of their thoughts are directed to where they will get their next *fix*. Parents who are

Example 1

Louise's father, an airline pilot, enrolled his four-year-old daughter in a childcare centre. Louise adjusted quickly and showed a great deal of independence and maturity. A very bright little girl, she quickly became a leader in her class and was eager to take on responsibility and help the staff.

Several weeks later the staff were surprised to hear that Louise's father was going through a divorce. He told the manager that Louise's mother was a substance abuser and had been through rehabilitation programmes four times but could not seem to overcome her addiction. He said his wife had been an alcoholic ever since he had known her, and that she went into rehabilitation programmes with the best of intentions. When she drank, however, she became abusive and violent. He said it did not matter to her right now whether he had Louise or not, so he was asking for sole custody. When the manager asked how Louise handled all of this, the father replied, 'Well, her mother has been sick all of Louise's life. It is just the way things are. We just keep telling her that Mum has to go in the hospital for a while to get better.'

Like many children of alcoholics, Louise compensated by being very responsible and independent. The staff responded to her situation by making sure Louise had lots of time to play, to be silly and just to act like a typical four-year-old. They also arranged lots of informal times to be with her so she could express herself. At this point, Louise is doing fine in the classroom and her dad appreciates the understanding and support he finds at the childcare centre.

addicted to drugs must first be supported in their recovery from addiction before they can focus on proper parenting of their young children. This does not mean that they do not love their children, but that the addiction dominates their thoughts and actions.

It is possible that carers are unaware of addiction problems in a child's family. People are skilled at hiding their addiction and family

Example 2

A staff member in her mid-twenties asked her manager if she knew of anyone she could talk to about her alcoholic mother. She said she had always coped well with her mother's alcoholism, and was proud of how she had taken care of her younger brother and had learned to cook at an early age. Caring for children in a childcare setting seemed to be a natural job for her. But now some of her childhood experiences were troubling her and she found it especially difficult to interact with parents she suspected of substance abuse. The manager put her in contact with the National Association for Children of Alcoholics, where she has been able to meet with others and work through some of her feelings.

members, even young children, learn to keep the secret. Some children, especially those who have taken on compensating responsibilities at home, do very well at school. School or childcare settings become the place where they feel safe and where they can shine for their abilities. However, these children also need special support from their teachers.

When there is substance abuse in a home, there are often other problems affecting the child such as physical and sexual child abuse, domestic violence, neglect, unemployment, poverty, or homelessness. Substance abuse is at the root of many of the most complex social problems.

Insights from Child Development

CHILDREN OFTEN FEEL THEY ARE TO BLAME for the family member's substance abuse. They may believe that the person is drinking or taking drugs because their behaviour upset that person.

THE CHILD SUFFERS A SUBSEQUENT LOSS OF SELF-ESTEEM because of guilty feelings. A child's self-esteem may also suffer because they believe, 'If daddy really loved me he wouldn't drink.'

Because substance abusing parents are inconsistent in their responses to children, children are often confused and frustrated.

LACK OF ATTENTION. Children who are raised in a home where substance abuse is present, even if only one parent is a substance abuser, often suffer from parents not being there for them. The substance preoccupies the adults. The lack of focused attention on the child can cause the child to have diminished self-esteem.

Children of alcoholics often do surprisingly well in school because it is the one place where they can thrive, and where there is consistency.

Keeping quiet. Children in alcoholic families usually learn very early not to express or even acknowledge their feelings.

If children have been prenatally exposed to drugs or alcohol they may suffer a wide range of **developmental problems** including learning delays, hyperactivity and behaviour disorders (*see also* Chapter 16).

When to seek help

— **Recurrent themes of drugs, alcohol or family violence** revealed in the child's dramatic play, stories or drawings
— **Signs of neglect;** child improperly dressed, dirty, hungry
— **Signs of physical or sexual abuse**
— **Excessive playing up**, *confirming* what the child feels to be other people's low opinion of them
— Lack of attachment to family members
— **Hyperactivity**
— The **child seems very non-expressive.** Some children learn early on: don't talk, don't trust, don't feel.
— **Regressive behaviour**
— **Frequent absence**

Who can help

Local groups of Alcoholics Anonymous (AA) or National Association for Children of Alcoholics (Al-Anon).
Local community drugs projects
Family doctors, health visitors
Family therapists, social services
Hospitals that provide detoxification and rehabilitation services
Look under *Counselling and Advice* in the Yellow Pages for a listing of local resources and treatment programmes.
Police drugs hotline number

How to respond

With the staff

Start with introspection. In today's society, many people have some form of substance abuse in their own families. It is important to be acutely aware of these issues so that you can moderate your responses to situations. It might be most helpful to do this in a staff meeting or workshop with someone specially trained in issues of substance abuse.

Find out about alcoholism. Read up on the topic. Possibly attend AA or Al-Anon meetings to know the dynamics of the disease and how it affects families.

Be aware of your mandated legal responsibilities if you suspect child abuse or neglect.

With the child

Develop consistency and security. Keep the daily schedule of routines stable and the number of staff members who interact with the child to a minimum. Maintain small group sizes.

Because the child may have inconsistency and broken promises at home, **be dependable.** Stick to any promises you make to the child. Let them know what to expect ahead of time.

If a child talks to you about a parent's substance abuse, reinforce that they are in no way to blame for the abuse. Also stress that they cannot stop the parent from drinking or using drugs.

Work to develop trust. Be careful about teaching a child to speak out against alcohol or drugs for it may backfire and create angry feelings in the adults at home. Rather, focus on giving the child a stable, accepting environment where they can feel free to play and trust.

Build self-expression skills. Provide many open-ended art experiences, block play, and opportunities to dictate stories of their own making. Let the children know you value their thoughts and think they have good ideas.

Encourage dramatic play. Provide opportunities for dramatic play, with dressing-up and housekeeping equipment, and with small dolls either in a doll's house or in the block corner. This gives children opportunities to play out scenes and put themselves in positions of power. While their play may be informative, avoid over-interpretations.

Do a lot of activities about feelings to show children that everyone has a range of feelings and it is okay to express them (see Chapter 24).

With the other children

Foster an atmosphere of playfulness. Life outside your classroom may appear very serious to the child. Use and encourage humour in the form of silliness and laughter (never teasing).

A child may have difficulty forming friendships and entering play with other children. Gentle coaching from the teacher can be helpful.

With infants and toddlers

Recognize vulnerability. Infants and toddlers of substance abusing parents are at extreme risk. Their emotional development may be greatly affected. When parents are addicted and *high*, or looking for their next *fix*, they cannot be responsive to their baby's needs and offer warm, nurturing care. The child fails to develop basic trust. The world is not a safe, predictable place for the baby. Neglect is common because the parent is distracted. Physical abuse is common because the parent's tolerance is lowered. Immediate and comprehensive intervention is necessary.

Children may have physical and neurological damage. Children who have been prenatally exposed to drugs and/or alcohol can suffer a whole range of effects, from invisible ones to severe physical and neurological damage. The impact on the child has to do with the particular drug, the amount, and the time and duration of the exposure during pregnancy. Effects are often long lasting and impact the child at each stage of development through adulthood.

Foetal Alcohol Syndrome

Prenatal exposure to alcohol can lead to Foetal Alcohol Syndrome (FAS). FAS can include the following characteristics in children:

— Mental retardation
— Hyperactivity
— Over-sensitivity to touch or other stimulation
— Facial and physical anomalies
— Problems in attention and learning
—Seizures

However, not all children prenatally exposed to alcohol will exhibit these characteristics.

Foetal Alcohol Effect

Foetal Alcohol Effect (FAE) exists when a child may have some of the characteristics listed above, but not enough to qualify for a diagnosis of FAS. Developmental delays and hyperactivity can be part of FAE.

Because there is such variability in how FAE or FAS effects individual children, each child needs to be looked at individually. Therapists, together with parents and teachers, should consider each symptom and work up an individual plan for the child.

With the parents

NOTIFY YOUR MANAGER IF YOU SUSPECT SUBSTANCE ABUSE IN THE FAMILY because of things a child reveals to you verbally or through recurring themes in dramatic play, stories or drawings. Decide together how the staff might be able to support the family to aid recovery.

RECOMMEND INFORMATION SOURCES. If other family members reveal to you that there is a substance abuser in the family, recommend information about addiction that they could read.

SUPPORT THE PARENT. If you have a friendly, supportive relationship with the parent, you might offer to go to an AA or Drug project meeting with them, or arrange for someone to accompany them.

Go to meetings first. If possible, visit such meetings first, so you can be sure you are recommending something that will be helpful.

Further Information

Resources for adults

Books

Health Education Board publications:

— *The Crunch: Negotiating the Agenda with Young People.* A training manual which aims to respond to questions raised by youth workers, teachers and managers about the principles of peer education.

— *The Facts of Drugs: A Parent's Guide.* A popular and easily understood guide listing commonly misused drugs, legal information and where to go for help.

Organizations and helplines

See your local telephone directories for information about locally based organizations.

Chapter Fourteen

Community Violence

Example

Five-year-old Jason returned home with his divorced mother after going to a film. When they entered their house, they surprised some burglars. Jason ran to a neighbour's house. After the incident, Jason went to live with his father who enrolled him in the local childcare centre, where he was given psychological counselling for a time. He stopped counselling when the psychologist felt he was doing fine, but his teacher is not so sure that this is the case. Jason told her that he feels bad because he should have fought the people who robbed his house but he was too scared. His father's girlfriend told her that Jason is afraid of the dark and to be in a room by himself and wakes up several times a night with bad dreams.

The Issue

Children are greatly harmed by their exposure to violence, either directly or indirectly. There is no argument about that. Teachers report that an increase in children exposed to violence is the greatest change in the last 20 years. They are seeing more fear, more rage, more aggressiveness, all of which interfere with learning, social adjustment and playing. All children today are victims, directly or indirectly, of the violence that pervades our society.

The examples of violence children see in the media are discussed in Chapter 15. Children also see role models in their lives, such as parents, people they know in the community and sports heroes who solve their problems by using violence.

Even though there is much media coverage and discussion about preventing violence with children, people do not often focus on young children and violence. Children are affected in different ways, depending on the type and amount of violence to which they have been exposed.

As we consider what to do, it is clear that the teacher cannot go out in society and solve these problems. Our question is, rather, how to respond to the individual children to boost their resilience, their ability to recover from the psychological impact and continue to develop in a healthy fashion.

Insights from Child Development

When children have witnessed a lot of violence, they are more likely to use violence themselves as a means to get what they want or to solve problems. Increased aggression is one symptom of a violent environment.

Being aggressive is also one way children compensate for feeling powerless in their lives.

Aggressiveness inhibits children's social development, being able to solve problems and get along with others. These things are vital for later learning and developing supportive peer relationships that build resiliency.

Examples of violent behaviour, plus a lack of examples for co-operative problem solving behaviour increases the likelihood of children acting aggressively, or bullying other children .

Children exposed to violence may be more explosive and quick to anger.

Children sometimes become *insensitive* to violence. They do not care, and do not empathize with the pain and suffering.

Children may become fearful and withdrawn and turn inward. They become emotionally numb to events happening in their lives that are otherwise overwhelming them.

Some of the greatest damage may be to infants whose major emotional task is developing basic trust and bonding to caring adults. When parents and family members do not feel safe and are emotionally distracted by community violence and its related social problems, they are often unavailable to babies and unresponsive to children's needs.

Problems in the parent-child relationship. Parents may be overprotective and restrict the child's opportunities for recreation and independent play. They may be harsh and punitive in an attempt to steer children away from violent behaviour or violent peers.

Adults who are stressed because of danger in the environment are less tolerant of the constant testing of typical toddlers. Harsh reprimands come more quickly, ultimately inhibiting a child's inclination to explore.

Children can suffer from post-traumatic stress, resulting from feelings of being overwhelmed and helpless.

When to seek help

Remember that all of the following may be present from time to time in all children. Knowing your children and their circumstances will help you determine when extra help is needed.

— **Overly vigilant**; the child feels very fearful, afraid to venture out to play and is frightened or overly wary of new people and new experiences. The child startles easily.

— **Overly sensitive** to sights, smells, sounds that remind the child of a direct experience.

— Nightmares and other **sleep disturbances.**

— **Memory impairmen**t, difficulty concentrating.

— **Regression.** Children often show signs of regression — such as thumb-sucking, returning to baby talk, loss of toilet training skills and throwing temper tantrums.

— **Emotional numbing.** The child seems flat, does not care.

— An excessive amount of **aggressive behaviour.**

— Repetitive play involving violent themes.

Who can help

Family doctor, health visitor
Child psychologists
Play therapists
The police
Concerned citizens in the community and Neighbourhood Watch groups

How to respond

Obviously, no teacher in the classroom is going to solve these problems. Yet, the teacher must respond in a professional way when one of the children in her charge encounters such an incident. The teacher can provide one safe haven where the child can relax, deal with fears, and feel capable and powerful.

With the staff

Staff meeting. You might start by having a staff discussion about how violence has affected you all personally. Sometimes these issues need to be dealt with first on a personal level in order to think clearly about our responses to children. Some of your staff may themselves be living in violent environments and may be suffering just like the children.

If your centre is located in a dangerous area, getting to and from work may be extremely stressful in the first place, and staff may feel like prisoners in the setting, afraid to go out for lunch or on breaks. Perhaps some creative problem solving might be possible.

With the child

In order to respond appropriately, you need to know what the child experienced. Find out as much as you can about what happened, what the child witnessed and how the child reacted. What was the child told? Who was there with the child?

Let the child talk about it. Do not pretend that nothing happened and go on as usual. Without prying or forcing the issue, let the child know that you know about what happened and that you are available to talk about it.

Depending on the type of incident, talk about how the child might respond or act if it happens again. What can they do? Where can they go?

Ask the child to make a list of people they can talk to about violence.

Help the child list places where they feel safe in their neighbourhood.

Encourage the child to draw the frightening things they have witnessed or are worried about. Very young children might just scribble, but you can ask the child to tell you about the scribbles and take dictation.

Encourage dramatic play. Young children often replay a traumatic scene over and over in their play. While a child does not need to replay the scene to recover from it, if they do, you can act as a soothing force.

Offer many calming activities. Find out what is comforting to this particular child such as playing with clay, sand or water, looking at books, doing puzzles or painting.

Include opportunities for self-expression. Activities such as squeezing clay, creative movement and dramatic play as well as verbal activities help the child express their dominant feelings (see Chapter 23).

With the other children

Find out what the other children know. If they are not aware of anything, consult with your supervisor about whether to tell them. Rumours among children spread quickly and often it is better to simply address the situation, state what happened and talk about it. If not, the rumours that children come up with can be more bizarre than what really happened.

TALK TO THE CHILDREN ABOUT THEIR CONCERNS. Depending on the situation, you may be able to help reassure them of their safety.

MAKE THE CHILDREN FEEL SAFE. Offer a stable, consistent routine with no surprises. The children need to know what to expect every day. That helps them feel secure (see Chapter 22).

REVIEW AND PRACTISE RULES FOR SAFETY. Frequently review and practise safety rules in neutral or pretend settings, such as acting them out in circle time, or letting children remind a forgetful puppet in your group meeting time.

DEVELOP FRIENDSHIP SKILLS. Support children as they learn friendship skills so that they can develop strong peer relationships.

INTERVENE IN PLAY when you notice verbal or physical aggression and the children do not seem to be moving in constructive ways.

BE A GOOD ROLE MODEL. Be very conscious of your interactions with other staff, parents and children, both in conflict resolution and in general social situations because a child may not have had appropriate examples in their life.

BUILD A SENSE OF GROUP AND BELONGING. Communicate in many ways that all the children in the group are valued and that you all care about each other. Talk with the children about a child who is absent, about how the class is looking forward to the child returning to the class.

INVITE A POLICE OFFICER TO COME AND TALK TO THE CHILDREN about how to stay safe in their neighbourhood. It is important that children learn to see police as people they can trust.

With infants and toddlers

Infants and toddlers are very vulnerable. Infants and toddlers are most affected by the reaction of the adults around them. If a trusted adult is traumatized by the violence, the child will feel it, become more tense and may develop eating and sleeping problems. This can, in turn, feed the tension in the family.

Remind parents that it is important to comfort and reassure babies and be as playful and interactive with them as possible.

Developmental delays are possible. In unsafe environments, toddlers and young children are often confined and unable to explore their environment, which is a vital step in cognitive development. They may have few opportunities to really play, engage in beneficial physical activities and have social interaction with other children. So there is a greater likelihood of developmental delays from simple lack of practice and opportunity. Be sure to offer them opportunities in your setting.

Help parents brainstorm and work out ways in which the child may receive the developmentally appropriate activities needed to thrive. Give ideas for adding safety to the environment for the child, simple activities to offer at home and places to take the child.

With the parents

Parents are undoubtedly feeling the same effects that their children are, if they are exposed to chronic violence. Feeling safe comes first on their needs list, before they can devote energy to their children. Be sure to link them up with any social supports that your centre or community offers.

Times of community violence are times when it is extremely important to reaffirm family bonds. Encourage parents to spend extra time with their children to let them know they are loved and cared for.

Become an advocate. Either individually, or as a whole staff, push to get the support in the community you need to provide a safe environment for children.

Further Information

Resources for children

Your local library should have a comprehensive list of appropriate children's titles.

Books

Morimoto, Junko, *My Hiroshima.* Angus and Robertson Children's Books, 1995.

Stones, Rosemary, *Don't Pick on Me: How to handle Bullying,* Piccadilly, 1993.

Burningham, John, *Avocado Baby,* Red Fox, 1999.

Hughes, David, *Bully,* Walker Books, 1995.

Browne, Anthony, *Willy the Wimp,* Walker Books, 1995.

Amos, Janine, *Bully,* Cherrytree Books (Chivers Press), 1994.

Sanders, P. and Myers, S., *What do you know about: Bullying?* Franklin Watts, 1993.

Cole, Babette, *Hurrah for Evelyn,* Mammoth, 1993.

Goffe, Toni, *Bully for You,* Child's Play (International Ltd.), 1991.

Jenkin-Pearce, S., *Rosie and the Pavement Bears*, Red Fox, 1992.

Wells, Rosemary, *Hazel's Amazing Mother*, Dial Books, 1992.

Resources for adults

Books

Organizations such as Kidscape have information about relevant publications. (*see* Appendix for further details).

Besag, Valerie, *Bullies and Victims in Schools*, Open University Press, 1989.

Elliott, Michele, *Bullying: a practical Guide to coping for Schools*, Financial Times Management, 1996.

Early Violence Prevention: Tools for Teachers of Young Children. Available from the Early Years Network.

Booklet

Children and Violence Newsletter. Published twice a year this booklet is available from The Forum on Children and Violence (Tel. 020-843 6309), which brings together a wide range of people committed to a non-violent society. The focus is on children because evidence shows that what happens to children in their early years determines their attitudes to violence.

Organizations and helplines

See your local telephone directories for information about other locally based organizations.

Victim Support. See your local *Yellow Pages.*

ChildLine. Tel. 0800-1111

Kidscape. Tel. 020-730 330

NSPCC. Tel. 0800-800 500

Parentline. Tel. 01702-514 1177

The Samaritans. Tel. 0345-909 090

Anti-bullying Campaign. See your local *Yellow Pages.*

The Forum on Children and Violence. Tel. 020-843 6309

Social Services. See your local *Yellow Pages.*

Citizens Advice Bureaux. See your local *Yellow Pages.*

CHAPTER FIFTEEN

Television Violence

Example

Matthew spent the morning aggressively chasing and threatening the other children, and several times his keyworker tried to slow him down. Finally, when she was at the other end of the yard, he hurt Martin by kicking him. She later asked him why he had kicked Martin. 'Because that's what they do on television,' he responded, showing no remorse.

The Issue

You only need to spend a few hours watching children's cartoons on television to see that in recent years the images they present to children are increasingly more violent, especially the action cartoon shows. Teachers report that children mimic the violence they see on television.

Weapon toys directly connected to violent television shows are now being actively marketed to children. These toys encourage violent play.

Many studies show that aggressive behaviour in children increases when they watch violent television shows, but those studies are no surprise to staff who deal with such behaviour on a daily basis. Across the country, staff are reporting a distressing change in the quality of socio-dramatic play. Instead of taking on pretend roles and acting out scenarios from their imaginations, children now are taking on roles of power figures they have seen on television. As a result, children today are losing much of the intrinsic value of socio-dramatic play (see Chapter 24).

Unfortunately, it is simplistic to say that parents should simply not allow their children to watch certain television shows. The images are so pervasive that children will be exposed to them through advertisements, toys and play with other children regardless of parental rules about television watching.

Insights from Child Development

FANTASY OR REALITY? Even if they live in a non-violent environment, young children who see violence on television can still be negatively affected by it because they may have difficulty separating fantasy from reality.

ADVERT OR PROGRAMME? Young children cannot distinguish adverts from programmes. In fact, many children's entertainment shows seem to be half-hour commercials for specific toys.

Children often re-enact frightening scenes in dramatic play in order to gain a sense of power and control over the frightening situation.

Even without commercially made war toys, **CHILDREN WILL OFTEN PLAY OUT BATTLE SCENES,** even creating their own weapons. Long before violent shows on television, children enjoyed monster play and other scary games. Through this type of play, children come to terms with their own feelings of aggression.

IMITATION OR IMAGINATION? Re-enacting scenes of violence witnessed on television does not have the same value as true dramatic play, where a child takes on a role and develops a plot with other children. Time spent in mere imitation play robs children, taking away the time they could spend on more valuable dramatic play.

TELEVISION AFFECTS CREATIVITY AND LANGUAGE SKILLS. Children who spend a great deal of time watching television have less time for playing, reading and talking with other children and adults. Language skills are best fostered through reading and active two-way participation in conversations and play activities.

CHILDREN NATURALLY IDENTIFY WITH THE POWER ROLES OF SUPERHEROES, which is not all bad. Children have little power in the world around them, and by pretending to have super powers, they can temporarily reduce some of their anxieties.

When to seek help

EXTREME IMITATION OF TELEVISION. When children's dramatic play seems to be mere repetition or imitation of violent scenes from television cartoon shows.

When war play escalates into actual hurting behaviour.

Who can help

Parents by:

— Limiting the number of hours of television that children watch.
— Selecting. Helping the child select shows that are appropriate for young children and have little or no violence.
— Watching television with their child and discussing what they see.
— Helping children think critically about adverts.
— Formulating policies. A parent group can have great influence by supporting your policies about war toys and encouraging other parents to monitor what children watch on television.

How to respond

With the staff

Discuss problem at staff meetings. This is a good focus topic for a staff meeting. Discuss specific incidents when the children have imitated television violence. Brainstorm responses and ways to extend children's play in creative ways.

Be aware of what the children are watching at home. Watch these programmes yourself so you are familiar with the characters and typical story lines. Then you can intervene more effectively.

Do not have a television in your early childhood classroom. In the case of childminders, where a television set is in most environments, limit it specifically to educational programmes designed for young children.

Many centres have a written policy that prohibits children from bringing toy guns and other war toys to the centre, even for show and tell.

Tell stories! Start by telling parents how their children's play is affected by what they watch on television. Be specific.

Raise awareness. Consider writing a story about this for your local newspaper to raise awareness.

Write to your MP. Share specific stories of children's violent behaviour caused by television and urge MPs to push for regulation of children's television programmes.

Become an advocate. Together with parents write to television when you do not like what you see in their programmes. Also let them know when you do like what they air.

With the children

Encourage imaginative dramatic play. Do not prohibit war play or superhero play, but expand and enhance the quality of the dramatic play by encouraging children to act out their own ideas.

Play with the children. You might join in by taking on a role yourself. Follow the lead of the children in the play theme, but ask questions or act out your role in ways that add depth to the characters and make children elaborate the plot.

Put limits on superhero play. Do not allow children to hurt or scare other children. Because this kind of play is very active in nature, it is easy for children to cross the line and really become aggressive. A pretend punch can easily become a real punch. The adult needs to stay alert to signs that the play is getting out of hand and help the children calm down.

Respect the child's role. Address children within their roles. Use the character or role names, not the children's names, to encourage them to be careful and to calm down.

See if you can get children to move beyond mere imitation of television scenes. Ask them about the character.

Discuss the positive side. Help children think about the positive side of the superhero's role, which involves protecting and helping others.

Have a discussion with children about adverts. Ask if any of them have ever been given a toy that they saw on an advert and were disappointed by it. How was the toy different from what they saw? Tell them that toy companies pay the actors they see on adverts to try to convince people to buy their toys.

With the other children

Create a safe place. Create a place in the classroom and outside where superheroes cannot go. This provides a haven for children who do not want to participate in this type of play.

During group time, teach the children to tell their friends when they do not feel safe. When you notice a child looking frightened or overwhelmed by superhero play, ask the child, 'Do you feel safe?' Then help that child tell the others.

With the parents

Think about developing a non-violent toy and book library. Parents can borrow from the library and suggest things to add to it. One teacher included a card with each toy or book telling how the child benefits when playing with the toy and how the adult can be involved in the child's play.

Further Information

Resources for children

Your local library should have a comprehensive list of appropriate children's titles.

Books

Burningham, John, *Avocado Baby,* Red Fox, 1999.

Hughes, David, *Bully,* Walker Books, 1995.

Browne, Anthony, *Willy the Wimp,* Walker Books, 1995.

Amos, Janine, *Bully,* Cherrytree Books (Chivers Press), 1994.

Sanders, P. and Myers, S., *What do you know about: Bullying?* Franklin Watts, 1993.

Cole, Babette, *Hurrah for Evelyn,* Mammoth, 1993.

Goffe, Toni, *Bully for You,* Child's Play (International Ltd.), 1991.

Jenkin-Pearce, S., *Rosie and the Pavement Bears,* Red Fox, 1992.

Wells, Rosemary, *Hazel's amazing Mother,* Dial Books, 1992.

Morimoto, Junko, *My Hiroshima.* Angus and Robertson Children's Books, 1995.

Stones, Rosemary, *Don't Pick on Me: How to handle Bullying,* Piccadilly, 1993.

Resources for adults

Books

Smith, Charles, *The Peaceful Classroom: Compassionate and Co-operative Activities for three to five-year-olds.* Floris Books, 1998.

Besag, Valerie, *Bullies and Victims in Schools,* Open University Press, 1989.

Elliott, Michele, *Bullying: a practical Guide to coping for Schools,* Financial Times Management, 1996.

Early Violence Prevention: Tools for Teachers of Young Children. Available from the Early Years Network.

Articles

'Superhero Play and very human Children.' *Early Years,* Volume 16, Number 2. Spring 1996 (Trentham Books).

Booklet

Children and Violence Newsletter. Published twice a year this booklet is available from The Forum on Children and Violence (Tel. 020-843 6309), which brings together a wide range people committed to a non-violent society. The focus is on children because evidence shows that what happens to children in their early years determines their attitudes to violence.

Organizations and helplines

See your local telephone directories for information about other locally based organizations.Victim Support. See your local *Yellow Pages.*

ChildLine. Tel. 0800-1111
Kidscape. Tel. 020-730 330
NSPCC. Tel. 0800-800 500
The Forum on Children and Violence. Tel. 020-843 6309
Parentline. Tel. 01702-514 1177
The Samaritans. Tel. 0345-909 090
Anti-bullying Campaign. See your local *Yellow Pages.*
Social Services. See your local *Yellow Pages.*
Citizens Advice Bureaux. See your local *Yellow Pages.*

CHAPTER SIXTEEN

Children with Special Needs

Example

'Birthday parties! That's what I want for my little boy. Birthday parties. I want him to be one of the gang. I want him to have friends. I want someone to like him who's not paid to like him.' This is what the father of three-year-old Stephen said when he enrolled his son in the centre. Stephen has cerebral palsy and cannot stand or walk or talk. He uses a wheelchair and a specially adapted chair and walking frame. The staff at the centre received some special training from Stephen's occupational therapist, who also helped the other children learn how to understand his way of communicating. A community agency also provided a volunteer in the mornings to help Stephen change positions and to be an extra pair of hands in the active classroom. Stephen's personality soon blossomed and the other three-year-olds quickly overcame the language barrier and were even skilful at telling the teachers what he wanted. And, yes, he was invited to many birthday parties.

The Issue

Having a child with special needs in your class is not a crisis, but a challenge. Handled well, it can be a positive challenge and everyone involved will benefit. In the above example, the child required special assistance. The centre approached the challenge positively, encouraging Stephen to take part fully in their activities. The idea of having a volunteer help with Stephen resulted from a staff problem solving session. However, many children who have special needs do not require extra adult assistance and can fit right in.

Childcare is a service often needed by families who have a child with special needs. Most early childhood centres or schools are enrolling at least one or more children who have developmental delays or some type of disability. This is no longer a remote issue. While including special needs children alongside typically developing children is now common, it is not always done well. However, with the right kind of staff training and support, it can be done well and benefit everyone involved.

Benefits to children with special needs

Increased potential. Children with special needs benefit from a group setting when they learn to feel good about themselves in relation to others. Their potential for social involvement is improved.

The child with special needs will benefit from the positive role models presented by peers.

Benefits to typically developing children

Developing tolerance. Typically developing children and adults learn to feel socially comfortable with people who have disabilities.

Many typically developing children will practise caring and nurturing skills as a result of interacting with peers who have special needs.

Barriers

Managing a classroom with diverse abilities can be challenging and require some special planning.

To be most effective, staff should work as part of a team by collaborating with the parents and other professionals involved with the child. This can be time consuming and require flexibility on everyone's part. These meetings do not always have to be face to face. Contact people by telephone, and take good notes.

Terminology

There has been much discussion about what to call individuals with special needs. Terms used in the past like 'handicapped children' and 'special education children' are no longer acceptable. The terms we use now attempt to focus on the whole child rather than the child's particular disability. Therefore instead of saying 'special needs child, put the adjective after the child and say, 'child with special educational needs;' instead of 'cerebral palsy child,' say 'child who has cerebral palsy.' Instead of referring to *normal* children, say *typically developing* children, because a child who has special needs may, indeed, be *normal* in many respects. Calling other children *normal* in contrast implies that the child with special needs is *abnormal.* All of this is done with the intent of treating individuals fairly and seeing them as whole, functioning human beings. Often the best thing is to ask the parents of the child how they refer to their child's condition and the terms they would like you to use.

Although this child may require some extra work until everyone gets into a comfortable routine, you will probably learn a lot from the experience. It will probably be an enriching experience for everyone involved.

Insights from Child Development

CURIOSITY AND OPENNESS. Young children haven't yet learned not to stare. They are likely to ask their questions right in front of the child with special needs. Or you may notice their interest and curiosity or fear in the way they look at the other child.

WORRIES ABOUT *CATCHING IT.* Young children worry that the condition may be catching and that if they play with a child wearing a brace, they may end up needing a brace as well.

FAMILIARITY WITH THE PROBLEM. Children may initially be afraid of the child with the disability, especially if the child looks different or has a special apparatus. The fear will disappear when the child becomes used to being around the child.

When to seek help

The following are signals that including children with special needs requires further intervention on your part:

— Typically developing children avoid contact with the child, showing fear or discomfort.
— Name calling, staring or excluding child from play by typically developing children.
— There is minimal or no social contact between the child with special needs and typically developing children.
— The child with special needs has great difficulty separating from their parent.
— The child with special needs fails to make progress or achieve goals.

Who can help

Child's paediatrician
Health Service therapy services (speech therapy, physiotherapy etc.)
Child psychologist, or other professionals who have worked or are working with the child
Your local professional association may be helpful in referring you to people who do workshops or staff training.
The child's parents
School services: advisory, visiting teaching services.

How to respond

With the staff

As a group, discuss your attitudes toward people with disabilities. Share any experiences you've had dealing with people who have disabilities.

In some cases, staff may need support to work with a child who has special needs. This support may come from the parents or other professionals, and may include training in how to manage special equipment or handling specific behaviours. All adults who are expected to interact with this child should be included.

START BY MAKING THE ENVIRONMENT ACCESSIBLE, even if no children with special needs are presently enrolled. Being prepared shows parents your willingness to include all children in your centre.

Guard against seeing the child only in terms of his disability. Instead, work hard to see the child as a whole person first.

While you are not expected to be an expert in all areas of special needs, you **SHOULD FIND OUT AS MUCH AS YOU CAN ABOUT THE CONDITION** affecting the particular child in your group. Start by asking the parents or other professionals working with the child if they can recommend some reading. Do not hesitate about asking the meaning of unfamiliar terms. Remember that there is a wide range of functioning with any particular syndrome or condition.

GUARD AGAINST GENERALIZATIONS. Realize that children with special needs are individuals and different from each other. Find out as much as possible about a particular child. What are their strengths? What frustrates them quickly? Where do they need help? Are there any particular ways you can adapt your environment to help this child?

With the child

LET THE CHILD GET USED TO THE CENTRE AND ACTIVITIES GRADUALLY. Encourage the child and parent to visit together for a short period of time. Then have the child stay for increasing lengths of time without the parent. Follow up by talking to the parent.

Do not do too much for the child. Give the child every opportunity to accomplish a task on their own, but be sensitive to when the child may be passing their tolerance for frustration.

Know when adult intervention is needed. The social benefits expected with inclusion do not happen without adult intervention. Facilitate friendships and social development. This may be the most important educational aspect of the programme (see Chapter 24). You might get the child used to interacting with just one other child in some very simple activity. Gradually involve the child in more small group activities, like blowing bubbles, that are simple and fun for everyone.

Practise acceptable behaviour. You might try playing with the child in view of the other children, even if it means getting down on the floor. A lot of games and activities that children enjoy can be done on the floor.

Include music in your provision. Music appeals to almost all children, even those with hearing impairments. Children enjoy it on several different levels. They can sit in a circle and use simple instruments such as shakers.

Include art in your programme. Manipulative mediums such as clay appeal to most children even those with motor impairments

Facilitate situations in which interactions with other children are successful and fun.

Plan opportunities that allow the child choices. Art activities when the child can select colours are especially good.

Build on what the child already knows and does well.

Children with special needs are often encouraged to be nice and not create problems. **Encourage them to just be themselves** and help them learn to express their feelings in appropriate ways. For example, if name-calling is a problem, help the child figure out the best ways to respond.

Put behaviour limits on the child, just as you would for all the other children. Sometimes adults, because they feel sorry for the child, will let them misbehave without consequences. This leads the other children to resent the child with special needs, and will certainly not help that child learn socially acceptable behaviour.

Look for books and pictures that show people with special needs

engaged in a whole range of activities. The child needs to see themselves reflected in at least some of the images present in the classroom.

Create a scrapbook for the child acknowledging every accomplishment made in your centre. This will help the child feel more confident and increase their self-esteem. Include photographs of the child participating and their accomplishments, but always ask the parent's permission to photograph the child. Even better, encourage the child to make their own scrapbook or portfolio of creative endeavours.

Be consistent with discipline. When children who have disabilities exhibit behaviour problems, work with the other adults in the child's life-such as parents and therapists to develop consistency in discipline techniques.

Practise special procedures beforehand. Prior to enrolment the manager should develop agreed written procedures for staff on safe procedures for handling medication and so on. Staff should be shown how to use equipment, and practise until they feel comfortable and competent. In some cases staff may not feels that they are competent or fit to carry out handling of the child, or medical procedures.

Have alternatives if the child's equipment should break or be damaged. Know who to call when repairs are needed.

Adapting your environment

Modify your classroom to optimize the child's ability to function. The following are general suggestions. Ask the parent and the physio- or occupational therapist working with the child for more specific suggestions.

Make materials accessible. If toys and materials are out of the child's reach, they may see this as a negative statement.

For children with motor challenges:

— You may need to widen the space between furniture to accommodate a wheelchair or other special equipment.
— Raise or lower tables.
—Make things easier to hold.

For children with visual impairments:

— Children with visual impairments may need the light level adjusted, either brighter or dimmer, according to their sensitivity.
— Round or pad corners on furniture.
— Use Velcro strips as guides for children with visual impairments.

— Have other tactile objects or clues in the environment for identification of areas and objects.

With the other children

MODEL ACCEPTABLE BEHAVIOUR. Without your support and encouragement, typically developing children may shun the child, eliminating the social benefits on both sides. You will need to help them learn ways to approach each other. Be supportive and empathetic. Lead the way. If you choose to sit by the child, play with the child and seek the child's opinions, the other children are more likely to do the same.

ENCOURAGE CHILDREN'S QUESTIONS. They may need to ask a lot of questions about the child with the disability. Answer questions simply and accurately, with a respectful attitude toward the special child.

Emphasize to the other children that although the special child is different from them in one area, they are like them in many other ways. Focus on what they all have in common. Perhaps you could make a chart of common interests.

Children often want to do too much for the child with special needs. Help them learn to ask if the child wants help and allow the child to do as much as possible for himself.

When a child with a disability is especially good at something, like singing or naming colours and shapes, **ALLOW THAT CHILD TO TEACH THE OTHERS.** This shows everyone that the child is a capable individual.

ASK PERMISSION BEFORE TOUCHING A CHILD'S EQUIPMENT. While children are curious about special equipment such as a wheelchair or a brace, they should be taught to ask permission (from the child or other adult) before touching it. Always supervise when a child touches another child's equipment because it may be expensive to repair or replace. Another option is to borrow or rent similar equipment for the other children to explore.

STOP ALL NAME-CALLING. Do not permit children to use words such as *cripple* or *idiot*. This is verbal aggression. Intervene immediately, just as you would with physical aggression.

DO NOT PERMIT CHILDREN TO EXCLUDE THE CHILD with special needs from their play because of the child's disability. If necessary, help the other children work out how to adapt their play so the child with special needs can be included.

INVITE ADULTS WITH DISABILITIES TO VISIT YOUR CLASS so children can see them as people who work, have families and live full lives. Make sure these adults are comfortable with children's direct questions and curiosity.

Invite adults with disabilities who have special talents such as art, music or acting to provide role models for children.

Develop children's empathy. Young children learn the concept of fair and unfair. Use this as a starting point when you try to help them empathize with people who have disabilities.

Help to identify any child in your group who might have an undiagnosed special need. You do not need to conduct formal assessments unless you have had specialized training. However, your experience with children in this age group will probably have helped you develop a sense of the norm for certain behaviour and skills. When you see a child who acts in an unusual way, pay attention. Ask yourself why this child seems different to you. Take some notes and observe the child's play and interactions. Ask another colleague to observe the child as well. Together, decide whether to mention something to the parent and recommend further professional assessment.

With siblings

Siblings of a child with special needs have their own special needs.

Children with special needs attract so much attention that their siblings might feel left out. This might cause feelings of resentment, which could be followed by feelings of guilt. Let the child know that it is okay to have all kinds of feelings and that people can feel many different ways about the same person.

They may play up to get attention. They might see the new environment as a place where they can get the attention they do not get at home. Be sure to give them lots of positive attention for the good things they do.

With the parents

Parents should be your prime consultants. They are the experts on this child and may know a great deal about the child's condition as well.

Understand that the parent of a child with special needs has been under personal stress, perhaps since the child's birth. They may be very assertive because they have always had to fight battles to ensure that their child gets needed services. They may also seem impatient.

Meet with the parents to find out specifically what their goals for the child are and together decide how you will proceed to meet these goals. Contact other professionals, such as speech therapists and occupational therapists, who may be working with the child. Try to follow their guidelines for consistency.

Ask the parents how they answer questions about their child, and use their explanation when discussing the child's condition with other adults and children who ask.

Invite the parent to talk to the other children about their child. They will probably be able to answer the children's questions in the best way. They can also share things about the child that the other children will be interested in-what their favourite toys are, what they like to do best.

Parents of children with special needs are often socially isolated because of the demands of caring for their child. They may appreciate social events where they can interact with the staff and other parents.

Suggesting to parents that their child should be evaluated for special needs is an extremely sensitive issue. Never do this without extensive discussion with your supervisor or manager. Do not guess what you think the problem is.

Be familiar with resources in your community. Refer parents when appropriate.

Other parents may fear that their own child will be afraid of the child with special needs, or won't get as much attention from staff. They might worry that their child will pick up behaviour of the child with special needs, or be injured by them. Usually it is possible to address these concerns to everyone's satisfaction. Tell the parents how their own children will benefit by being in a class with the child, and explain your plan for classroom management so that everyone will benefit fully from your programme.

Further Information

Resources for children

Books

Your local library should have a comprehensive list of appropriate children's titles.

Resources for adults

Books

Hansmann, H., *Education for Special Needs.* Floris Books, 1992.Luxford, M., *Children with Special Needs.* Floris Books, 1994.

Lindon, J. *Working with young Children.* Hodder and Stoughton Educational, 1997.

In their own Right: Early Years Participation (Early Years Network).

Green, Dr C. *Toddler Taming.* Vermilion Press, 1992.

Green, Dr C., and Chee, Dr K. *Understanding ADHD: Attention Deficit Hyperactivity Disorder.* Fawcett Crest, 1998.

Stobbs, P., *Making it work together,* National Children's Bureau, 1999.

Council for Disabled Children, *Help starts here: A Guide for Parents of Children with Special Needs,* National Children's Bureau, 1997.

Organizations and helplines

Many disabilities are supported by national associations which you can call for resource materials. See your *Yellow Pages* for details listed *under Charitable and Voluntary.* The child's doctor or local hospital libraries will also probably have information about local branches of these associations.

DIAL. UK network of disability information and advice services. Tel. 01302-310 123

Disabled Living Foundation. Tel. 020-289 6111

RADAR. The Royal Association for Disability and Rehabilitation. Tel. 020-250 3222

Royal National Institute for Deaf People. Tel. 020-296 8000

Guide Dogs for the Blind Association. Tel. 0118 983 5555

Royal National Institute for the Blind. Tel. 020-388 1266

Asthma Helpline. Tel. 0845-300 0336

British Stammering Association. Tel. 0845-603 2001

SCOPE (Cerebral Palsy) Tel. 0800-626 216

Epilepsy. Tel. 0800-309 030

British Diabetic Association. Tel. 0800-834 247

Disability Benefit. Enquiry Helpline. Tel. 0800-882 200

Health Information Service. Tel. 0800-665 544

Social services. See your local *Yellow Pages.*

Pre-School Alliance. Tel. 020-833 0991

National Children's Bureau. Tel. 020-843 6000

Local Education Authority. See your local *Yellow Pages.*

CHAPTER SEVENTEEN

Racism and Prejudice

Example

Theresa, the carer of three-year-olds, overhears blonde, blue-eyed Elizabeth announce in the doll corner: 'I don't want to play with that black doll. She's ugly!' Nicole, a shy African-American child, looks on. Theresa knocks on the door of the play area and creates a role for herself. 'Hi, I'm your neighbour. Thank you for babysitting my beautiful little girl,' and goes over and picks up the black doll. 'How is my little girl with the beautiful brown skin? Did you have a good time playing with our neighbours today?' Later, with everyone gathered around the lunch table, Theresa points out the many beautiful colours of skin the children have and comments positively about every one.

The Issue

Young children generally play with each other regardless of skin colour. While they notice skin colour or racial differences, they usually do not attach the same importance to these differences. However, their attitudes are forming and they may begin to develop a kind of 'pre-prejudice' that will eventually turn into racism.

Racism can be defined as any action or attitude, conscious or unconscious, that subordinates an individual or group based on skin colour or race. Racism is about power and who has access to privilege and opportunity, and is at the root of many societies' problems.

Children form attitudes about race early in life, learning from the important adults in their lives. An educator's goal should be to take advantage of children's natural curiosity and help them see differences in individuals as interesting, exciting and enriching. Unfortunately, children will be confronted with racist messages and images. If important adults such as parents and carers take a proactive stance against unfair and hurtful practices, they can help prevent the development of racist attitudes.

It is important not to over-simplify when we speak of differences and focus only on race. A family's culture, economic status, education, presence of extended family and community supports, religion and many other variables help determine a child's sense of themselves and their self-esteem.

One thing is certain: society is becoming more and more multiracial. Being tolerant and respectful of people of different ethnic backgrounds and races is essential in our society.

Insights from Child Development

Children know about fair and unfair, and about hurt feelings.

Inclusion and exclusion. These are themes in all childhood, regardless of race.

Self-esteem, so vital in learning and later success in life, is very much connected to competence. Young children must feel valued for who they are. A favourite teacher has an important role in helping a child believe they are beautiful and competent.

Young children, in establishing their own identity, are busy sorting out the world. They notice and talk about physical characteristics such as skin colour, eye shape and hair type.

Contrary to popular belief, young children do notice physical differences associated with racial identity.

Skin colour words. Words which adults use are confusing to children. *Black* skin isn't black, *white* skin isn't white, *yellow* skin isn't yellow, and *red* skin isn't red.

As children get older they tend to seek out friends who are as much like them as possible. This can lead to the hurtful exclusion of others. If they have early, positive experiences with all kinds of people, they will be more flexible in their thinking and more accepting of children who are different.

Special issues for children of mixed racial heritage

Children who have parents of different racial or cultural background are becoming more and more numerous. While they share similar developmental processes with all children, they also face some specific issues.

To develop their self-identity, they have to sort out more pieces in relation to their racial background and may feel confusion about where they fit.

To develop a clear sense of identity, mixed race children need consistency between home and school in the naming and supporting of who they are.

Parents of mixed race children may choose different ways of thinking about their child's identity. Some choose to focus on one heritage. Other parents consider all aspects of their background to be equally important and want their child to have biracial identity. Some parents are not sure, or disagree about what identity they want their child to develop and may need support to make their own decisions.

Mixed race children are raised in varying contexts: some by both parents, some by one of their parents, some with support from both extended families, some with support from only one extended family, some by adoptive parents of a different racial background. All can provide their child with a strong identity, but each context has its own dynamics and specific challenges.

When to seek help

Although racism and prejudice are on-going problems in our society, the following situations indicate when specific intervention is needed.

— Negative behaviour and statements of children become a problem.

— A child excludes another child from play because of colour or culture.

— Children refuse to sit next to a child because of colour or culture.

— Children say racist things such as, 'I don't like her. She has ugly skin.' 'His eyes are funny. He's weird.'

— Direct ethnic slurs and name-calling.

Who can help

Trainers from colleges, advisory services, organizations such as Save the Children and the National Children's Bureau.

How to respond

With the staff

Encourage training and awareness. This issue merits special attention by staff.

The Anti-Bias Curriculum (see the resource section at the end of this chapter) offers specific staff training and discussion topics.

Encourage staff members to think about their own first awareness of racial differences and experiences with prejudice.

Through storytelling, encourage staff to identify the important underlying values and rules of behaviour they learned from their families and what aspects of their culture give them strength and support.

At regular staff meetings encourage people to bring up difficult situations they have encountered, especially if they were unsure of how to respond. Discussing the incidents in a supportive environment can give people insights to use in future situations.

As you plan themes and curriculum activities, **be sure not to reinforce stereotypes.** Be on guard for stereotypical images in purchased classroom materials or decorations. Watch for these images especially in books and festive decorations.

Work on this issue every day. Countering early racism and prejudice should not be a theme or a unit, but rather a philosophy woven into your everyday interactions with children.

With the children

Be alert for comments that reveal racial misunderstandings on the children's part either about themselves or others. Use these teachable moments. Do not ignore them.

Prejudicial statements need immediate contradiction by the adult present.

Alert children when their remarks might hurt someone's feelings, and remind them that it is not okay to say such things.

When you sense that children's remarks are racial slurs purposely meant to hurt another child, treat this as you would any other type of aggression. Intervene, comfort the victim, address the situation and state strongly that it is not okay to hurt people with words or with actions in the classroom or at home.

Admire differences. Speak openly and with interest and admiration about people's different skin colours, eyes and hair. If you ignore race or change the subject when it comes up, children may believe that it is something to be ashamed of or avoided.

Give accurate, positive information. Even if you hear no remarks about racial identity, bring the subject up. Children may hear racial comments at another time or place. They need accurate, positive information.

Use puppets or dolls with different skin colours to talk to each other or the children about how their feelings were hurt when someone would not let them play, or said unkind remarks about their skin colour. The children can talk about how it was unfair. This type of activity builds empathy in a neutral setting, without embarrassing anyone.

Be sensitive to children's feelings. As children approach school age, they try very hard not to be different. If only one of the children in the group is of a different race, avoid singling that child out for observation. Instead, talk about everyone's skin colour. Comment positively on all the children's skin colour.

Notice with wonder different skin colours. Collect photos and magazine pictures of people with many different colours of skin. Make a book or a collage that you can look at often with the children. Let them compare their skin colour to those in the photos.

Notice the great variety of skin tones. In all classrooms there is a great variety of skin tones, eye and hair colour.

Invite people of different races to visit your class, especially if all of your children are of the same racial group. Find out if these visiting adults would let the children compare their skin colours and talk openly with them about the differences they see. If these visitors can do something fun with the children, like play an instrument, cook something or play with blocks, the children will quickly learn that they are no different than anyone else.

Ask all the children to bring in pictures of their immediate family and other relatives if possible.

Collect pictures showing eyes of different shapes and colours. Your interest and appreciation for the variety will foster children's positive attitudes.

Create a body tracing for each child. Let the children choose the colours of paint or crayons they feel is closest to their own skin, eye and hair colour. Put the tracings on the wall with a title, *We Come in Many Colours.*

Collect samples or pictures of different types of hair. Perhaps people you know will donate little snippets of their hair for a poster. If not, you might make a book of photographs showing hair of many colours and textures.

Classroom materials should reflect the children. Children should see images of their own race as well as other children's races reflected in the posters, books, toys and other materials in the classroom.

Collect pictures of adults of different races at work. Include all types of jobs. Perhaps put the pictures in a book about occupations.

Collect children's books that have beautiful illustrations of children of different races as main characters, but are first and foremost good children's literature. After enjoying the story together, ask the children, 'Do you think she'd be fun to play with? Wouldn't it be fun to have her in our class?'

If you hear children say that brown or black are ugly colours, collect beautiful things that are black or brown. Let children know by your words and actions that you think all shades of brown and black are beautiful.

Children may have misconceptions about skin colour and think that it was coloured or painted on, or more commonly, that dark skin colour is dirty. You need to correct such misconceptions. One simple explanation is that people get their skin colours from their birth mother and father.

Avoid complicated explanations. Explaining skin colour to children in terms of geography or melanin can be difficult. Introducing the concept now will do no harm, and children will understand it better when they are older.

Discuss adopted children. When an adopted child is of a different race than her family members, children may ask for an explanation. Say that the adopted child was born to people who look like them.

With the parents

It is important that parents know how you address issues of racial bias with children so that messages at home are consistent with what children are hearing at school or in the childcare setting.

Communicate your philosophy. Either in a handbook, newsletter or parent meeting, explain to parents that you believe in talking about all races in positive terms and addressing related issues with their children. Have a copy of your Equal Opportunities Policy available for parents to read.

Have a parents' meeting on ways to prevent prejudice. Share with parents some of the typical questions and issues that can come up in an early childhood classroom and brainstorm appropriate responses. Describe how children develop negative attitudes and misconceptions about race, and what adults can do to overcome them. Also describe strategies for building tolerance in children, such as providing opportunities for positive interactions with people of different races and talking with children when you notice examples of unfairness and prejudice.

CONSULT THE ANTI-BIAS CURRICULUM. Chapter 11 of the *Anti-Bias Curriculum* listed in the resource section at the end of this chapter gives useful strategies for a parent meeting.

BUILD POSITIVE ATTITUDES. Some parents may respond, 'They're so young and innocent. Do we have to burden them with this so soon?' You may need to let parents know that children as young as two notice and comment on different skin colours and other racial characteristics, and that now is the time to build positive attitudes towards people who may look different.

USE FAMILY PHOTOS. Encourage parents to send in family photos so that children can see that they get their colours from their families.

Ask parents how they have explained ethnicity to their child so you can be consistent. Be sensitive to the needs of adopted children and children of mixed race.

Invite parents who represent different races and cultures to visit your classroom and interact with the children.

INVOLVE PARENTS WHEN DEALING WITH PREJUDICIAL REMARKS. Involve them whether their child is the victim or the offender. Describe what happened, and how you responded. See if you can figure out together how best to handle the situation. Discuss how the parents will handle it at home so you can reinforce each other's efforts.

Remember that few problems are solely related to race. Resist ascribing the child's or the family's problems to their racial or cultural heritage. In reality, very few of their problems may be related to race or culture.

Further Information

Resources for children

Your local library should have a comprehensive list of appropriate children's titles.

Books

Bradman, T. And Brown, E., *In a Minute,* Mammoth, 1991

Pragoff, Fiona, *What Colour?* Victor Gollancz, 1987.

Coles, Robert, illustrated by George Ford. *The Story of Ruby Bridges,* Scholastic Inc., 1995.

Hamanaka, Sheila, *All the Colours of the Earth,* Morrow Junior Books, 1994.

Johnson, Dolores, Now Let Me Fly: The Story of a Slave Family. Aladdin Publishing Co., 1997.

Lacapa, Kathleen, illustrated by Michael Lacapa. *Less than Half, More than Whole.* Northland Publishing, 1998.

Mockizuki, Ken, illustrated by Dom Lee. *Baseball Saved Us,* Lee and Low Books Inc., 1995.

Nikola-Lisa, W, illustrated by Michael Bryant. *Bein' with you this Way,* Lee and Low Books Inc., 1994.

Polacco, Patricia, *Mrs. Katz and Tush.* Dell Publishing Co., 1994.

Rosen, Michael J. illustrated by Aminah Brenda Lynn Robinson. *Elijah's Angel.* Harcourt Brace and Company, 1997.

Shelby, Anne, illustrated by Irene Trivas. *Potluck.* Orchard Books, 1994.

Wild, Margaret, illustrated by Julie Vivas. *Let the Celebrations BEGIN!* Orchard Books, 1991.

Resources for adults

Books

Henderson, Ann, *Equal Chances,* Pre-School Learning Alliance,1996.

Epstein, D. And Sealey, A., *Where it really matters,* Development Education Centre (Birmingham), 1990.

Elfer, P., *With Equal Concern,* National Children's Bureau, 1995.

Abbott, L. and Rodgers, R., *Quality Education in the Early Years,* Open University Press, 1994.

Denman-Sparks, Louise, *Anti-Bias Curriculum,* Association for the Education of Young Children, 1993.

Pugh, Gillian, *Contemporary Issues in the Early Years,* Paul Chapman Ltd., 1992.

Commission for Racial Equality, *From Cradle to School: A Practical Guide to Race Equality and Childcare,* 1989.

Miller, Judy, *Never Too Young.* Booklet published by the National Early Years Network, 1997, and spiral-bound book published by Save the Children Fund, 1996.

Ford, Clyde W., *We Can All Get Along: 50 Steps You Can Take to Help End Racism at Home, at Work, In Your Community,* Dell Publishing Group Inc., 1994.

Paley, Vivian Gussin, *White Teacher.* Harvard University Press, 1990.

Curriculum materials

Crayons and paints reflecting a wide range of skin tones. Available from most school suppliers.

Dolls and puppets for dramatic play, puzzles and posters that represent people of different races are available from most school suppliers.

Organizations and helplines

Commission for Racial Equality. See your local telephone directory.

Equal Opportunities Commission. Tel. 0161-833 9244

Multi-Cultural Education Resource Centres. Contact your local education department for information.

National Early Years Network. Tel. 020-607 9573

National Children's Bureau. Tel. 020-843 6000

Pre-School Learning Alliance. Tel. 020-833 0991

CHAPTER EIGHTEEN

Sexism

Example

Four-year-old Jimmy, Justin and Tommy, usually kings of the block corner, were lured into the housekeeping area by beautiful, new dressing-up clothes the staff had brought in that morning. They giggled and pranced around in feather boas, sequinned evening dresses, silver high heels and broad rimmed hats, admiring themselves in the mirror. Their carer, Debbie, was so proud of them for crossing the barrier between *girls' play and boys' play* that she took a photograph of them proudly modelling their finery for the class scrapbook. Tommy's father arrived at that moment, and Debbie was dumbfounded when Tommy's father was outraged to see his son in women's clothes. 'What are you trying to do to my son?' he shouted. He told Tommy, 'Take that stuff off. You look like a sissy.' Later, at a private parent meeting, Debbie tried to explain to Tommy's parents that when children are four-years-old they often enjoy trying different roles and engaging in fantasy play. However, her remarks seemed to make no impression on the parents, although they did not try to argue with her. The point was clear to Tommy. He never ventured near the housekeeping area again.

The Issue

The example above reflects an attitude that is prevalent in our society. A staff member is in an uncomfortable dilemma. Her decision to talk to the parents in a private meeting is wise. Even though she felt she was not effective in getting Tommy to feel free to dress up, she made an effort to defuse the anger of the parents and to understand their feelings. She can still make sure Tommy has many rich dramatic play opportunities in different settings.

Parents (and grandparents, siblings, aunts, uncles) sometimes feel that they must nurture 'boyishness' or 'girlishness' in their children in order for them to develop the proper sex role identification. They may do this without consciously thinking about it. From the beginning, girls and boys may be treated differently by parents. Girls may be perceived as delicate and fragile, boys as robust and strong. As they progress through the toddler years, girls may be praised for how they look, while boys are praised for their accomplishments.

On the other hand, it is a mistake to pretend that boys and girls are just the same except for their physical differences. Boys do seem to gravitate towards playing with vehicles and blocks. The nurturing side of girls shows up early in their play with dolls and stuffed toys. It is hard to say how much of this is due to the roles they see in their families and the type of toys they have been given, and how much of it is biological.

It is important to bear in mind that both boys and girls generally like all kinds of play. Even if they spend more time in one area than in others, they should always have a wide variety of options. Boys enjoy dramatic play, if not always in the housekeeping area. Girls enjoy constructing things. Make sure that your classroom or home environment does not develop *exclusion zones.*

Showing respect for the opposite sex is a problem in our society. Whether it is sexual harassment lawsuits or sexual discrimination in the job market or individuals limited because of gender, sexism is an aspect of society.

Some gender differences are a reality, and we need to be aware of them to make the curriculum work well for boys as well as girls.

Insights from Child Development

Sense of identity. Sometime in their second year, young children work out that they are either a boy or a girl and are then intent upon determining what makes them a boy or girl and how the rest of the world fits into these powerful categories. They do not realize that body parts determine gender.

MISUNDERSTANDINGS. Hair styles, clothing and activities are highly visible to young children, so they tend to think that these are the distinguishing characteristics of gender.

Children may not realize that they will always be a boy or girl, and that changing hair length or clothes does not constitute a sex change. The understanding that gender does not change over time also has to develop.

Young children, with their limited experience, are quick to stereotype based on examples they have been exposed to. They may ignore, or at least resist, evidence that does not agree with what they have personally experienced. Cognitive development takes care of some over-stereotyping, but the role of teachers and parents in encouraging multiple perspectives is important.

ROLES FOR MEN AND WOMEN. Young children are rather rigid in what they believe men and women can or should do. This is due to their recent acquisition of the concepts 'men' and 'women.' They are actively sorting out who goes with what. Three-year-olds in particular ascribe very traditional roles to adults, and as they gain experience of diverse roles, they expand the list of what they consider to be acceptable roles for men and women.

Children, once they are beyond the age of two, may develop strong preferences for playing with same-sex peers. Since this tendency seems to occur across different cultures, there might be a biological basis. Perhaps boys and girls are more comfortable with same-sex peers because of similar play styles. This play preference can become a problem when children are excluded by those of the opposite sex from joining in their play.

When to seek help

Since sexism is endemic in our lives, it should be addressed on a daily basis. The following are a few warning signs indicating that additional intervention is needed:

STRONG EXCLUSION STATEMENTS, 'Girls can't climb,' 'You can't play here because you're a boy,' indicate that you need to devote some specific attention to this issue.

A child is reluctant to try anything not strictly in traditional sex roles. Boys will not try cooking, for instance, or girls will not use tools at the workbench.

A child may bully, trying to solve all problems by dominating others.

A child may seem very timid, unwilling to try new things, passive, whining often, afraid to get dirty.

Some parents tell their children what is okay to play with and what is not, especially warning boys to stay away from *sissy* activities.

Who can help

Experienced early childhood professionals

Children's librarian to help you find resources and children's books that counter stereotypes

How to respond

With the staff

Observe children's play patterns. Start by observing the play patterns of the children in your group. Who likes to play where, and with whom? Take some time to formally observe your classroom. Every five minutes during free playtime write down who is playing where. Review your notes. You might be surprised.

Show play that is not typical of your own gender. If you are female, play in the block corner or at the woodworking bench and show that you enjoy the materials. If you are a male, play with dolls and dishes. Your example shows children it is okay to play with everything in the environment.

With the Children

Staff need to be proactive on this issue, not just intervene when they hear some stereotypical comment from children. You may have to show children over and over again that certain activities and roles are not just for one gender or the other.

Emphasize to children, who may think that dress, length of hair or play preferences are what makes them male or female, 'What makes you a boy is that you have a penis. What makes you a girl is that you have a vagina.' If you are uncomfortable using the terms *penis* and *vagina*, say *boys' private parts* and *girls' private parts.* Accurately illustrated children's books and anatomically correct dolls are useful.

Children should be told that, no matter how they dress or wear their hair, they will always remain a boy or a girl because of their special boy or girl body parts.

With input from the children, create the rule for your classroom or childcare home: Everyone can play with everything.

Intervene quickly, directly and tactfully when you hear children being excluded from an activity because of their gender. This is really a form of aggression — verbal aggression — and you should treat it as you would treat physical aggression. Comfort the victim, discuss the situation and help the children solve problems without hurting anyone.

COMMENT ON MIXED-GENDER PLAY. When you see boys and girls playing co-operatively with each other, say something like 'Manuel and Julia are making a city in the sand box.' Pointing them out to the class gives the message that you approve of this type of play.

SOME CHILDREN WILL NEED SPECIFIC ENCOURAGEMENT or an invitation to try certain activities. Engaging in parallel play with them also helps them feel more comfortable.

PRESENT TRADITIONAL AND NON-TRADITIONAL ROLE MODELS. Look for and present to children examples of capable, confident, caring individuals in traditional and non-traditional roles. Find these examples in children's stories, illustrations, photos and magazine pictures.

Invite visitors who work in non-traditional roles, such as women electricians and male cooks, to visit your classroom or centre. Start with parents to find such examples.

Encourage children to think beyond stereotypes. Point out exceptions.

COUNTER CHILDREN'S STEREOTYPICAL STATEMENTS with contradictions from their own experience. 'Girls can't fix things.' 'Miss Marsha is a girl, and she just fixed our toilet.'

SELECT AND READ BOOKS THAT CHALLENGE STEREOTYPES. This gives you a chance to tell children that it is okay for boys to play with dolls and that lots of boys like to do this. Also encourage girls to talk about the *boys' toys* they like to play with. Talk about what you liked to play with when you were a child that might not fit into the stereotype.

RIDING TOYS AND DRAMATIC PLAY. Make sure girls have equal access to riding toys outside. Create dramatic play settings outside that attract both boys and girls and that can incorporate riding toys.

MAKE A CLASS BOOK about activities that the children's parents do in and out of the home. Then point out and talk about the diversity of roles.

MAKE SURE THAT BOYS AS WELL AS GIRLS HELP THE STAFF. All children should have the privilege and responsibility of helping the staff with classroom chores, such as cleaning up and setting the table.

ARRANGE THE CLASSROOM. For example, placing the doll corner furniture right next to the block corner can encourage more co-operative play between boys and girls.

Place the woodworking bench next to the art area. Encourage children to blend the materials. Both boys and girls will be drawn to it.

Create dramatic play areas around themes such as a restaurant, a grocery shop, a hardware shop, a hospital, a fire station. Diverse props attract diverse children.

How to make your seating more comfortable and challenging for all children:

Limit time spent on activities such as circle time where you require children to sit still and pay attention. Instead of always reading to a large group, for instance, read with one or two children in a cosy corner.

Look for books that will appeal to active learners — books about construction, workers and tools, vehicles, imagination and adventures.

PROVIDE LANGUAGE ENRICHMENT ACTIVITIES. Bring language learning into the block corner. Offer to take dictation from the children about what they built. Provide writing materials so they can create signs.

Enlarge the block corner to make room for more boys and girls.

Set up a workbench.

PROVIDE DRESSING UP CLOTHES FOR MALES AND FEMALES. Hats of all types are popular. Also include capes, belts, and workmen's props such as toolboxes, lunch boxes and clip boards.

With the parents

Discuss how children benefit from different kinds of toys. Bring up the subject at parent meetings and in newsletters.

Encourage parents to get a nurturing object toy for their sons and daughters — if not a doll, then a stuffed toy that they can tenderly care for and play with, give rides to and pretend to feed. Encourage dramatic play.

STRESS THE IMPORTANCE OF PLAY CLOTHES. Encourage parents to dress both boys and girls in play clothes that can get dirty.

DEVELOP A COLLECTION OF MALE AND FEMALE STEREOTYPICAL IMAGES from magazines and cards. Use this to raise parents' awareness of images their children are seeing, even if they are not modelling this in their own lives.

HELP PARENTS TO COUNTER STEREOTYPING. Suggest words they can use to counter male and female stereotyping which they encounter in the media and books, or on toy packaging, greeting cards.

Further Information

Resources for children

Your local library should have a comprehensive list of appropriate children's titles.

Books

Hoffman, Mary, Illustrated by Caroline Binch. *Amazing Grace,* Frances Lincoln. 1998.

Danish, Barbara, *The Dragon and the Doctor.* The Feminist Press, 1995.

Hudson, Wade, illustrated by Culverson Blair. *I'm Gonna Be!* Just Us Books, 1992.

Phelps, Ethel Johnston, illustrated by Pamela Baldwin Ford. *Tatterhood and other Tales.* The Feminist Press, 1979.

Zolotow, Charlotte, illustrated by William Pène du Bois. *William's Doll.* HarperCollins, 1985.

Resources for adults

Books

Henderson, Ann, *Equal Chances,* Pre-School Learning Alliance,1996.

Epstein, D. And Sealey, A., *Where it really matters,* Development Education Centre (Birmingham), 1990.

Elfer, P., *With Equal Concern,* National Children's Bureau, 1995.

Abbott, L. and Rodgers, R., *Quality Education in the Early Years,* Open University Press, 1994.

Denman-Sparks, Louise, *Anti-Bias Curriculum,* Association for the Education of Young Children, 1993.

Carlsson-Paige, Nancy and Levin, Diane E., *Who's Calling the Shots: How to Respond Effectively to Children's Fascination with War Play and War Toys.* New Society Publishers, 1990.

Edwards, Carolyn Pope, *Promoting Social and Moral Development in Young Children: Creative Approaches for the Classroom Environment.* Teachers College Press, 1986.

Miller, Karen, *The Outside Play and Learning Book: Activities for Young Children.* Gryphon House, 1989.

Paley, Vivian, *You Can't Say You Can't Play.* Harvard University Press, 1993.
Thomas, Marlo, illustrated by Christopher Cerf. *Free to Be You and Me.* Running Press Book Publishers, 1998.

Curriculum materials

Community helper figures for block play in non-traditional sex roles.

Puzzles that picture non-traditional work roles.

Anatomically correct dolls.

Organizations and helplines

The Equal Opportunities Commission. Tel. 0161-833 9244

National Early Years Network. Tel. 020-607 9573

National Children's Bureau. Tel. 020-843 6000

Pre-School Learning Alliance. Tel. 020-833 0991

Local Education Department. See your local *Yellow Pages.*

CHAPTER NINETEEN

Children from Different Cultures

Example 1

Four-year-old Pedro and his parents had just arrived in Massachusetts from Portugal. Both parents found work immediately, so Pedro was enrolled in the local childcare centre. His teachers, Karen and Vivien, did not speak Portuguese, but the assistant manager at the centre was Portuguese and acted as an interpreter for the staff while they showed the family the classroom and explained what Pedro's days would be like. The assistant manager also translated notes home describing what Pedro did each day. Vivien explained to the other children that Pedro could not understand them and talk to them yet, but he would learn and they could help. On the first day, Karen read them a funny picture book story, and Pedro laughed at one of the pictures. Another child announced happily, 'Pedro laughs in English!' An outgoing child, Pedro happily joined in all the play options of the classroom and especially enjoyed building with the other boys in the block corner and playing outside. Karen made time each day to settle down with Pedro and one or two friends to do a language activity, like identifying pictures in a book. Everyone was amazed at the speed at which Pedro picked up English. He started with words of greeting and routines such as 'Hi!,' 'Bye-bye!,' 'Go outside,' 'Clean-up time,' and 'Lunch!' He was especially proud when his mother came and cooked with the other children one day. After six months, Pedro's language developed rapidly.

Example 2

Barb enrolled her four-year-old daughter, Melissa, in a pre-school. On visiting, she found a chaotic situation. About half of the children in the class were Japanese. The fathers of the children were on a year's exchange with executives from a local company. Since the carer had no idea how to communicate with the Japanese children, there was no order or routine in the classroom. The carer was at her wit is end. Also, Barb observed that the local children and the Japanese children did not play together. She sensed that there were many missed opportunities. So Barb decided to form a mothers' club. With the aid of one Japanese mother who spoke both English and Japanese, she invited everyone for tea at her house while the children were in school. They talked about the problems in the classroom and devised ways to help. The Japanese mothers had not realized that they would be welcome to volunteer and help in the classroom. Many of them knew a little English but were shy and did not want to make mistakes. The carer later assured them that they would be most welcome and that their help was much appreciated. Barb also encouraged the other mothers to invite one Japanese child and mother to come over to their house to play after school, thus building friendships between the children and the parents. Before long, the Japanese mothers were actively sharing their culture in the classroom, and everybody benefited from their unique situation.

The Issue

The challenge is not just linguistic, communicating with the child and the family, it is also cultural. You need to make a special effort to make the family feel welcome, and recognize and value their culture. Often the child's family is in transition. They have left their homeland, sometimes under dramatic circumstances and are trying to start a new life. Even in the best situation the family will probably be under stress.

The parents may find it difficult to trust you. When people search for childcare, they instinctively look for people as much like themselves as they can find, who reflect their own values and culture. Some parents fear that if their children learn English, they will forget their native language and will not want to identify with their native culture and values.

This situation is a marvellous opportunity to enrich your curriculum and your life, but it will take some extra effort at first.

Insights from Child Development

A child from a different culture is likely to experience strong separation anxiety. Not only are they being left with strangers, but you might look different from people they know. You certainly sound different! The food might taste different, and nobody can comfort them and reassure them that their parent will return.

The child may also reflect the considerable anxiety many parents feel leaving their children with someone they do not know, have not yet learned to trust, and with whom they cannot communicate.

Remember that words are only one part of communicating. Tone of voice, intonation, facial expression, body language, gestures and touch are all important ways with which human beings communicate with each other, and even very young children understand these things very well.

Young children have an amazing capacity to learn language. Be aware that receptive language — hearing and understanding words and phrases — comes first. Productive language, producing words and phrases to communicate, is usually harder and comes a little later. In other words, a child understands more than they can speak.

Young children have little understanding of cultures, but they do notice differences. If the new child not only sounds different, but looks different from the other children in the group, you need to talk about it with the other children. Be open as you talk about skin colour, hair type, the colour of eyes and other differences. Collect pictures of people from different cultures. Invite visitors to the class who represent different cultures, if you do not have a diverse population in your class or centre, so children become comfortable with diversity (see Chapter 17 on racism).

Do not allow people to talk about the child or the family (especially if there are problems) in the child's presence, thinking the child does not understand. Even though the child may not understand every word, they will probably sense that you are talking about them and will pick up on the tone.

When to seek help

Extreme separation anxiety. The child may continue to exhibit extreme separation anxiety for a long period of time. Do not ignore this situation because it may not resolve itself without your help. If the child cries and clings to the parent and then clings to you all the time instead of participating, and the parent seems anguished, talk with the parent. Home visits often help a great deal in such situations. You will have to judge each situation individually to decide how long normal separation anxiety behaviours can go on, and when it needs more attention. Discuss it with your supervisor.

Social interactions. The child may be withdrawn, aggressive, or have trouble making friends. This behaviour may be related to language development, feeling isolated, insecure or frustrated. Work with the child to ease social interaction.

Irregular attendance may indicate family anxieties. Be proactive. Reach out to find out why the child is absent and what else you might do to make the parents and child feel more comfortable.

Who can help

English as a Second Language (ESL) teachers and advisors in your local education district.

The education department at a local university or college may also be a resource.

Someone who speaks English from that child's cultural community. It is ideal if your centre can locate someone who is well respected in that community who can act as an interpreter and liaison for you and the parents. Unless there is no other alternative, avoid using an older child as an interpreter.

How to respond

With the staff

Read about the family's culture. The local librarian can help you find resources. Then check details with the family. 'I read this about your culture. Is it true? Tell me more about it.' Parents will react warmly when they sense that you are trying to learn more about them.

Learn key words and phrases in the child's language. Nobody expects carers to be multi-lingual, but you can learn greeting, parting and social words, *like hello, good* *morning, good-bye and thank you.* Survival phrases are important for you to understand, such as *hungry, tired, thirsty* and *go to the bathroom.* You might develop a list of these phrases, written out phonetically, to have in the child's file.

If many children come from a particular culture in your centre, it is ideal if you can add a staff person or volunteer from that culture.

With the child

BE THE CHILD'S *ANCHOR*. Like all new children in your centre, the child needs to develop a trusting relationship with one adult first and then extend this trust to others. The child may need a lot of holding and comforting. Stay close. Like a toddler in a new environment, the child will eventually venture out and play a little, and come back to touch you at intervals, to make sure you are still there. If you provide this extra accessibility when it is critically needed at the beginning, the child will develop confidence and independence more quickly.

MAKE SURE THE CHILD'S CULTURE IS REPRESENTED in pictures and materials that you have available in your classroom. Perhaps the family can be of help. Ask them to save food boxes or dressing up clothes for the housekeeping corner. Try to find pictures, books, music and other items representative of the culture.

If possible, find recorded music from that child's culture to play to the whole class.

BE A GOOD LANGUAGE MODEL for the child. Speak slowly, simply, and clearly (but not more loudly), and in full sentences. Describe what you are doing, and what the child is doing.

TALK TO THE CHILD AS THOUGH THEY UNDERSTAND YOU, and help them to understand you by doing what you are talking about. For instance, say, 'Peter, it is time to go to the table and eat lunch.' Then take him by the hand and lead him over to the table and sit down with him.

Extend the child's single word utterances when they start. If they say, 'Shoes,' and points, say, 'Yes, I see you have new red shoes on today!'

PLAY SIMPLE LANGUAGE GAMES that involve understanding (receptive language) while also involving other children to develop the child's social contacts. For example:

Puppet packs his suitcase. Have a puppet tell the child and a friend or two, 'I'm going to Grandma's house, and I need to put some things in my suitcase to take with me.' Then make the puppet name things from the room and ask the children to go and get them for him. The puppet can talk about each object before it is put into the suitcase. 'Here's a nice red, shiny lorry.'

Puppet unpacks his suitcase. When the puppet *returns from Grandma's* the next day, he can bring the packed toys as well as a few other objects out of the suitcase to talk about. 'Here's the red lorry. You can put it back now. Thank you.' 'Look what Grandma gave me, a nice, soft pillow.

Find a picture book with many pictures on a page. Magazines and catalogues work well too. Ask the child, 'Where is a cat?' 'Where is a television?' Let the child point to the objects. If they do not know, take their finger and put it on the correct picture and say, 'There is the cat!' Then a few questions later, ask them to find the same thing again. An English-speaking friend will enjoy playing along and praising the friend for getting the correct answer, or helping them to find it.

Cut out pictures of objects in your room and mount the pictures on cards covered with transparent self-adhesive paper. Hand the card to the child and a friend. Say, 'This is a ball. Take the picture to the real ball.' Later the child will be able to do this independently. Before long, you will be able to point to the object or the picture and ask, 'What's this?,' and the child will be able to name it in English.

Cut out a number of pictures of common objects and back them with felt, sandpaper or Velcro. Place them in front of the flannelgraph. While working with a small group of children, ask them to pick up the picture of a certain object and put it on the board one at a time. With the child who speaks limited English, choose something you are sure they know, or have them pick up the last one and put it on the board. Take the pictures down again in the same fashion.

Build vocabulary. Cleaning up time can be a great vocabulary builder. Simply stay with the child and name the things you are putting away together. Or let a puppet help.

Read familiar books again and again.

Create simple rituals. Often the first words a child says out loud are social words such as *hello, bye-bye* and *thank you.* Encourage all the children to say *hello* or *good morning* and *bye* when someone leaves, and *thank you. Yes, no* and *okay* are other common early words. Think about including other ritual phrases.

Interpret early efforts to communicate. Read the child's non-verbal communication and supply it with words. The child points at the jug and makes a noise. 'Oh, do you want more juice? I'll be happy to pour you some juice.' You are helping the child connect useful words to feelings. 'Maria is sad because she can't find her hat.'

Songs with repeated phrases are good to use. *E-i-e-i-o* is easy to master, and fun to sing. Singing is much easier than talking. The words usually come out more slowly and are more predictable. It is good practice with productive language (speaking and producing words). Musical games involving body parts, such as the *Hokey Cokey* are ideal. Perhaps the child, with a parent, can teach the other children familiar songs like *Happy Birthday* in their own language.

Use firm, gentle guidance and consistent limits. Whatever the culture, children will feel most secure with firm, gentle guidance and consistent limits. Sometimes children will pretend not to understand messages long after they really do understand. Remember, non-verbal messages of a discipline situation are always understood, so make your tone of voice and facial expression match your words. If a child is doing something unacceptable like taking a toy away from another child, simply get down on the child's level, hold his shoulders, look into his eyes and shake your head while saying, 'No, that's not okay.' Use the same positive techniques you use with the other children of praising good behaviour and redirecting unacceptable behaviour.

Increase open-ended activities. Luckily, many of the activities in a typical early childhood curriculum do not require strong language skills on the part of the child. Like all the other children, the child who does not speak English will need many experiences of success and fun to develop a feeling of self-worth. So, provide plenty of experiences using art materials, clay, playdough, blocks and dramatic play. Children pick up language from their parallel play with other children, and you can describe with interest what they are doing.

Let the child help you create their own word book. In a home-made book, put pictures or drawings of words that the child knows in English. You might also say the word in the child's native language. It is a good idea to do this in a loose-leaf binder so it can grow and grow!

Record progress. Keep a record of the new words and phrases the child learns. It will be interesting to see what comes first, probably some of the things most important to the child. Also make note of what the child enjoys doing and with whom the child likes to play. Keep the parents well informed and share the pleasures and successes.

With the other children

Encourage interaction. Talk to the other children about how their new friend cannot understand their words, but does understand what their bodies are saying. Let them think of ways they can use their bodies to *talk* to their friend such as smiling, nodding or shaking their head and taking the child's hand.

Interpret interactions. Help the other children to *read* their new friend's gestures. 'Mariko is shaking her head. She doesn't want to go with you right now.'

Encourage friendships. Brainstorm with the children how they can be a friend to someone without being able to talk to them. The children might think of things like sharing playdough, sitting next to each other, playing with dolls, looking at pictures in a book together, playing follow the leader, holding hands and greeting their friend with a warm hug.

Let the new child teach words from their language to the other children. The English-speaking friends will enjoy learning greeting words in another language as well as the words for common objects in the room. The child who does not speak English will probably enjoy teaching these words, possibly with the help of a parent, and it shows respect for the child and their culture.

With infants and toddlers

Parents may have greater anxiety leaving an infant or toddler than when leaving an older child. They may feel that the child is particularly vulnerable because they are so young and cannot express themselves. Have an adult interpreter present to facilitate communication with these parents, if possible.

Note how the parent interacts with the child. Notice how the parent holds and comforts the baby and try to adopt that style yourself.

Invite the parent to spend the day with you and the baby, caring for the child. Try to imitate the parent's gestures and ways of communicating with the baby.

Arrange for a consistent carer. Having the same, consistent primary carer is especially important for babies from a different culture so that they only have to get used to one new thing at a time.

With the parents

MAKE THE EFFORT TO BECOME ACQUAINTED WITH THE FAMILY and help them feel comfortable. Take your time with the intake interview. Use this as the first opportunity to make the parents feel welcome and supported.

INVITE THE PARENTS TO SPEND A DAY OR MORE IN THE CLASSROOM, with or without the child, to see what goes on and to become comfortable with you. They might then have more specific questions. Assure the parents that they do not need to know English to be welcome in your classroom.

Visit the home, if this is agreeable to the parents. You can learn a great deal about the child and about the culture. Plus, meeting them in their home, you develop a sense of ease and friendship with the family. It might be easier for a mother to express her concerns and fears, as well as her hopes and wishes, when she is sitting in her own kitchen.

MAINTAIN A WARM SOCIAL RELATIONSHIP WITH THE FAMILY. Be conscious of your facial expressions, body language and tone of voice when you see parents. Greet them warmly and with respect. Share the joy of their child. Laugh. Develop and attend social events for families like events and parties that include the children. When you have a social rapport with parents, it is easier to talk about any conflicts or concerns that arise, and you avoid creating mountains out of molehills.

FIND AN INTERPRETER FROM THEIR CULTURE to be present at all meetings and get-acquainted sessions with the family. All of the centre's written policies should be translated for them into their language.

Encourage parents to bring in pictures of their families, family celebrations, vacations or other events, as well as pictures of their homeland, if possible. It gives the new child some comfort in a strange situation, as well as sharing the culture. Do this with all of your children. It is also a good idea to send home pictures of you and the children in the class. If they do not have pictures, offer to take photos of the family yourself. Explain how you will use them.

Invite family members to come in and spend time with you, and as much as they are able, share their culture. A cooking project is fun. Perhaps a family member could teach a children's song from their country. If they know some English, they might be able to tell the children one of their folk tales, or show them a children's picture book from their country and tell the other children what it says on each page. Again, make them know that you would welcome their participation, even if they cannot speak English. A non-English-speaking parent could sit at the clay table and play with the children, or look at picture books with them. The child will be proud that their parent visited.

Translate the lunch menu. Send a translated version of the lunch menu home a week ahead of time. Talk to the parents about the child's food preferences and introduce new foods gradually. Allow parents to bring in substitute food items when they do not think their child will eat what is planned.

Establish a daily routine that you can share with parents so that they can prepare the child. Knowing the routines is comforting to the child.

Help parents understand the calendar. Make a special effort to ensure parents understand events on the calendar (especially when school might be closed).

Further Information

Resources for children

Your local library should have a comprehensive list of appropriate children's titles.

Books

Martin, Bill, illustrated by Eric Carle. *Brown Bear, Brown Bear, What Do You See?* Hamish Hamilton Children's Books, 1997.

Mitsumasa, Anno, *Anno's Journey*, PaperStar Books, 1997.

Bradman, T. And Brown, E., *In a Minute*, Mammoth, 1991.

Pragoff, Fiona, *What Colour?* Victor Gollancz, 1987.

Coles, Robert, illustrated by George Ford. *The Story of Ruby Bridges*, Scholastic Inc., 1995.

Hamanaka, Sheila, *All the Colours of the Earth*, Morrow Junior Books, 1994.

Johnson, Dolores, *Now Let Me Fly: The Story of a Slave Family*. Aladdin Publshing Co., 1997.

Lacapa, Kathleen, illustrated by Michael Lacapa. *Less than Half, More than Whole*. Northland Publishing, 1998.

Mockizuki, Ken, illustrated by Dom Lee. *Baseball Saved Us*, Lee and Low Books Inc., 1995.

Nikola-Lisa, W, illustrated by Michael Bryant. *Bein' with you this Way*, Lee and Low Books Inc., 1994.

Polacco, Patricia, *Mrs. Katz and Tush.* Dell Publishing Co., 1994. Rosen, Michael J. illustrated by Aminah Brenda Lynn Robinson. *Elijah's Angel.* Harcourt Brace and Company, 1997.

Shelby, Anne, illustrated by Irene Trivas. *Potluck.* Orchard Books, 1994. Wild, Margaret, illustrated by Julie Vivas. *Let the Celebrations BEGIN!* Orchard Books, 1991.

Resources for adults

Books

Ramsey, Patricia G., *Teaching and Learning in a Diverse World: Multicultural Education for Young Children.* Teachers College Press, 1998.

Henderson, Ann, *Equal Chances,* Pre-School Learning Alliance,1996.

Epstein, D. And Sealey, A., *Where it really matters,* Development education Centre (Birmingham), 1990.

Elfer, P., *With Equal Concern,* National Children's Bureau, 1995.

Abbott, L. And Rodgers, R., *Quality Education in the Early Years,* Open University Press, 1994.

Denman-Sparks, Louise, *Anti-Bias Curriculum,* Association for the Education of Young Children, 1993.

Pugh, Gillian, Contemporary Issues in the Early Years, Paul Chapman Ltd., 1992.

Commission for Racial Equality, *From Cradle to School: A Practical Guide to Race Equality and Childcare,* 1989.

Miller, Judy, *Never Too Young.* Booklet published by the National Early Years Network, 1997, and spiral-bound book published by Save the Children Fund, 1996.

Ford, Clyde W., *We Can All Get Along: 50 Steps You Can Take to Help End Racism at Home, at Work, In Your Community,* Dell Publishing Group Inc., 1994.

Paley, Vivian Gussin, *White Teacher.* Harvard University Press, 1990.

Curriculum materials

Crayons and paints reflecting a wide range of skin tones. Available from most school suppliers.

Dolls and puppets for dramatic play, puzzles and posters that represent people of different races are available from most school suppliers.

Organizations and helplines

Commission for Racial Equality. See your local telephone directory.

Equal Opportunities Commission. Tel. 0161-833 9244

Multi-Cultural Education Resource Centres. Contact your local Education Department for information.

National Early Years Network. Tel. 020-607 9573

National Children's Bureau. Tel. 020-843 6000

Pre-School Learning Alliance. Tel. 020-833 0991

Chapter Twenty

Poverty and Unemployment

The Issue

People are poor for many different reasons — bad luck, substance abuse, job losses, teen pregnancy, divorce, etc. Poverty is one of the most complex issues discussed in this book. At best, it is possible only to look at the effects of poverty. The childcare provider cannot be expected to solve a family's financial crisis, but good childcare can be one factor that helps a family climb out of poverty.

It is important to distinguish between poverty and neglect. Both may lead to a child not having the basic necessities of life, such as food, clothing, shelter and medical care. However, the interventions and supports needed are different for each. Neglect is a form of child abuse (see Chapter 10) that you are required to report to your local child abuse agency. Neglect indicates the *emotional absence* of the carer and is extremely devastating to a child's development. Although many neglected children are from poverty-stricken families, not all poor children are neglected. Many are loved and emotionally valued by their families. A family living in poverty often receives social supports such as job training, food and housing benefit. While poverty and neglect may exist together, this is not always the case.

Poverty is often a *blame the victim* situation in our society, but one thing is certain — children do not deserve the circumstances of poverty that often deprive them of the opportunities they need to overcome life's hardships.

Insights from Child Development

Increased stress in the family. The very circumstance of poverty in a child's life almost always translates to an environment of high stress in

Example

Beth had a rough year. She discovered that her husband was a substance abuser, which explained why there never seemed to be enough money to pay the rent and buy food for her four-year-old son, Jamie and three-year-old daughter, Sarah. After their divorce, Beth applied for social security to help her with childcare and other living expenses while she went to college to become a bookkeeper. She also worked part-time at a local shop in the evenings while a neighbour watched the children. Jamie and Sarah were small for their age and somewhat listless, and both exhibited extreme separation problems in the morning. They were also often unkempt and hungry. When the staff made a home visit, they came away feeling that this was a mother who loved her children but who was simply at the end of her tether, trying desperately to put some stability into her life.

After a few months at the centre, the children began to thrive. They clearly benefited from the good nutrition at the centre, and from the relationships they formed with the staff and with their peers. The staff made friendly contact with Beth, reporting the many positive experiences her children were having and noting their progress. Beth later told them that the support she had from them was the boost she needed to regain her self-esteem and climb out of her depression.

A year later she found a bookkeeping job but lost the social security that covered her childcare expenses. She now had to pay for childcare, and was only a few pounds ahead of where she had been. However, there was a huge improvement in her state of mind and in the well-being of the children. She still got their clothing at a local charity shop, but knew that things would get better in a few years once the children were at school. She felt confident that she could handle things and appreciated the ongoing friendship and support of the staff at the childcare centre.

the family. High stress may lead to increased domestic violence, child abuse, neglect or substance abuse.

SELF-ESTEEM AND POVERTY. As children get older and compare their circumstances to those of peers, they may feel that they are not as good as others. This may be reinforced if their peers look down on them unfairly.

DELAY IN SOCIAL AND ACADEMIC AREAS. Poverty can exclude children from many enriching social and educational experiences. The child may begin to lag in social and academic skills.

DIVORCE OR SEPARATION may often plunge a family into poverty. Children will need your help in coming to terms with their feelings of abandonment and worthlessness, especially when the custodial parent is feeling depressed and therefore not as emotionally available to the child.

CHILDREN MAY FEEL LESS WORTHY THAN THEIR PEERS. They may learn to think of themselves and their families as losers. Frustration turns into hopeless resignation, and they stop trying.

When to seek help

The child lacks basic necessities; food, clothing, shelter.

The child is tired, falls asleep during the day.

The child is insecure, fearful, possessive, clinging to a coat or any small possessions.

Owing to enormous stress, the parent may be emotionally unavailable to the child. The child may become withdrawn and depressed.

Who can help

Social security offices
Local social services
Job centres
Job training programmes
Rights offices
Citizens Advice Bureau

How to respond

With the staff

Childcare workers may themselves be part of the working poor. The issue of poverty may be painfully close to home for many. Staff should join and support their professional organizations to improve salaries and benefits.

MAKE SURE STAFF MEMBERS ARE AWARE OF LOCAL RESOURCES for assistance with food, clothing and shelter in case parents need this information.

With the child

Address hunger first. If you have children who may be hungry and you do not normally offer breakfast or other meals, see if you can arrange to do so. Perhaps these children can go to another room to eat so they will not be embarrassed. Hunger impacts on every other aspect of a child's experience. Good nutrition must be the starting point.

Provide a special place. Children need a place of their own in the classroom to store their possessions.

Since children from poorer families often live in unstable, even chaotic environments, take extra steps to make your environment feel stable, safe and predictable for the child.

Understand possessiveness. A child may be very possessive about toys and materials, and sharing may be more difficult. This requires sensitive intervention on your part. Do not always insist that a child has to share. Sometimes the need to *own* a toy, even for a little while, outweighs the social value of learning to share.

With the other children

Encourage children to include everyone. Try to prevent children from being excluded from play with others because they are dressed differently.

Discourage showing off. Eliminate the *bring and brag* type of show-and-tell from the daily routine.

Build on children's talents. Many skills do not depend on material possessions. Offer many opportunities to use art materials, for instance.

Offer your support. The support and encouragement of one adult can make a difference. When a child feels respected by a caring worker, they will be more secure and optimistic.

With the parents

Help put parents in contact with community agencies and services that offer various forms of support. Find out about services that exist in your community, what they offer, who can take advantage of them and what people must do to participate.

Parents need to feel your respect, empathy and support before they can fully benefit from the services of your programme. Your friendship, pleasant greetings and sharing of good news about their child can be very encouraging to them. Knowing that their children are well looked after, they can put their energy into job training or other activities that will help them pull things together for the family. There will be one less worry, one thing that is going right in their lives. They can build on that.

Further Information

Resources for children

Your local library should have a comprehensive list of appropriate children's titles.

Books

Ackerman, Karen, illustrated by Catherine Stock. *By the Dawn's Early Light.* Aladdin Paperbacks, 1999.

Altman, Linda Jacobs, illustrated by Enrique O. Sanchez. *Amelia's Road.* Lee and Low Books Inc, 1993.

Covault, Ruth M., illustrated by Francisco *Mora. Pablo and Pimienta.* Northland Publishing, 1998.

Mills, Lauren, *The Rag Coat.* Little, Brown and Company, 1991.

Sonneborn, Ruth A., illustrated by Emily A. McCully. *Friday Night is Papa Night.* Puffin Books, 1987.

Thomas, Jane Resh, illustrated by Michael Dooling. *Lights on the River,* Hyperion Books for Children, 1994.

Resources for adults

Books

McLoyd, Vonnie, C. and Flanagan, Constance A. (Eds.), *New Directions for Child Development : Economic Stress.* Jossey-Bass Inc, 1990.

Organizations and helplines

Social Services. See your local *Yellow Pages.*

Citizens Advice Bureaux. See your local *Yellow Pages.*

Shelter. Tel. 0800-446 441

National Debtline. Tel. 0645-500 511

The Samaritans. Tel. 0345-909 090

ChildLine. Tel.0800-1111

ParentLine. Tel. 01702-559 900

NSPCC. Tel. 0800-800 500

Save the Children Fund. See your local *Yellow Pages.*

Barnardo's. See your local *Yellow Pages.*

Chapter Twenty-One

Homelessness

Example

Marguerite was very surprised to find herself classified as *homeless* when she landed in a shelter for battered women with her three children, aged 18 months, three and six. She had always thought homeless people were mentally ill or substance abusers. Through her own experiences, she found out that people are homeless for many reasons. Abused by her spouse, frightened, and with nowhere to go in her small community, she fled to a large city. She could not afford the deposit on an apartment and had no job. The shelter that took her in offered childcare while she looked for a job. The shelter helped her apply for social security and got her into transitional housing while she attended job training. She says that she feels stressed and overwhelmed much of the time. She is also annoyed by the stigma she feels from being homeless, that others look down on her. She has had quite a hard time with her children. Much to her amazement, they say they miss their dad! The older one especially misses his toys, friends and other relatives and is often belligerent and hard to handle. The baby seems okay, but somewhat listless. The three-year-old is very quiet and withdrawn but is starting to play with other children at the childcare centre run by the shelter.

The Issue

Homelessness is a growing problem. People are homeless for many reasons. It may be a temporary situation, as in the example described above, as women escape from situations of domestic violence and try to get their feet on the ground, or relocate to other areas and start all over again. Or wage earners lose their jobs and are evicted because of the inability to pay the rent. Some homeless people are college students who run out of funds. And yes, there are those who have emotional problems, mental illnesses and problems with addictions.

Some of the following common characteristics are associated with parents in homeless families (a large percentage of them single mothers). Keep in mind that these are generalizations and by no means indicate that all homeless parents have these characteristics:

— Maternal drug and alcohol abuse and psychiatric problems are much greater than among mothers living in public or private subsidized housing.

— A history of abuse as children, and battering as adults.

— Homeless parents may have few, if any, long term support networks.

Homeless parents desperately need and want respect. They need a lift, a break; they need support, humour and friendship because they are looked down upon, even by some of the very people who help them. These parents and especially their children, are often innocent victims of life's circumstances. Many may be escaping abusive situations and are desperately trying to make positive improvements in their lives. Not all homeless people are substance abusers or mentally ill. Those who have been affected by these problems may be trying hard to make changes.

Do not confuse the deprivation they experience as a family with the issue of child neglect, a form of child abuse. Both situations require intervention.

Many parents are afraid that their children will be taken away from them, so it may be difficult to develop warm, trusting relationships with them.

In addition to stable housing arrangements, families need help finding permanent places for their children in early childhood centres and schools. They may need job training and parenting and counselling sessions. This is not a one-dimensional problem. The growing problem of homelessness requires a multifaceted social response.

The childcare centre can be an enormous positive influence in the life of the family. The child may have his first opportunity to play, paint, dig, have friends and feel safe. The parent may feel supported for the first time and, consequently, feel optimistic about the future. With children well cared for, parents can look for work and take advantage of job training, counselling and other services to get their lives on track. Your friendship and respect for the parent and for the child can have a subtle yet great impact.

Insights from Child Development

The child may suffer from extreme separation anxiety.

Changes in a child's life add stress. The child has gone through a lot of changes lately, none of which they had any control over. This may make the child insecure and frightened.

The child may have been a witness to violence or have had other traumatic experiences. Try to find out as much as you can about what the child has been through so you can respond sensitively and interpret behaviour.

A child who has witnessed domestic violence may identify with the aggressor and be aggressive themselves. The parent is likely to be very stressed, tired, and perhaps finding it hard to focus on the child.

The child comes from a frightening, serious world where there is little opportunity for humour or play.

Owing to difficult life circumstances, **homeless children have a higher percentage of special needs** than children in the general population. Since they have lacked a nurturing, stimulating environment, they may be suffering from developmental delays and language delays.

The child may have difficulty sharing. Homeless children can lack a sense of permanency, fearing that everyone and everything in their lives will disappear. Hoarding toys and the inability to share are common behavioural responses.

General characteristics of homeless children.

The following characteristics of describe the general population of homeless children compared with children who are not homeless (taken from various research studies):

— Higher levels of behavioural problems
— One or more developmental

delays serious enough to warrant referral
— Severe depression, anxiety and learning difficulties
— Sleep problems and extreme resistance to napping
— Shyness and withdrawal
— More aggression
— Severe separation problems
— Severe anxiety interfering with the ability to participate in routine activities
— Poor quality (superficial) relationships
— Short attention span
— Signs of emotional disturbance, including severe tantrums, dangerously aggressive and destructive behaviour, extreme withdrawal, elective muteness, violent mood swings, and aggressive and manipulative behaviour
— Gross motor developmental delays
— Speech and language delays
— Cognitive developmental delays

These characteristics are not surprising considering what life has been like for many homeless children. Bear in mind that this does not mean that all homeless children embody all of the above characteristics. One thing, however, is certain. Children from homeless families and their parents have suffered extreme amounts of stress and trauma. Life has been very, very hard for them.

Also remember that children are quite resilient and with consistent and sensitive help, they can make amazing improvements. You are the starting point.

When to seek help

Most of the time, staff know when homeless children are enrolled. So, the warning signs you look for are those that indicate that the child has suffered some severe psychological or developmental delays from his life circumstances. Be aware of the characteristics described above and sensitive to any behaviour that indicates that the child needs more help or more specific intervention.

Who can help

Community agencies that provide services for homeless families
Social services
Social security offices
Shelter and other refuge agencies (see your local Yellow Pages)

How to respond

With the child

Since this is a family in transition, you may only have the child for a few weeks. This is not much time to establish trust and build a relationship. Nevertheless, try hard to establish trust on the part of the child. Be there for the child. Spend as much one-on-one time with the child as possible.

Take a photograph of the parent to **HELP EASE SEPARATION ANXIETY.** The child can keep the picture with them all day. It might also help if the child can also keep some small thing that belongs to the parent.

ESTABLISH A CONSISTENT AND STABLE ROUTINE. Provide consistency and stability in the childcare environment. A few full time, stable adult carers is better than a host of part time staff and volunteers. Use the same room all the time and keep the furniture in the same arrangement for an extended length of time. Maintain great consistency in your daily routine. These things allow the child to predict the future and have a sense of safety and control.

GIVE THE CHILD MANY OPPORTUNITIES TO FEEL IN CONTROL, to make choices, to decide what will happen. Free playtime is important, when the child can decide where they will play, with what, with whom, and for how long. Avoid making all the decisions for the child.

HOMELESS CHILDREN NEED REINFORCEMENT OF THEIR SELF-ESTEEM. They may be feeling helpless, worthless, confused or insecure. You have an opportunity to make them feel valued and special. Greet them warmly, talk with them, play with them, ask for their help, and show pleasure in their ideas and positive interactions.

Give the child many opportunities to express themselves with beautiful, open-ended, creative art materials.

HOMELESS CHILDREN HAVE A SPECIAL NEED FOR PLAY. They may not have any other opportunities to play in their lives. Provide rich opportunities for dramatic play and block play; tactile play with water, sand, clay and playdough; play with toys; riding toys and active outdoor play.

HOMELESS CHILDREN OFTEN NEED EXTRA HELP WITH SOCIAL SKILLS. Because of the chaos in their lives they often have not had the experience of forming friendships with peers.

SOME CHILDREN MAY NEED SPECIAL HELP SOLVING PROBLEMS in ways that do not involve physical aggression.

Rethink what you do about birthdays and other celebrations if there are homeless children in your group. Asking parents to bring in baked goods presents a real hardship. And if these are the only families you do not ask, the children may be embarrassed or made to feel different.

Since homeless children are still in transition they are likely to be with you for only a short time. When the family establishes permanent housing and the child is being transferred to another early childhood setting, make an effort to prepare the child for the move and even talk to the next teacher. It is especially helpful if you can maintain a friendship with the child and the family.

Further Information

Resources for children

Your local library should have a comprehensive list of appropriate children's titles.

Books

Bunting, Eve, Illustrated by Ronald Himler. *Fly Away Home*. Clarion Books, 1993.

Chalofsky, Margie *et al*, illustrated by Ingrid Klass. *Changing Places: A Kid's View of Shelter Living*. Gryphon House, 1992.

Goble, Paul, *The Lost Children*. Aladdin Paperbacks, 1998.

Guthrie, Donna, illustrated by Dennis Hockerman. *A Rose for Abby*. Abingdon Press, 1998.

Resources for adults

Books

McLoyd, Vonnie, C. and Flanagan, Constance A. (Eds.), *New Directions for Child Development : Economic Stress*. Jossey-Bass Inc, 1990.

Organizations and helplines

See your local telephone directories for details of locally based organizations.

Social Services. See your local *Yellow Pages*.

Citizens Advice Bureaux. See your local *Yellow Pages*.

Shelter. Tel. 0800-446 441

Women's Aid. See your local telephone directory.

Homeless outreach projects. See your local telephone directory.

National Debtline. Tel. 0645-500 511

The Samaritans. Tel. 0345-909 090

ChildLine. Tel .0800-1111

ParentLine. Tel. 01702-559 900

NSPCC. Tel. 0800-800 500

Save the Children Fund. See your local *Yellow Pages*.

Barnardo's. See your local *Yellow Pages*.

Part III: Crisis and Curriculum

CHAPTER TWENTY-TWO

Curriculum Provision and Design

Create a stable routine

To help children feel safe in the classroom environment, try to create a stable routine. Children whose lives at home are unpredictable will find this reassuring.

Make events predictable

Think about the regular events in your daily schedule, such as arrival and greeting time, circle time, free playtime, cleaning up time, snack time, outside time, lunch time, rest time and closing and departure time. Do these things in the same order each day. If snack time always comes after cleaning up time, and going outside always comes after circle time, the child begins to feel secure. Other suggestions include:

Create a chart where children can read together the regular routine of the day. Use photographs of children engaged in all the various aspects of the daily schedule. If you arrange these from left to right, you are also reinforcing a reading skill. Place this at the children's eye level.

Review the chart frequently with children. It is a nice way to open a conversation with a new child in your centre.

If you have planned some modification in the routine on a particular day, such as a special visitor, go over to the chart and point to the place where the change will occur.

Review the chart each morning. Describe for the children all the things that will happen within the normal routine — what play choices there will be, what will be served at snack time.

Create routines

Children like routine — doing certain things in certain ways every day. Although some children might seem rigid in their need for routine, remember that routines give them something to hang on to and help them feel secure. These can be very simple things, such as saying the same greeting poem as soon as everyone is gathered for circle time, singing a certain song together before you eat lunch, or having one book and one stuffed toy at rest time.

You may notice that some children create their own routines. For instance, every morning a child might put their coat in their locker, say hello to the pet guinea pig and draw a picture. Give the children power. Let them help you create the group's routine. You could develop a special greeting together and decide what the signals will be for various routines of the day. You might ring a bell, sing a song or clap a pattern to indicate a change of routine. These are all subtle ways to give children power and a sense of control.

Keep special events to a minimum

Field trips, exciting visitors and other special events should probably be kept to a minimum when you have traumatized, insecure children. Even happy events like birthday parties should be low-key because they, too, can cause stress for some children.

Do not create events that are stressful by their very nature, like having children sing in front of parents, or speak before a group of strangers. Parent functions are important but should be informal and fun.

Invite parents to come to the centre with their child. Let each child show their parents around the room. Encourage parents to participate in their child's favourite activities, such as painting, clay, dressing up or block building.

Tips for the daily schedule

Greeting time

Greet each child warmly and make physical contact as soon as the child comes in. Touch the child with a pat on the back, a handshake, a hug, an arm on the shoulder — whatever the child seems to prefer. This human contact tells the child that they are valued and acknowledged.

Some teachers find it helpful to begin the day with structured activities and allow more freedom as the morning progresses. Instead of having all the centres open, for instance, you might have just a few enticing, calm play choices set out on table tops for the child to select. Suggestions include warm playdough with interesting objects to press into it on one table, special construction toys saved just for this time of day on a second table, and drawing materials on a third table.

Have a brief group greeting ritual soon after all the children have arrived each morning. You might sing the same greeting song every time. Do one or more activities that mention each child's name, such as singing a song or having a pet puppet come out and greet each child. The puppet could also describe plans for the day.

A fun way to take attendance that builds a feeling of group cohesiveness is to fill a box with individual photographs and then take them out, one at a time. Ask, 'Who is this?' Describe the child in the photo in complimentary ways: 'Here is a girl with pretty black hair and blue eyes. Who could this be?' When a child identifies the photo, they hang it on a *Who's Here Today?* chart. Also identify the children who are not present and express concern for them. 'I hope Tara will get better soon.' This builds a feeling of belonging as you indicate that each friend is important.

Morning group time can also set the tone for the day. Tell children what activities will be available that day, and anything else that will be happening.

Free playtime

Knowing what is expected of them makes children feel comfortable and secure. They should know where they can play, what they can do with the materials and how to put things away again.

Some children have a difficult time choosing where to settle down. You may notice that a few children prefer to watch others play at first. Give them the time to do this. Later, when they are used to the routine, help them make a choice.

You may decide to limit the number of children who can play in one area at a time to avoid overcrowding the space. Do this with care and only if you feel it is really necessary. It can be extremely frustrating for a child when they have finally made a choice and then are not allowed to go there. This child may then need your help to choose an alternative play choice. A waiting list helps. Put the child's name, photo or symbol on a sign-up board so you remember that they are waiting for a turn. Be sure to let the child know when there is a space.

Cleaning up time

Cleaning up time may be a new experience for some children who do not have a cleaning routine at home. In addition, many children resist any change in activities, especially if they are not ready to stop what they are doing. Have something fun to do next to increase motivation. Food works best!

Give children a two or three minute warning before cleaning up begins so they can finish up what they are working on and feel prepared for the change. The block corner may need a little more time to clean up, so you can get them started earlier. (See the section on block play in Chapter 23 for more specific cleaning up strategies.)

Develop a sense of pride in the room. When everything is picked up, look around and admire the good job they did and say how nice everything looks.

There is a real value in developing orderliness in your environment to counter chaos in children's lives. Having a labelled place for everything and special containers that are easy to find and use makes cleaning up go more smoothly.

Snack time

Food is very important to children under stress for several reasons. Aside from its nutritional value, food symbolizes nurturing. Some centres have developed a snack centre where snack foods are put during free playtime and where children can help themselves. This works fine for many children. However, some children who are very insecure or very hungry, or who have problems with sharing or hoarding, may tend to grab or guard their food. In that case, a more formal snack time may be best. The main thing is to have plenty of food and to keep things relaxed.

Going outside

Parents often marvel at how staff can get hats, coats and boots on a whole group of children in ten minutes. One approach is to encourage each child to do it by themselves. Also, teach children to ask each other for help. This allows a child with skills to feel competent and valued. Cut down on passive waiting time as much as possible. Try to have one adult available to go outside with the children who are ready first so they do not have to wait. Otherwise, have something for the waiting children to do like looking at a collection of greeting cards or laminated pictures.

Lunch time

Sitting down at the lunch table and enjoying a meal together may be another new activity for some children. Develop a lunch time routine to help children feel secure. Whatever serving routine you choose, try to keep it the same every day. Although it may be more convenient to have the food dished out before the children get to the table, this may cause the children to miss some important opportunities. A better option is to introduce the food, describe what is in each bowl and then pass it around. Let children help themselves and tell them how much they can take for their first helping. You can also tell children to put at least a little bit of everything on their plates.

It is very important for adults to eat at the table with the children. Although you do not need to stress manners, you can be an example of good manners for children. You can also be the social director, keeping pleasant conversation going and talking about what the children did that day or what will happen after rest time.

An important part of the lunch ritual is what happens when the children have finished eating. It is not advisable to make everyone stay at the table until the last person has finished eating. Too much waiting time invites restlessness and trouble. Develop a routine for what they should do — scrape and stack their plates, put their utensils in a special container, throw their napkins away.

Lunch to rest transition

Find the sequence of events that works for you and for the children. Some centres have one adult who settles down for a calm story time, perhaps using a puppet that is very sleepy and keeps yawning, while the other adults clean up the lunch table. That carer then calls one or two children at a time to use the bathroom, wash hands and brush teeth before settling.

Rest time

This will not apply to all settings, but will to those who have very young and/or full day children.

Although some children like napping, others find it very difficult. It may just be a matter of temperament, but children who are experiencing trauma in their lives may be particularly resistant to falling asleep. It takes trust to allow yourself to slip into a subconscious state in a room full of people! If you have a child who strongly resists napping, consider the individual and what is going on in their life.

Keep the atmosphere calm and comforting. Sing each child a lullaby, incorporating their name into the song while you rub their back, for example. This is the time to bring out special security toys brought from home.

If a child does not fall asleep after about thirty minutes, have a place where the child can get up and play quietly, ideally in another room. Quiet play choices such as reading books or putting together puzzles are good.

Closure

It is good to have a closing ritual before children go home. Schedule a late afternoon group meeting when all the children are still there. You can talk about what you did that day, what was the most fun, new accomplishments or what is planned for tomorrow — always emphasizing the positive. Again, mention each child's name, and perhaps sing a special song or hold hands in the circle. This is your final way of acknowledging each child in the group and building a sense of belonging before everyone goes home.

Rethink circle time

Large group time, or circle time, is such a traditional aspect of the early childhood curriculum that sometimes people engage in it automatically without truly examining its values. It warrants a good look.

Challenges of circle time:

The adult is less available

When the carer is conducting circle time, they are not very accessible to individual children. They are intent on controlling the whole group and keeping everyone focused and engaged. Because each child is unique, it may be difficult to reach all the children at the same time. The more time you spend in circle time, the less time you have to spend with individual children.

Behaviour problems emerge

Circle time is often the least successful time of day for troubled children who may have difficulty paying attention, sitting still and blending into the group. They may not want to feel like part of the group. Much of their behaviour cries out, *Notice me!* Often emotionally needy children will get negative feedback from adults trying to get them to settle down during this part of the daily routine. Consider making circle time optional or not worrying if a child chooses not to sit down with the others as long as they are not disruptive and can still be supervised.

Value of circle time

This is not to say that circle time has no value for children or that you should discontinue it. There are some major advantages to circle time.

A sense of belonging

A major value of circle time is to develop a sense of belonging or togetherness. Circle time builds a sense of community for the children.

A neutral arena

You can bring up sensitive topics in a neutral, non-threatening way using books, puppets, pictures or the flannelgraph. In this way, children learn that they are not alone in their experiences.

The joy of music

Music activities, which are important opportunities for self-expression, are often best taught and enjoyed in group time. Knowing the same songs makes children feel like they belong to a group. Do not be surprised if you hear the children singing these songs spontaneously while they play.

Shared pleasures of language and literature

During group time, you can share a poem or picture book with the children. You can read aloud in a way that emphasizes the rhythmic flow of sounds or words.

Problem solving
This can also be a valuable time for group problem solving. Be sure to use this time to congratulate each other when a problem is finally solved.

Should this be a circle time activity?

For everything you plan to do in circle time, get into the habit of asking yourself, 'Does this really need to be done with the large group? Would it be more effective with one child at a time or with an informal small group during free playtime?' Often it is much more effective to read a book to two or three children snuggled together on your lap, for instance, or to use a puppet to talk to an individual child.

The importance of the child-centred curriculum

Make the most of free playtime

The greatest learning takes place during free playtime, when children choose or initiate the activity. That is when you will see children exhibiting concentrated attention. This is also a time when questions emerge and communication skills are practised. More importantly, for our purposes, you are able to settle down with a few children at that time, rather than being in charge of the whole group.

The child centred curriculum

There has always been some confusion about the term *child choice* or *free play*. We now refer to free play as the *Child Centred Curriculum*. This term 'is used to refer to the framework of planned activities and experiences based on the different aspects of children's development: emotional, physical, social, intellectual, along with communication and language, aesthetic experience, and attitudes and values,' (From *Education of Children under 5 in Scotland*, Scottish Office Education Department). Some people think that during free playtime staff sit back and do nothing while the children play. However, for free play to be a learning experience staff have to plan carefully, observe play and interact with to develop skills and interests further. Planning the child centred curriculum so that children develop necessary skills is a daily and/or weekly essential team activity. Staff will plan to develop children's noted interest as well as the areas of development outlined previously. Plan your environment so that activities support the full range of children's developmental needs. Plan which materials will be available to the children and how to display these materials so that they are easily accessible and encourage independence.

How do staff ensure that children develop skills as they play?

During free play time, the staff member is able to settle down with a small group of children, either facilitating a project such as an art or cooking activity, or observing children's play, noting how children interact with each other, what issues they work on in their play, how they use language to express themselves and which materials each child seems to enjoy most. At times, the staff member may join in the play but should always follow the children's lead.

During free playtime, the staff are available to talk to a particular child, read a book to one or two children or just play with a small group of children, making them feel valued and accepted.

In short, it is during free playtime that the staff member can truly concentrate on what is happening with individual children and build relationships with them.

Why is the child centred curriculum valuable?

The main premise behind free playtime is that children almost always choose the very activity that is just right for them on that given day, provided the environment is rich and varied with many appropriate choices. So make it truly child choice time and do not try to rotate children from one area to another or force them to do everything. Allowing children to choose how they want to spend their time respects them as individuals and gives them a sense of power. Remember that children learn from everything in your environment. Trust them to select what they need!

Keep things interesting by including a variety of choices, including puzzles and construction toys, dramatic play accessories, books and a wide assortment of materials for creative expression and sensory play. Vary what is available. However, it is also good to have consistency, making many of the same materials and favourite toys available from day to day. This makes children feel safe; they know what to expect and where to find favourite things.

Plan special projects such as cooking or art experiences to be a choice during free playtime. Although many children may choose to participate in the specially planned project, allow those who do not to play somewhere else.

If all the children are new to the setting, or many of the children are easily distracted (one outcome of excessive stress in their lives), it is best to start with a limited number of play choices so you do not overwhelm them. Let them have a chance to get to know each new toy or material without feeling pressured to move on to the next thing.

Make the most of outdoor time

do not forget that outdoor time is a valuable part of play when different types of play and learning can occur. Staff often neglect outside time. They may fail to involve themselves in the play or maximize the possibilities for valuable, expressive play. More sociodramatic play goes on outside than inside, especially for boys. Sand and water play opportunities outside mean less mess to clean up and give children chances for free expression. Active, gross motor play allows children to release energy and feel powerful. Plan in order to make the most of this valuable portion of your day.

Resources

Curriculum planning

Bruce, Tina, *Time to Play,* Hodder and Stoughton Educational, 1991.

Denman-Sparks, Louise, *Anti-Bias Curriculum,* Association for the Education of Young Children, 1993.

Bruce, Tina, *Early Childhood Education,* Hodder and Stoughton Educational, 1997.

Drummond, M.J., Lally, M., Pugh, G., (Eds.), *Working with Children: Developing a Curriculum for the Early Years,* Published by the National Children's Bureau and NES Arnold, 1989.

Starting with Quality, The Rumbold Report, Her Majesty's Stationery Office.

Bredekamp, Sue. (Ed.), *Developmentally Appropriate Practice in Early Childhood Programmes: Serving Children from Birth through Age 8.* (Ed.). Specialist Early Childhood Publications, 1993.

Classroom environment

Smith, Charles, *The Peaceful Classroom,* Floris Books, 1998.

Edginton, Margaret, *The Nursery Teacher in Action,* Sage Publications Inc., 1998.

Hurst, Victoria, *Planning for Early Learning,* Sage Publications Inc., 1997.

Working with under 5s, PE635, The Open University.

Greenman, Jim, *Caring Spaces, Learning Places: Creating Environments That Work,* Exchange Press, 1988.

Outside play

Smith, Charles, *The Peaceful Classroom,* Floris Books, 1998.

Petrash, Carol, *Earthwise: Environmental Crafts and Activities with young Children,* Floris Books, 1992.

Moyles, Janet R., *Just Playing?* Open University Press, 1989.

David, Tricia, *Under Five — under educated?,* Open University Press, 1990.

Miller, Karen, *The Outside Play and Learning Book: Activities for Young Children.* Gryphon House, 1998.

Chapter Twenty-Three

Curriculum Ideas and Activities

Section 1: Dramatic Play

Dramatic play is an extremely important part of the early childhood curriculum and is often undervalued by both staff and parents. Perhaps this is because children who have spent a morning engaged in dramatic play or pretend play have nothing to show for it — no concrete product. In our results-oriented adult thinking, that may be viewed as wasted time. On the contrary, the kind of play where the child takes on a role pretending to be somebody else, and interacts with other children from within that role, is very valuable.

Value of dramatic play

Relief from emotional tension

When adults experience a traumatic event in their lives, like the death of a friend or relative or witnessing a terrible accident, they may cope with it through conversation, retelling the event over and over. Children, however, tend to replay the event in their dramatic play rather than talk about it.

If a child attends a funeral, they are likely to *play funeral* afterwards with friends, dolls and stuffed toys. Children who have experienced a fire like to play *fire*, making the blocks rumble and running for cover. If a child witnesses a car accident on the way to school, they might spend the morning in the block corner making toy cars collide with each other, or crash their tricycle into someone else's.

Children feel powerful

When children re-enact frightening experiences, they usually put themselves in a position of power. They often choose the role of mummy or daddy, the most powerful people in their lives. When they play *fire* they are the ones who make the fire start and stop. When they play *hospital*, they are the ones who give the injections. Children often feel powerless, especially when faced with a crisis. This leads to extreme frustration, fear and feelings of dependency and helplessness. In pretend play, all things are possible. A child can punish the aggressor they are afraid of in real life. Wishes can come true.

Empathy and social interaction

Dramatic play offers children valuable opportunities to see things from someone else's point of view. When they have make-believe experiences where they have put themselves in someone else's shoes, they become better able to do it in real life. This role-playing ability is especially useful in developing conflict resolution and problem solving skills.

When children interact with each other in their roles, they also learn to negotiate and work together. You may hear much discussion about who is going to do what and how.

Language development

Language development is fostered by dramatic play. Expressive language is augmented when children are motivated to make their wishes known to other children and speak from within their roles. It may be in the dramatic play area that you hear your first real expressive language from shy, withdrawn or frightened children. Receptive language is also enhanced as children pick up vocabulary from other children.

When children have had many experiences acting out the story line of their own dramas, they become better able to follow the sequence of events in a picture book. They learn about sequential thinking, realizing that events take place in a certain order.

Use of symbols

When children have many opportunities to create and use symbols of their own making, they gradually become better able to use other symbols, like letters, words and numbers. For younger children, or children who have not had much experience with pretend play, the props available have to be very concrete. The object has to look like a telephone for a two-year-old child to use it like a telephone. A four-year-old child, however, who is experienced in dramatic play, can use a block or even a hand gesture to represent a telephone. A doll is a symbol for a baby, or even the child themselves. A paper plate might become a steering wheel. Pieces of paper become money. A stick or extended finger becomes a gun. A piece of material tied on their back becomes a cape symbolizing supernatural power.

Sorting out fantasy and reality

It is obvious that dramatic play helps children to sort out fantasy and reality when they announce, 'I'm just pretending!' When they are sure that everyone present knows this, they feel safe to explore the possibilities of the role. You will also hear them change their voices into exaggerated inflections as a signal that they are playing a role.

The role of the adult

Provide time

The key element is to provide enough time for children to become deeply involved in their play. Children need time to decide what they are playing, who has what roles, what dressing up clothes and props they will need, and how to negotiate the action. If they are frustrated in their attempts to get started, they may be discouraged from engaging in dramatic play. Generally, playtime of 45 minutes to one hour at a stretch is needed to foster good play.

Provide space and materials

TYPICAL HOUSEKEEPING EQUIPMENT. This should include a table and chairs, stove, refrigerator, sink, dishes, telephones, dolls, doll beds and standard home accessories.

DRESSING UP CLOTHES for both traditional and non-traditional male and female roles.

Whenever possible, **PROVIDE PROPS RELEVANT TO THE CRISIS** the child is experiencing, such as a pretend vet's office if the child's pet has died.

Provide objects and materials that children can use in many different ways when engaging in dramatic play. For example:

— Suitcases
— Containers of all types, such as shopping bags, boxes, barrels
— Telephones in different styles, walkie-talkies, beepers
— Large pieces of fabric, tablecloths, or blankets
— Writing materials, such as paper, note pads, marker pens, tape
— Art materials they can use to create other props they need.

Help children plan

Involve children in gathering and creating props for their play. Later on, they will do it for themselves. 'What do we need to make a hospital?' 'What could we use?' 'Do you think we could make that out of something?'

WHAT DO THEY WANT TO PLAY? Find out which children want to play pretend. Ask them what roles or situations they think they will want to act out. Help them to decide what things might happen (enriching the theme), what props they will need and where they can play so they will not disturb the other children. You do not want to take away their spontaneity, but you do want to encourage them to organize their thoughts so their dramatic play will be a better experience.

When the children have finished playing, talk to them informally about what they played. Can they describe the scene and the action? Were there any problems? Do they think they will play this again or add some variation the next time? This builds self-awareness and problem solving on the part of the children and also tells them that you are interested in play that comes from their own ideas.

Observe the action

Observe children's play and think about how each child is involved.

Favourite themes. What kinds of pretend situations does the child seem to prefer?

Does the child engage mostly in solitary play or is he able to include others?

With whom does the child usually want to play?

Does the child simply use the props in front of them, or are they creative in making their own props or improvising?

Discuss and negotiate? Does the child discuss the play with others and negotiate what will happen and who will do what?

Is the child a leader or a follower in deciding play themes and determining the action?

Extend the play

Do not edit. The play belongs to the children and they should be able to play out themes of interest to them, with the exception of sexual activity or exploitation. In that case, stop the play and involve the child in something else (see Chapter 11 on sexual child abuse).

Ask the children what they are playing. See if they can describe the situation to you. Ask them questions that might further define roles. 'Is the bad person always bad?'

Ask questions that will extend play. 'How will someone know your shop is open?' 'Will your passengers need any money?'

Sometimes adding a simple prop related to the play theme will make it more interesting for the children.

Take on a role. On occasion, play with the children and use your role to support the other players. Do not take the dominant role. Be a passenger rather than the driver, a patient rather than the doctor. Follow the children's lead and do not dictate the action. You can even ask them how you should act. 'Should I pretend to be afraid?'

If you notice that the play is imitating violent television shows, you could either take on a role yourself to redirect the play, or ask questions to give the play more depth. 'It looks like that person is hurt. Should we call 999?' (see Chapter 15 on television violence).

A good time for you to take on a role is when a child becomes fixated on a particular role or plays the same thing in the same way over and over again. As a fellow player, you can help the child develop new roles and subplots.

What to do if the topic troubles you

Be careful not to over-interpret. When you see troubling play themes such as beating up a doll or acting out some form of substance abuse, do not assume they signify a real problem. The child may, for instance, be re-enacting something seen on television or in the play of other children.

Ask questions or make a comment. 'It looks like the mummy is really angry with that baby.'

Be careful with the child's feelings. If you feel the need to stop the play or change its theme, tone down the intensity of your response so the child does not feel ashamed.

Observe over a period of time. If the troubling play themes continue in spite of your efforts, talk to your supervisor about the problem. You may decide to seek the advice of other professionals such as a child psychologist or social worker.

If the play gets rough, you can ask the players, 'Do you feel safe?' Then remind the players that everyone has a right to feel safe in the classroom.

Stop hurtful play. If the play involves sexism or hurtful words or actions, make a statement that affirms everyone's rights and dignity. 'In our classroom, play cannot hurt someone's feelings.'

Superhero play. For a discussion of superhero and war play, see Chapter 15 on television violence.

Miniature play

Another kind of pretend play that has great value is the kind that goes on in the block corner, the sand box and the doll's house. In this type of play, the child literally becomes a giant, able to create a miniature world and manipulate all the characters within it. Is it any wonder that this type of play has such appeal to children?

Value of miniature play

The child assumes a position of total power, which may relieve feelings of frustration that come from being powerless in an adult world.

Miniature play gives children a way to tell their stories. Many children do not have the language skills to tell their stories any other way.

Use of symbols. Miniature people and objects symbolize real people and objects for the child. In some cases, the child creates their own symbols to add to the other available objects. Blocks are used to build rooms or highways. Boxes become rooms. Pieces of fabric become tents or roofs.

Creativity and imagination. The child learns that their ideas are valued. As they create props and scenes, they use materials in new ways. They learn to ask the question, 'What could I use for...?'

Problem solving. The child learns to experiment with ways to create a certain scene or effect.

Solitary or group play. The child can play alone or with others. When playing as a group, children will practise language, negotiation, communication, and conflict resolution skills.

Character identification. This doll is me, the child thinks. Through this type of play, they can put themselves in the middle of a situation in a non-threatening way.

More control than dress-up play. Miniature play gives the child even more control than dressing up because the child can take on several roles simultaneously.

Block play

People usually think of play with wooden unit blocks as constructive play, and that is certainly one aspect of their use. Children use blocks to construct things, and in doing so gain all the benefits of that type of play; developing problem-solving skills, absorbing mathematical concepts, and learning concepts of space, size and location. However, depending on the accessories available, dramatic play is equally dominant. In fact, the block corner is where the indoor dramatic play of most boys takes place.

To enrich the dramatic play potentials in block play, provide a variety of accessories.

Purchased accessories

Early childhood suppliers offer a wide variety of high quality, durable accessories for block play. It is best if solid blocks are mathematically accurate in relation to each other as those sold by Early Learning Centres and specialist educational suppliers. Toys designed for use in the home are usually not durable enough to stand up to rough use by many children, they may also be stereotypical. Be careful what you make available.

— Cars, lorries, fire engines, police cars, ambulances

— Accessories relevant to the children's culture. For example, saris, crockery, utensils, hats, turbans.

— It is possible to order small wooden or plastic people with different skin colours from school suppliers. Also, look for figures that represent both men and women in various work roles. Small, flexible doll's house families also make good block corner accessories.

— Small animals. Beautifully made and sturdy replicas of farm and wild animals are available. Farm accessories such as barns and fences are also available.

— Dinosaurs. Although young children may not have a true understanding of dinosaurs and prehistoric times, toy dinosaurs are valuable because they symbolize frightening things. By using them in their play, children can confront danger and conquer frightening situations.

Improvised accessories

There are many kinds of objects that can add to children's play in the block corner. Again, involve the children by asking them what they might need to create something and help them locate materials. Also bring abstract props into the block corner and ask the children, 'How do you think you could use these?'

— Shoe boxes and other small containers
— Cardboard tubes
— Flexible plastic tubing
— Coffee can lids
— Canning rings
— Aluminium foil
— Large pieces of fabric
— Plastic fruit baskets
— Torches
— Wool
— Masking tape
— Writing materials

Dressing up clothes

Adding a few items for the child to put on as they play can enhance miniature play. Perhaps dressing up helps the child to concentrate and put themself into the role.

— Workmen's hats including hard hats
— Head phones
— Beepers and pretend mobile phones

Tips for cleaning up time

One reason the block corner can be an unpopular place for teachers and some children is the hassle of cleaning up time. Here are some tips:

MAKE SURE THE CHILDREN HAVE HAD ENOUGH TIME TO PLAY. When children feel like they are right in the middle of a project, they will be more reluctant to dismantle it to put the blocks away.

KEEP TRACK OF WHO PLAYED THERE. Children may spend most of the play period in the block corner and then suddenly change activities at the very end, just before cleaning up time. They can be told to go back and help clean up.

NOTICE THEIR CONSTRUCTIONS. Children are often reluctant to tear down something that they have made. It may help to take a photo or make a drawing of the construction first. Sometimes it is enough if the teacher just takes the time to look at the construction and discuss it with the children.

Give block builders a few extra minutes for tidying up. Start them a little earlier than the others and give them a few minutes of warning so they can put the finishing touches to their building project.

CONSIDER LEAVING THE CONSTRUCTION UP. You probably cannot do this all the time, but every now and then you might put a 'Please leave this up' or 'Please do not disturb' sign on the building so the child can go back to it during the next play period. Make the children put away the extra blocks they did not use.

OUTLINE THE BUILDING. Make a masking tape line around the perimeter of the building so that the children can attempt to rebuild the structure in the same place during the next play period.

A sock or other type of puppet that can pick up things with its mouth or hands can be a useful helper and elicit eager co-operation from children. The puppet can pick up blocks, ask children to hand them other blocks and talk about how much fun tidying up can be when everyone pitches in.

Create an assembly line. This can turn drudgery into fun. Position a child who is good at organizing and recognizing shapes next to the shelf. Make the other children form a line from that child to the block corner. They should be spaced an arm's length apart. Then make the children pass the blocks down the line. The child by the shelf stacks the blocks according to shape.

Divide and conquer. Put one block of each shape into a box or bag. Make each child reach into a box and pick out a shape to put away. One child puts away all the triangles, another all the squares, etc.

Use a small wagon or big lorry. Children enjoy filling the back of a lorry or trailer with blocks, then pushing it over to the shelf and unloading it.

Express admiration and appreciation for a job well done! Comment on how nice the block corner looks with everything in order. Talk about the reason for this as well. 'Now you will be able to find things easily when you play there again.'

When a child seems *stuck* in the block corner

Teachers may worry when a child spends all of their free playtime in the block corner, but this is really not a cause for concern. The learning potential of block play is so great that there is almost no place else a child could settle that would be more beneficial. Add variety to the experience by bringing in different props and creative materials like writing and art supplies for making signs and props. Bring books or measuring tools and scales to the block corner.

Provide enough unit blocks

In my experience, early childhood centres usually do not have enough unit blocks available for children's play. They are an expensive purchase when setting up a nursery, and there are many other demands on the budget. However, without an adequate supply and variety of blocks, the value of the play will be diminished. It is worth a fundraising effort to augment the supplies of blocks available in the block corner.

Doll's house play

Doll's houses are very useful to have in classrooms where children are experiencing trauma or crises in their lives, since so many crises centre around the family. A doll's house gives the child a setting to play out scenes and control the drama.

Unfortunately, doll's houses made for home use and the furniture and accessories that go with them are generally not sturdy enough to withstand the play of many children in group settings. So it is definitely advisable to buy doll's houses and accessories from early childhood suppliers where the materials are designed for childcare and early childhood education settings.

Children can create their own rooms using blocks. If you do not have a doll's house and cannot afford one, ask the children to help you create rooms from cardboard boxes. Wallpaper the rooms with patterned self-adhesive paper or wallpaper samples and glue a carpet or flooring sample to the floor. Add windows, curtains and other trimmings. The children will have fun looking through magazines and finding little pictures for the walls that they can cut out and add. A series of small boxes could even be arranged by the child to make their own house configuration or neighbourhood.

Use sturdy, purchased doll's house furniture in these home-made rooms, or let older children make the furniture from small boxes, paper cups and other materials of their choosing.

Represent different races and cultures. School suppliers all carry doll's house families representing different races. Provide doll's house dolls that represent all the children and families in your group.

Make home-made doll's house dolls. These can be made by bending and twisting pipe cleaners and then wrapping this wire frame with adhesive tape. Make the heads from fabric stretched over cotton wool balls. Features can be drawn on with permanent markers. Sew on some wool hair.

Sand play

The outdoor sand area or indoor sand tray can be a great setting for miniature dramatic play.

Sand that is a little damp can be moulded into shapes more easily. It also keeps its shape as roads, rivers and mountains are built. Try giving children spray bottles with a small amount of water so they can dampen their own sand.

In addition to traditional sand toys like shovels, spoon, and buckets, provide children with some of the miniature play accessories such as little people, animals, plastic fruit basket, fences, vehicles and even doll's house furniture. Plastic dinosaurs are particularly popular. Children like burying and digging them up and creating attack dramas. Indoors and out, use objects from nature such as pine cones and sticks to create trees and other landscape features.

Display accessories. Indoors, keep a group of miniature accessories on a shelf next to the sand tray. Let children help themselves to the accessories they want to use rather than dumping everything into the tray.

Other opportunities for miniature play

Table top play

Play with water, cornflour, clay and other materials can easily involve miniature people and accessories.

Shaving cream on table top

Smearing large, soft, fragrant gobs of shaving cream on a table top is a favourite activity in early childhood classrooms. Increase the fun by adding plastic animals and dinosaurs, fruit boxes, plastic vehicles and other small accessories. Give each child a Styrofoam or paper cup and show them how to invert it and push it through the shaving cream to create roads.

People dolls

Take a photo of each child in your group (whole body, not just face), or cut out pictures from magazines and catalogues representing different types of people. Include people of different races and ages. Let the children help you search for suitable pictures. Cut out and mount the photos or magazine pictures on sturdy cardboard or thin wood and laminate. These figures can be made to stand up in lumps of modelling clay or play dough. For a more permanent result, mix up plaster of Paris and pour it in spray can lids. Then stick the people figures in this and allow to set. Children might use these like stick puppets, making them talk to each other, or they might move them around in a doll's house or block setting.

Spontaneous miniature play

You will see children engaging in this type of play in every imaginable setting, planned or unplanned. A child might *drive* a crayon up one arm and down another, crashing in various places along the way.

Role of the staff member in miniature play

Observe, do not edit. The play belongs to the child and they should be allowed to play out any theme they wish with the materials provided. Make note of the play themes that might bother you and discuss these with your supervisor if you feel you need to.

Provide materials and help the child gather what they need.

Organize materials so they are easy for the child to find.

Make creative art materials available in case the child needs to create something to enhance the scene.

Help the child think about the play. Ask the child to describe what they are playing. Ask extending, open-ended questions. Usually a child is eager to describe the action to an interested adult. But be careful not to be intrusive. You will not want to do this every time the child plays.

Offer to be a recorder for the child. You could take dictation as the child describes what is going on. Later, the child might like to illustrate this description of their own play. Perhaps it can be something to share with parents.

Section 2: Creative Art

Children need many ways to tell their stories, express their emotions and influence their environment. Dramatic play and playing with blocks are some of the ways children can express themselves in an early childhood education environment. Painting, scribbling, drawing, playing with clay, singing, dancing, making things and using words are other ways. Words are important. Young children grow rapidly in their ability to express themselves verbally, but verbal expression is often not a child's most effective way of communicating.

The staff's challenge is to offer children many different ways to express themselves and many interesting materials to use. Another challenge is to allow children freedom of expression, and to be accepting of that expression.

Open-ended activities

Resist suggesting to children what they should draw or make. If a staff member tells a child to draw a dog and it does not end up looking like a dog, the child will feel that they failed and will be less interested in trying things in the future. If a staff member produces an example of what a craft project should look like, and the child's efforts fall short, the child again feels like a failure. This can erode self-esteem.

However, when a child is given interesting, beautiful materials and encouragement to express themselves, they have an opportunity to feel successful and to develop potential talents. Do value the product a child comes up with on their own, whether it is a block building, a clay animal, a painting of abstract shapes, a new way of moving to music or an elaborate drawing. Show children you value their work in many ways.

Show interest. Look with appreciation at what they did. Comment on the physical characteristics of what you see. 'I see you used mostly rectangle blocks and made both sides the same.' 'You used lots of yellow today.' 'You used round stickers for the wheels of your car!'

Be careful with their work. If children make something such as a painting or collage, help them find a place where it can dry or be stored without being damaged.

Display children's work attractively. An ever-changing display of children's art near the entrance of your classroom will show children and visitors that you value the work. If a child insists on taking their artwork home, try asking them to make another one for you to put up in the room because you like it so much. A child is often proud to comply with such a request.

Invite (but do not insist) the child to tell you about their work. Offer to take dictation and create a descriptive label for it.

Sometimes teachers are tempted to alter, improve or correct a child's work. Avoid doing this. A child should not be made to feel that their work is not good enough.

Help others, especially parents, notice and appreciate the child's work. Describe how children benefit from such an activity. A photo of the child engaged in the process of creating it is especially meaningful.

Occasionally photograph non-permanent creativity. Catch a child involved in creative movement. Surprise actors in the middle of their dramatic play with a camera. Take a snapshot of that great block building before it has to be put away. Display these pictures or put them in your class scrapbook for parents to see.

All of this tells the child, 'I think you are interesting. You have good ideas.' This builds self-esteem and encourages the child to communicate more.

Creative art

The process of creating art can help build a sense of self-worth and identity in a child. When they make a drawing, sculpture or collage, they put something of themselves into it. They have made a mark, altered the world a little bit. Sometimes children are able to work out unconscious feelings through artwork, either through the physical motion of smearing paint across the page, which can serve as a release of tension, or through using symbols.

Play therapists have long used children's drawings to try to work out their emotions. Early childhood teachers are not usually trained in this skill, and I caution you against over-interpreting children's artwork. A child may be using a lot of black and red in a painting because they are feeling depressed, or have a lot of rage, or because they really like bold colours! They may draw themselves tiny when they draw their family because they feel small and insignificant, or because they did not think they had left enough room on the page. Do not worry about interpreting children's drawings, although you might save some in the child's file. Creative art is therapeutic. It has value all by itself without any interpretation. It is fun. It makes pretty colours. It feels good.

When planning art activities, bear in mind that the child should be able to do the entire project by themself. If the adult has to do any part of it, question if it is really appropriate for this age.

Do not use colouring books or pre-drawn patterns for children to colour or paint. The object is to get children to express themselves, and these items inhibit self-expression. It is the illustrator's ideas that are on the page and not the ideas of the child. Colouring book patterns also inhibit creativity in other ways. Children are less likely to draw things in their own way when they have seen the example in a pattern. There is a greater possibility of failure and comparison. It is very difficult for young children to stay within the lines. Other children might be quick to point out where a child went out of the lines. Children do not learn anything at all about the object depicted in a two-dimensional line drawing, so there is virtually no learning value to colouring books and reproduced patterns.

Help-yourself art and craft

Certain materials should always be available for children to express their ideas with. The particular items you make available on a daily basis might vary from group to group, but they should be consistent for that group. The older and more capable children should have a greater variety of items to choose from.

A HELP-YOURSELF ART AND CRAFT SHELF MIGHT CONTAIN:

— Writing implements
— Pencils, black and coloured
— Ball-point and felt-tipped pens
— Wide-tipped felt markers
— Paper
— Newspaper
— Scrap paper from offices and printing shops
— Construction paper in various colours
— Sticking agents
— Several types of tape
— Glue pens
— Paste
— Small bottles of white glue
— Children's round-tipped scissors
— A collage box with a variety of interesting materials to glue
—Cardboard, paper plates and other things to use as collage bases

Work to build children's independence with art and craft materials

When you teach children to work independently with art and craft materials, you make them feel more capable. You also give yourself more free time to interact with the children because you do not have to oversee everything.

Show children how to use materials properly. You could do this as a circle time activity. For instance, you could demonstrate how to dip a brush in paint, wipe it against the side of the cup to remove excess paint, use it on the paper and then return it to the same paint cup.

Teach children to put materials away properly. Each item should have a specific spot on the shelf. It helps to label the spot with a picture of the object.

Teach children to put on their own aprons, or ask a friend for help.

Older children can learn to put paper on the easel, remove it when they are finished and take it to a drying rack.

Gather interesting materials

Another way you can show children that you respect them is by giving them beautiful, high quality materials to work with. Offer children a wide variety of materials, including standard items that are always available. Be on the lookout for interesting materials the children might enjoy. If a certain item is a big hit, budget to purchase more in the future so that it becomes a standard item.

Mix paints well. If you use powdered paints, be sure to mix them well. Try using baby powder as a paint extender. It creates a creamy consistency and sparkles a little when dry. Discard paint that becomes muddy from mixed colours.

Have a range of colours for children to use. Let them choose the colours they want to paint with from a wide assortment.

Include different skin tone colours. Paint, crayons and marker pens now come in many different skin colours.

Collect interesting brushes and rollers for children to use in their painting projects.

Collect paper scraps. Print shops often have scraps of interesting paper to give away.

Visit a recycling centre. Staff can pick up unique industry rejects that can be used for art projects and other activities in your classroom.

Basic processes

Drawing

Some children will begin representational drawing as young as three years of age, telling the adult proudly what it is they have represented on paper. Other children will simply experiment with lines and patterns. Young children should not be pressured to make or draw something that looks like a particular person or object.

Very young children enjoy the pure pleasure of scribbling. They are learning that they can make marks and are discovering the relationship of their arm and hand movements to where the marks go. It takes a lot of scribbling practice before children can control their movements and make marks that are more systematic. Also, it is difficult for children under three to do two different things with their hands. Since drawing requires the child to hold the paper with one hand and move the drawing implement with the other, it helps to tape the paper to the table top, wall or easel.

Crayons have distinct advantages for young children over other drawing materials. Crayons are the only medium that responds to the pressure the child exerts. Light pressure makes a fine, pastel line and heavy pressure makes a dark, bold line. Children can use the tip and the broad side of a crayon. Old and broken crayons can be peeled, melted in baking trays in a warm oven and cooled to make *hockey puck* crayons. Plus they come in every colour imaginable. Have both fat and thin crayons on hand so that children can experiment to see which is the easiest to use.

Felt-tipped marker pens are also interesting to use because with very little pressure they make a bright, vivid line that is very satisfying to children. Use them on finger-paint paper or coated shelf paper. However, if the child wants to press hard with the markers,they will quickly destroy them so in some cases they are inappropriate. Supervise the use of marker pens with very young children because they sometimes like to suck them. Safety note: Pen and marker caps are just the right size for choking. Discard pen caps. Sink marker caps, open side up, into wet plaster of Paris poured into a small container. Place the caps so they stick up about half an inch above the surface of the plaster of Paris. These caps now cannot be swallowed, and you will not lose them.

Suggestions for supplies to include in a drawing centre:

- — Fat and thin crayons
- — Wide-tipped felt markers
- — Fine-tipped marker pens

— Coloured and white chalk and a blackboard
— Various types of pencils and rubbers
— Coloured pencils
— Oil crayons
— Ball-point pens
— Several types of paper
— Small writing pads
— Clip boards

Painting

Children who are under stress often find painting to be a very satisfying release. Try to make this activity available each day. Control messiness by teaching children how to use the paint and brushes properly. Teach the children to put on an apron and be independent in the process. Children often love the job of washing out the brushes at the sink under a running stream of water, watching the colour come out and gradually fade.

Some children will really thrive on consistency; having the same kind of paint and the same colours available all the time. However, if you sense that the children need a change, add variety to the painting process by changing the medium, the tools or the surface used to paint on. Here are some ideas.

THE MEDIUM:

— Offer different combinations of colours.
— Mix the paint thickly one day, thinly the next.
— Use block paints.
— Mix different things into the paint. For example, baby powder, coffee grounds, sawdust.

THE TOOLS:

— Standard easel brushes
— Short-handled paintbrushes from the hardware shop
— Wide house-painting brushes
— Fine, watercolour brushes
— Make-up brushes

— Sponges of various textures
— Small paint rollers from the hardware shop

The surface:

— Easel paper and lining paper
— Aluminium foil
— Plastic wrap
— Wax paper
— Cardboard boxes of all shapes
— Wood scraps

Finger-painting is a valuable process to offer children. It is messy and requires supervision and planning. Some children will be reluctant to try it and get their hands dirty. These children might be more comfortable finger-painting with shaving cream on a table top. Make sure children are wearing aprons and have their sleeves pushed up. Coated finger-paint paper works best, allowing the smooth paint to glide across the glossy surface. Coated shelf paper can also be used. You might consider allowing children to finger-paint directly on the surface of the table or on a baking sheet.

Face painting is wonderful fun and a good self-image activity. Place a long mirror sideways on a table top and position chairs and paints in front of it. Let children sit side by side and paint their own faces with small paintbrushes. Use specially bought face paints for safety.

Collage

Children enjoy all kinds of cutting, pasting and gluing activities. The main challenge is to gather a rich variety of materials with different shapes, textures and colours for children to use. The greater the variety of materials, the more imaginative children's productions will be. Keep a large divided collage box on the art shelf, or create a separate Collage Area. As you collect things, think about three variables:

— the bases to which children can stick things
— the things that they can stick on
— the sticking agent.

Suggestions for a collage area:

BASES:

— Pre-cut pieces of heavy cardboard
— Paper plates
— Plastic coffee can lids
— Corrugated cardboard
— Cardboard boxes
— Small, flat pieces of wood

STUFF TO CUT AND STICK:

— Old greeting cards
— Old magazines
— Ribbon scraps
— Wool scraps
— Lace scraps
— Fabric scraps
— String
— Wire
— Buttons
— Fake fur pieces
— Coloured paper scraps
— Odd puzzle pieces

STICKING AGENTS:

— Small bottles of white glue
— Paste
— Glue pens
— Masking tape
— Sellotape
— Coloured electrical tape

In addition, provide children's round-tipped scissors. Children might also use some of the writing materials to add lines or colour to their collages.

Sticky wall

Attach a large piece of self-adhesive paper, sticky side out, to the wall at the children's height. Remove the backing. Add a border if you like. Hang a bucket of fabric scraps and other interesting things like yoghurt container tops in front of it. Let the children stick the objects on to the wall and peel them off again. You could also attach a photo of each child to a yoghurt top so the children can put their friends' pictures on to the sticky wall.

A few more thoughts about creative art

There are, of course, many more art techniques besides those described here. Just remember to search out interesting techniques and materials that you think your children might enjoy. Refrain from telling them what to make and any form of patterned work where everybody's product ends up looking the same.

Art should be offered to children individually or in small groups when they also have plenty of other play choices. Never sit the whole group down at once to do a project as this does not respect children's individual interests. Children will be much more relaxed in a small group and have more opportunity for conversation with you about what they are doing, and there is less wasted time. If children have a hard time waiting for their turn to do an art activity, offer them a sign-up sheet so they can be sure they will have art time too.

Also bear in mind that sometimes boys stay away from art activities. If pressed, they will do one quick sample to please the staff and then head somewhere else. To entice reluctant boys, invite several to the art area at the same time. Try taking art outside where children can make a mess with great abandon. A different setting may attract children who are reluctant to paint indoors.

Finally, do not feel pressurized to offer something new and different every day. Children enjoy doing the same process again and again. A child who has done seven paintings in a row gets more out of the experience than the child who is forced to move on after only one painting. Some children just like to sample an art activity, while others want to repeat it many times.

Save samples of children's creative artwork and date them. It is exciting to see scribbles turn into suns and spiders and people. This is one concrete way to share the child's progress with parents. A child's artwork might also be of interest to a psychologist or play therapist who is working with the child.

Woodwork

Many staff members are hesitant to include woodwork in their classrooms. So woodwork benches sit unused in many classrooms. Although you might not choose to offer this type of activity to children who have severe problems with aggression, it can be a very satisfying creative activity for children if there is proper planning and set-up.

If possible, wait to introduce woodwork until all the children are familiar with each other and with routines, and you feel that you know individual children well. Open the woodwork area when you are free to supervise and are not deeply involved in other activities. There should be written safety procedures for staff to follow in relation to the use and supervision of tools. No child should be left unsupervised.

Value of woodwork

Banging and making a loud noise in an acceptable way can relieve physical tension caused by stress.

It offers a good alternative. Pounding at the woodwork bench can be a satisfying alternative when a child is inclined to hit another.

A child feels powerful as they make dents and cuts in wood.

A child enjoys using real tools and develops fine motor skills in the process.

Set-up

Place a child-sized woodwork bench in a corner of the room where noise will not disturb others. It should not be near the library or other quiet area, for instance. You might put it next to the art area because children often like to use art materials such as glue, paint, string and various collage materials along with the wood.

To reduce the noise, try carpeting the workbench by nailing on carpet samples. These can easily be replaced.

Keep a good supply of small wood scraps in a box nearby. Provide a variety of shapes and sizes. Ask a secondary school woodwork teacher if their students could cut up their scraps into small pieces for your class. Lumber yards and cabinet or furniture making shops are other good places to find wood scraps.

Store tools in a toolbox, or hang them on hooks near the workbench.

Limit participation to one or two children at a time. Create a sign-up system if necessary.

Introducing the children to woodwork

Children should be *checked off* on each tool before they are allowed to use it. To *check off* a child, show them how to use the tool safely and properly, then make them demonstrate the tool's use to you. At the same time, make the child show you that they know how to put the tool away properly.

Learn how to use the tools yourself first. You may need to find someone to teach you how to use them.

Start with simple hammering

Just pounding directly on wood (without nails) is very satisfying for children. You might start by letting them hammer tree trunk blocks, first using light wooden mallets, then later using real hammers.

Hammering with nails

To prevent children from hammering their thumbs, punch a nail through one end of an index card. Let them position the nail where they want it, then hold the other end of the card while they hammer. Short nails with large flat heads are best to use.

After they have had some experience with the index card, show them how to hold the nail and tap it lightly to make it stick in the wood. Tell them to let go of the nail and hold the side of the board before pounding it in further.

Sawing

You need either a vice or a C-clamp to firmly attach the board to the workbench before a child can use a saw effectively. Show the child how to put the wood into the vice and screw the vice shut. This can be fun. Then show them how to use the saw and how to keep it at a proper angle.

Taking things apart

Children enjoy using tools to take things apart, although screwdrivers may not be easy to use safely. Collect telephones, radios, alarm clocks and other small machines that are no longer usable for children to take apart. This builds fine motor skills, sparks curiosity and makes children feel powerful.

Don't worry about final products

Young children are very satisfied just using the tools and seldom care if they have a finished product at the end. They like making noise, seeing nails sink into wood, feeling the saw's vibrations and touching the pile of sawdust that accumulates. Sometimes a child will want to make something specific, like a sign for a block structure, and may even ask for help. Act as an advisor and help where needed, but allow the child to do as much as possible for themselves.

Music and movement

Music and movement is an essential part of any early childhood classroom. The benefits of music and movement for children in crisis are as follows:

It is another form of expression, a way for children to show emotions without having to use words.

Moving to music allows an acceptable release of energy.

It strengthens cultural identity when music from the child's culture is included in classroom.

It encourages children to feel happy. Singing and dancing is fun and can lift the mood of the children.

Music develops a sense of belonging, a sense of being part of a group. Singing is something people do together. When children know the words to the same songs and enjoy them together, they feel that they are all part of the same group. That is one reason to let children enjoy singing the same songs over and over, all year.

Sing anytime

There are certainly many fine children's recordings on the market, but do sing along with the recordings, and do not always use recordings. Children need real live examples to learn to sing. Use music as a handy tool, something you can pull out any time without the use of a tape recorder or record player. It is one of the best things in life and it is free! Here are some ways to encourage spontaneous music making.

Make up songs for various routines of the day. Weave children's names into the song as they perform the routines.

Make up songs or simple chants to sing when there are special events. Simply fit words to familiar tunes. For example, sing the following to *Mary had a Little Lamb.*

Henry got new shoes today,
Shoes today, shoes today.
Henry got new shoes today,
He likes them very much!

Encourage children to make up their own songs and sing them for you. You might record them on a cassette tape or invite the child to teach the song to the group. This is a great activity for increasing self-esteem.

When you hear a child chanting, as some children will do spontaneously, chant along with them.

Sing anytime. If you have to wait between activities, if lunch is late, or if it is a beautiful day and you're outside, just start singing one of the songs you all know and see who joins you.

Develop a collection of favourite songs. These could be made-up songs, songs from recordings or songs from songbooks. As you teach these to children, write down the words and add them to a loose-leaf notebook called *Our Songbook.* Illustrate the songs, or add children's illustrations. Place this book on a low table or in the music area. It will not take long for children to learn these songs if they can read the words as they sing. Parents may like a copy to use with the children at home.

Songs about feelings

There are many good children's songs about feelings, starting with *If You're Happy and You Know It.*

Make stick puppets that illustrate facial expressions for various emotions that children could hold up as they sing.

Mood music

Search for instrumental music that reflects various emotions. Classical music offers a wide range to choose from. Of course, you'll find plenty of examples in popular music as well, but sometimes the words in the songs are not appropriate. Occasionally put on one of these recordings and ask the children, 'Listen to this music. How does it make you feel?' You might invite children to scribble or paint while they listen.

Use lullabies at rest time

Soft recorded lullaby music is nice to play at rest time. There are a number of good recordings available. This does help drown out background noise and reduce distractions as children try to relax. It is especially nice if you offer to sing each child a special lullaby. Have several to choose from.

Haul out the band

Some teachers avoid using rhythm instruments because they can create chaos. That need not be the case. Using rhythm instruments with children gives them a legitimate opportunity to express themselves, but they do need training in the proper use of instruments.

Here are some hints to get the most value out of these materials:
In the beginning of the year, use rhythm instruments without any other music so children can concentrate on the sound they make. Also, use rhythm instruments as a small rather than large group activity.

Start with the body as the first instrument. Explore how it sounds when you all clap your hands, hit the top of your heads, open and close your mouths while tapping your cheeks, slap your thighs, stamp your feet or tap a table with your fingertips.

Let children practise controlling the sounds they make using their bodies. See if they can clap going from soft to loud to soft again. Then practise going from slow to fast and back to slow again.

Start by giving all children the same instrument. There will be less competition for favoured instruments and the children can concentrate on just one sound. Introduce the instruments to a small group of children.

Add one more instrument at a time. Create groups of two, then three different instruments. See if children can start and stop playing their instrument when you give them a signal like a bandleader. Later children can take on this conductor role.

When children have learned about the sounds of all the different instruments, add music.

Home-made instruments are fun to add. They include everything from coffee can drums to hollow tubes to wooden blocks.

Dancing to all kinds of music

Moving to music is another way to express oneself. Dancing is a good large group activity. Collect a wide variety of recorded music that is fun to move to, such as classical ballet music, marches, polkas and rock and roll. Do not bother with choosing partners or teaching dance steps. Keep it as free and open-ended as possible. Simply invite children to move in any way the music makes them feel. Bring out scarves, paper streamers or pompons to use when dancing.

Resources

Music and movement

Curry, Suzanna, *Little Folk,* Floris Books, 1996. Cassette tape.
Beall, Pamela C., and Nipp, Susan H., *Wee Sing Silly Songs,* Putnam Publishing Company, 1997.

SECTION 3: PLAY WITH SENSORY MATERIALS

This kind of play involves things that squish, drip, ooze and pour. These materials feel wonderful, and are especially good for children in crisis for the following reasons.

— A child can make things happen. A child can mould these materials, and this makes them feel powerful.

— The child has a legitimate way to make a controlled mess.

— These materials offer easy social interaction. They are especially good for children who are not very skilled at making friends or playing with others. When children play near each other, they may share ideas, comment on each other's projects and occasionally practise sharing and taking turns.

— These materials encourage the child's use of imagination. Listen for the stories that might emerge.

— Tactile materials offer cognitive benefits. By playing with these materials, children gradually absorb the concept of conservation of matter; that the amount remains the same even though the shape may change.

— The activities provide fine motor practice as the children fill and pour.

Another benefit of tactile materials is that they are often soothing and calming. The child focuses less on what is happening in the environment and more on the sensations in their fingertips. If you sense that a child is very tense, this might be a good way to help them settle down.

Tactile materials lend themselves to miniature play. Children might even create stories with them.

When you join in the play with sensory materials, copy the children's actions rather than showing them what to do. Be sure to show the proper way to handle the materials, such as not throwing sand, keeping the water in the water table.

Some children like tactile materials. Other children may have tactile sensitivity and not like the feel of certain kinds of materials. Never force tactile materials on children. A better strategy is to set them up in the classroom and let the children decide if they want to use them.

Try to offer at least one of the following tactile play options as one choice during every free playtime.

Water

Setting up

Some people hesitate to set up water play because cleaning up is too much work. Even with the rule, 'Keep the water in the water table (or sink, or saucepan),' some drips are inevitable. But remember that the children might actually enjoy using a mop to help clean up.

Protect children's clothing with waterproof aprons. Hang aprons nearby at the children's height. Show them how to put the aprons on themselves or ask a friend to help.

Start with fresh water for each play session. During cold weather, keep children with runny noses away from this play choice.

Place water play accessories on a nearby shelf. Let the children choose for themselves which accessories they want to use that day.

Also remember that water play is a great outdoor activity on a warm day.

Possible water play accessories:

THINGS FOR POURING:

— Plastic containers of different shapes and sizes
— Small plastic pitchers
— Funnels
— Plastic bottles

THINGS FOR EXPERIMENTING:

— Turkey basters
— Clear plastic plumbing tubing pieces
— Plastic eyedroppers
— Sponges of several types
— Collected junk for float and sink experiments

— Spray can tops and jar lids
— Containers with small holes punched in the bottom
— Plastic flower pots

THINGS FOR DRAMATIC PLAY:

— Little people
— Plastic boats
— Plastic plates to create islands
— Plastic animals and dinosaurs

From time to time, offer to add other things to the water, such as fluffy islands of shaving cream, food colouring or ice cubes. Let the children decide what to add.

Blowing bubbles

Blowing bubbles is one variation of water play that the child who avoids tactile play might enjoy. The deep breathing required to blow out the bubbles helps relieve tension. Bubble blowing usually puts children in a good mood. Bubbles are beautiful! The children are thrilled at their shapes and rainbow colours.

Bubbles can also be an exciting, tension-raising activity, depending on what you do with them. If you blow bubbles across the room and encourage children to catch them, you raise the activity level and create competition and sometimes collisions. You might want to do this type of activity when the children seem sluggish or in need of exercise. In that case, let children chase bubbles outside on a windy day.

A good bubble solution is about eight tablespoons of washing-up liquid to one litre of water. You can add a little glycerine to create stronger bubbles, but this really is not necessary.

Start by showing children how to blow through a straw rather than suck it. Get all the children to demonstrate that they can do this. Then give each child a small dish containing about one quarter of the bubble solution. Let them blow a big froth of bubbles.

Later let children experiment making bubbles using a variety of different materials.

Dip the end of a kitchen towel tube in the solution and blow slowly and steadily on the other end to make a big bubble.

Cut out the inside of a plastic coffee can lid to make a ring. Dip this in the solution and wave it through the air to make a long tube-like bubble.

Let children twist pipe cleaners into loops of various shapes, dip them in the bubble solution and blow on them.

Pour the bubble solution into a large baking tray. Twist a wire coathanger into a circle and dip it fully into the solution so that the whole space is covered with bubble film, (this might take several attempts). Then wave this through the air to make a really huge bubble.

Experiment with other things that have holes. Plastic fruit boxes, slotted spoons, tea strainers, key rings and funnels are just a few ideas.

Yes, bubbles are messy! Little puddles of soapy water will get all over the place and the floor might get slippery. So limit bubble blowing to a certain area of the classroom, and give the children have the pleasure of cleaning the floor when they have finished.

Sand and more sand

Sand play has many of the same benefits as water play and the set-up can be very similar. Even the accessories are similar, except you can add toy vehicles and sieves. Provide a broom and dustpan and brush in place of the mop for cleaning up.

There are a couple types of sand to consider, as well as offering wet and dry sand. Fine, soft sand, like beach sand, feels wonderful falling through your fingers and pours easily through a funnel. It is very soothing. On the other hand, it is not very good for moulding, sculpting or making roads. Coarser sand, like builders use for making concrete, is great for making roads, mountains and tunnels. Perhaps you could put one kind of sand indoors in the sand tray and another type outside in the sandbox.

Many different things can be put in trays besides water or sand. These include birdseed, paper *holes* from hole-punches, confetti, cottonwool balls, packing materials like shredded paper, or huge mounds of shaving cream. Each provides a different texture to explore. Involve the children in deciding what to put in the tray from week to week. Avoid any other substance that children can choke on, such as Styrofoam beads.

Create mud

It is fantastic to have mud days in the summer and flood part of the playground. Children can wear bathing suits and spend the whole day outside playing with hoses and sprinklers, creating lakes, mud puddles and rivers. However, it is also possible to give children a more controlled mud play experience any time of year, indoors or outdoors.

Use an empty sand tray and water tray — one filled with water and the other filled with sand and dirt. Let children experiment on their own combining different quantities of water, sand and earth. Also supply play dishes, large spoons and containers for scooping and pouring.

Clay

Try potters clay! It is a natural product — cool, soft, and recyclable. It comes in several different colours. It is *clean* dirt. Store it in a plastic rubbish bag inside a bucket with a lid. To keep it moist, add a little water to the bag, twist the bag closed and put the lid on the bucket. If it gets too gooey (not necessarily undesirable), let it dry out a bit in the open air. If it hardens into solid pieces, these can be reconstituted by putting them into a bag with water. Clay cleans up easily with wet sponges. You will find this kind of clay in school supply catalogues or. It comes either in powder form or in pre-mixed blocks. I recommend the pre-mixed blocks.

Put clay on the sensory table and simply cover it with plastic when not in use, or let children use it on a table top. To minimize mess, let children play with the clay on baking trays or plastic draining trays.

Some children love to pound clay with their hands. This is a good release of tension.

Many people make the mistake of encouraging children to create permanent objects out of clay to take home. Clay is very fragile when it dries and must be fired in a kiln. Even the oven-bake variety is still fragile after it is fired. The objects break easily. Remember that young children are not as interested in the final product as they are in messing around with the materials. Do not put pressure on them to make something. Instead let them enjoy poking, punching, squeezing and rolling. They are learning that they can change the shape of certain things. It is the pure sensory pleasure of the material — the way it feels when you play with it — that is its major value.

When joining children who are playing with clay, imitate what they are doing; poking, patting and rolling.

Fun accessories to include with clay are textured objects that leave an interesting pattern when pressed into it, such as onion bags and plastic fruit boxes, as well as plastic knives, pastry cutters, lollipop sticks to carve with, and plastic people and animals to stand up in it. Remember, though, that clay is fun to play with using no accessories at all.

Plasticine

Plasticine, or modelling clay as it is sometimes called, is a common early childhood play material. It comes in many bright colours and does not dry out. Although it is cleaner than potter's clay, it can get stuck in crevices of textured things and cannot be washed out as easily as potter's clay. It is difficult and frustrating to use when it is cold, and only becomes malleable when children have held it in their hands for a while. For all these reasons, clay is preferable to plasticine.

Playdough

Playdough, the early childhood classroom standard, is wonderful for its variety. In addition to the commercial product there are many different recipes for satisfying playdough, each with a slightly different texture. You can add food colouring and powdered gelatin mixes for colour and fragrance, or various cooking extracts and plastic glitter for variety.

Although people automatically bring out rolling pins and pastry cutters for accessories, playdough is great fun to use with the toy shredding machines that squeeze the dough through a shaped hole. Use a garlic press for a similar effect. Younger children love poking things into playdough, such as plastic drinking straws and birthday candles.

Make a huge amount of playdough and let children combine it with small plastic people, animals and vehicles to create miniature dramatic play scenes.

Gooey stuff

The following materials are favourites of many teachers and children. They are soothing and allow children to use their imagination. You can see the tension drain from children as they play with these materials and utter sounds of delight.

Shaving cream

Is it safe to let children play with shaving cream? The cans say, 'Keep out of the reach of children.' The manufacturers and poison control people I contacted said that once it is out of the can it is simply soap. If a child were to consume great quantities of it, they would only get stomach-ache. (I have never seen children take more than one little taste.) Like any soap, it can irritate the eyes. If a child's eyes come in contact with it, wash them out with water. Be sure to supervise the use of shaving cream. Push up children's sleeves so that the substance does not stay in cuffs and irritate the skin underneath. Avoid using the mentholated kind.

Some things to do with shaving cream:

— Let children finger-paint with it directly on the table top. Later, add a little food colouring or powdered paint to create pastels.

— Give them little people and animals to use with the shaving cream.
— Invert a styrofoam cup and scrape it along the surface where they have spread the shaving cream. This will create *roads*. Then give the children small vehicles to drive along these roads.
— Let them finger-paint with it on an unbreakable mirror. They like covering and uncovering their reflections.
— Make *islands* of shaving cream that float in the water tray.

Make *aggression bags*

Help the children fill small, zip-closure plastic bags with shaving cream. Now let each child choose two different colours of food colouring. Put a squirt of each into the bag and zip it closed. If desired, tape the bag closed with tape. Now let the child squeeze the bag to mix the food colouring into the shaving cream. This makes beautiful pastels, and squeezing it is very satisfying and soothing.

Cornflour and water goo

Pour a box of cornflour into a large bowl or dish. Mix in just enough water to make it the consistency of yoghurt. This magic substance can be picked up and squeezed. It will become warm and more solid when the child squeezes it. When the child releases their hand, it will become liquid again and dribble between their fingers.

Finger painting

Mix decorators paste to a thick consistency. Add powder or liquid paint for colour. Use large plastic trays and let children make patterns with their fingers. Lay a clean piece of painting on top of the patterns if children want to make prints. Hand and even foot prints are fun to do on large sheets of paper. Make sure that the children's clothes are well-covered with aprons or overalls.

SECTION 4: LANGUAGE ACTIVITIES

Books and stories

The wide variety of excellent children's books available today is a valuable resource. In addition to the children's books listed in these chapters, the children's librarian at your local public library can suggest books on particular topics.

Reading a book about a topic you know a child is struggling with can be an ideal way to open up a conversation without prying. The child may spontaneously bring up the parallels in their own life. Or, depending on the situation, you could ask, 'Do you feel that way sometimes? '

Although books are very helpful, they are not a substitute for proper conversation with the child about a situation. Do not assume that the child has come to terms with the topic just because you have read the book or they make no comment about it.

Books can help children make the discovery that they are not the only ones who have ever had a particular problem. They may feel relieved to discover this.

As well as books on specific problems, find books and stories that display role models.

Some hints

You will have to make the decision whether to read the book to a group of children or to one child in a more private setting. Books about feelings, general problems and adventures are good for everyone. A book about a particular situation or a sensitive issue might upset a child if read to the whole group.

Choose a time and place when it will be easy for the child to concentrate.

Read the book before you read it to the children.

If necessary, modify the book as you read it, simplifying the language or leaving out certain concepts you feel the child is not ready to hear. Or, use the framework of the book to tell your own story.

Allow the child to interrupt and make comments or ask questions. Take your time.

Make story cassettes available, or record books yourself. Read the story and make a sound signal when the child should turn the page. Children can take the cassette player, cassette and book into a corner and listen to it by themselves. It is best, of course, to read the book to the child in person. However, children like to hear stories over and over again, so this allows that to happen even when you are busy.

Things to do after reading books

After children are quite familiar with a particular book or story, try some of these activities.

Invite the children to act out the story. Assign particular character roles to children in the group. While you read, they can act out what the character is doing. Gather any necessary props ahead of time.

Create stick puppets for the main characters. Older children might even enjoy illustrating the characters. With the help of the children, cut them out, mount them on cardboard and attach them to short sticks. Give the stick puppets to the children. (You could have multiples of the same character). As you read the story, each child holds up their stick puppet when they hear you read about that character.

Create a flannelgraph representation of the story. Mount pictures of main characters and objects in the story on cardboard and put Velcro on the back. Let the children help you place these illustrations on the flannelgraph as you read the story. Leave these out in the book area during free playtime.

Invite the children to change the ending or other details of the story if they wish. Then read their versions.

Substitute a child's name for that of the main character.

Storytelling

Storytelling is the most direct art form. There is nothing that comes between the teller and the listener, and it is the ultimate way to customize the curriculum! If you are an active example of storytelling, soon the children will become storytellers as well. You are also giving them a valuable tool for self-expression; a critical skill for all children, but especially those in crisis.

When listening to a story, children have no pictures for cues, so they stare intently at your face while forming pictures in their minds.

You do not have to be a master storyteller to tell stories that children will enjoy. There are some great, easy techniques to get children involved in the telling.

The story of our day

Simply frame the morning's events in story language. Settle down with the children and announce that you have a story to tell them. Use a special storytelling voice. Make eye contact with everyone. Then start, Once upon a time, on a *(your weather)* day in April in the little town of *(your town)*, there was a teacher named *(your name)* in a school called *(your centre).'* Then simply describe the events that actually happened during the day. 'Timmy was the first to arrive, just as Miss Susan had finished mixing the paint for the easel. He said, 'Guess what, Miss Susan ...' Describe the rest of the day or morning, mentioning other children. End your story with, 'And they all lived happily ever after.'

Your children will not mind the weaknesses in the plot. They will love hearing their names in the story and might even correct details as you go.

Depending on the situation and the children's sense of humour, you might add funny details from your own imagination. 'Nicholas walked over to the wall, walked up the wall, and then walked across the ceiling upside down!' 'Katie was running so fast outside, suddenly the wind picked her up and she started to fly!' Some groups will want you to stick strictly to the details of the truth, while others will love flights of fantasy.

Real-life heroes

Tell true stories about children in the class who bravely survived some ordeal (only if it is appropriate to talk about, of course). 'Once there was a little boy named Derek. One morning he woke up feeling very, very ill. His mother felt his forehead and said, "I think we better take you to the doctor."'

A funny thing happened on the way to the office ...

Tell the children about something you saw on the way to work, or something funny that happened at home. If you tell stories like this, children will start telling you stories as well. First they have to know what a story is.

Offer to take dictation

When you pull out a pencil and a pad of paper, children's stories become more elaborate. They feel important and valued. Invite them to tell you their stories.

Vivian Paley, a nursery teacher who has written many wonderful books about teaching, writes down children's stories every day. She sits at a *story table* where children can come during their free playtime and dictate their stories to her. Later in the day, she invites these children to act out their own stories, with their friends taking on roles.

Fill-in-the-blank stories

This is great fun. You supply the story framework, the connecting phrases and the transitions, and the children provide the details. You can do this individually or with a small group. Use a tape recorder while you do this and write the story down later. These will become some of the children's favourite stories to hear again and again! One possibility is:

Teacher: Once upon a time there was a...
Children: Bear (or whatever the children say)
Teacher: This bear was very, very...
Children: Clumsy (tired, hungry, ...)
Teacher: He was so clumsy that he couldn't even ...
Children: Stand up (climb a tree, run...)
Teacher: Now this bear realized he had a problem! So he decided to call his good friend ...
Children: The hummingbird (the giraffe, Miss Smith...)
Teacher: Hummingbird said, 'Mr. Bear, why are you so upset?'

Continue the story until you run out of time or ideas.

These stories are great fun, and every one is different. You never know where they are going. Best of all, the adult must follow the lead of the children. The only difficulty is that sometimes they are hard to end! Don't worry, the character can always fall asleep.

Tell a story, then read it

Find a good story in a children's book that the children have not heard before. Learn the story and tell it without using the book. Then pull out the book. 'Look. Here's a book of the same story I just told you. I'm going to read you the book now.' Read it and show children the pictures. Then ask them, 'When you had to see the pictures in your mind, how were they different from the pictures you see in the book?'

By doing this, you reinforce the idea that the pictures they make in their own minds are just as good as the pictures the illustrator thought up.

Parallel stories

Start with a simple story that the children all know, *like The Three Billy Goats Gruff* or *Goldilocks*. Invite them to help you retell the story by changing all the details. You might end up with four gentle rabbits and a wolf who live under the bridge. Again, with this process, you are valuing children's ideas and showing them that they have something interesting to say.

Create your own album of collected stories

Children love to hear their own stories over and over again. Make little books out of each story, or write them down and keep them in a large binder. Some of the children might be motivated to illustrate their stories.

Puppetry

Everyone knows that puppets are magic. What starts out as a small piece of cloth and scraps suddenly takes on a personality and a life of its own. They add charm and fun to a classroom, and it is truly amazing what a child will tell a puppet!

Puppets are also great teaching tools. They are extremely good at holding children's attention, possibly because children are trying to work out what is fantasy and what is reality. With puppets, you can present social and emotional concepts in a neutral way.

Puppets for children to use

It is good to have puppets on hand for children to put on and use during their playtime. By talking for the puppet on their hand, children learn to put themselves in someone else's shoes and consider a different point of view. A shy child sometimes talks more freely through a puppet because everyone's eyes are on the puppet instead of the child. A child who stutters may be able to make a puppet talk without stuttering. A child who is afraid or worried might be able to express fears through a puppet. A child's puppet can have a conversation with an adult's puppet. Two or more children will enjoy making their puppets interact. So it is good to have a nice variety of puppets for children to choose from.

Early childhood suppliers now have a great variety of multiracial puppets depicting all types of people and occupations. Home-made sock puppets and animal puppets are great additions, too.

Children will also enjoy making their own fanciful paper bag puppets. Perhaps they could create puppets to go along with a particular story.

Stick puppets are easy to make by cutting out magazine pictures of people, gluing them to cardboard backing and attaching them to short sticks. Ask the children to find characters for stick puppets.

Puppets for adults to use

There are special benefits to having a Pet Puppet that is only for the teacher to use. A puppet can be like a teaching assistant, doing all sorts of useful chores for you. They are not human, so they can make silly mistakes for the children to correct. They can discuss problems they are having, allowing you to address children's problems without becoming personally involved. They can introduce new concepts and ask children questions, giving them a valuable review of experiences. They are wonderful poets, musicians and storytellers, and if they sing off key or forget part of the story, the teacher does not feel like a fool. Best of all, they add an element of humour and imagination to the classroom.

Pet Puppet activities

Give the Pet Puppet a special name, voice and personality. Although you can have other puppets for the children to play with, do not let them play with the Pet Puppet. Keep the personality of the Pet Puppet strong and consistent. Children will also pay attention to the Pet Puppet if he only comes out at special times. There are many wonderful ways to involve the Pet Puppet in the classroom. Here are some suggestions:.

Morning greetings

The puppet takes attendance by calling each child's name in turn. When the child hears their name, they go over and gets a kiss from the puppet. If they want to they can give the puppet a hug. Even very young children enjoy this game. It helps them learn everybody else's name.

Describe each child

After the Pet Puppet comes out in the morning, he can suggest that you play a guessing game. He describes one child at a time, in admiring ways, and the children have to guess who he is describing. 'I see someone who has long, brown braids and beautiful, brown eyes. She's wearing pink trainers and has buttons on the front of her shirt. Who is it?' 'Right! It's Flora.' This builds vocabulary and enhances self-esteem and a feeling of belonging.

Forgetful puppet

In a variation of the above, Pet Puppet is forgetful and embarrassed that he cannot remember the children's names. So you ask him to describe the person he cannot remember until the children are able to tell him who he is thinking of.

Or, Pet Puppet asks you who a particular child is. You describe the child. 'Manuel has black hair and brown eyes and today he's wearing a shirt with green stripes.' The puppet can then examine each child, out loud, until he comes to the right conclusion. 'Let's see. This person has blond hair, so that can't be Manuel. This person has black hair, but he has on a blue shirt so that can't be Manuel. This person has black hair and big brown eyes, and a shirt with green strips, so this must be Manuel! Hi, Manuel!'

Shy puppet

This puppet is very shy and afraid of loud noises. He peeks out and then ducks back in his bag. You coax him out and he shakes in fear. You ask him what the matter is. He whispers something to you. You say aloud, 'You're afraid of these children? Why?' He whispers something else to you. You say, 'Because they're so noisy? You'll be quiet won't you, boys and girls?' The puppet can then proceed to whisper a series of questions to you that you can then relay to the children. If the children ask him a question, he can respond to you in a whisper. He never talks to them because he's so shy. You never have to be a ventriloquist, and the children usually stay quiet and strain to hear what he is whispering. This can be a calming activity when the children have been noisy.

Review the morning

Your puppet has been asleep all morning and has missed out on everything that went on. So he asks the children, one at a time, what they did that morning. He can ask questions to get the children to expand on their remarks. 'You played with blocks? What did you build? What shapes did you use? Was anyone playing with you?'

Make silly mistakes

The puppet can show misunderstanding of a basic concept. For instance, he can pull a ping-pong ball out of his bag and announce proudly that he has a great big ball. If the children do not correct him immediately, you can call their attention to his mistake. 'Is that really a big ball?' Then you can say to the puppet, 'You don't seem to understand the difference between big and small. We'll help you.' Then you can make children teach the puppet by finding things in the room that are big for one pile and things that are small for another. You could do this with many concepts: colours, hard and soft, round and square.

True and false game

The puppet can make a series of statements and the children call out whether the statement is *true* or *false*. 'Cars have tyres.' 'Cars drink milk.' 'Cows say, *Moo.*' 'Cows live in hen houses.' The sillier the better!

Where is it?

This is a good receptive language game. It can be used to find out what words the children understand but do not speak. The puppet challenges children to find certain things in the room. 'Where is there a picture of a dog in our room?' 'Where is there a flower in our room?'

Puppet packs a bag

On a Friday, our puppet arrives with a small suitcase. (Children are fascinated by suitcases.) He is excited because he is going to visit his Grandma, but he wants to take some things with him because there are not many toys at Grandma's. So he asks children, one at a time, to go and get certain things in the room for him to borrow over the weekend. This is an excellent receptive language game, because the children simply have to understand what he wants. For older children, you could make this more advanced by making the puppet forget the name of the toy and describe it instead. Or he could describe certain attributes.

Puppet's surprise bag

Pet Puppet returns from visiting Grandma and is excited because he has something special from her house in his bag. He can bring out any common object — a rubber glove, hand mixer, wire whisk, wallet or book — and discuss it with the children. 'What is this? Do you know what it's for? Guess which room in her house I found it in.' For older children, make a guessing game out of it. The puppet gives hints or clues about the object and challenges the children to guess what it is before he pulls it out. Or, the object is in a cloth bag and the children can guess what it is by feeling through the bag first.

Guess what...

The puppet can lead simple guessing games. Every time Pet Puppet comes out this could be part of his ritual. 'Guess what I did this morning! It has to do with food.' Or the simple, *I spy* game. After you have played this type of game many times with children and they are thoroughly familiar with it, ask the children to think of something that the puppet has to guess. 'Guess what we did this morning.' It may be difficult for children to come up with clues that do not give it away, so play this with older children.

What do you know?

Use Pet Puppet to ask children questions about a topic to see what they already know about it. This can be very useful before you go on a field trip or at the very beginning of a theme unit. 'Tell me about fire engines. What are they for? Why do they make so much noise? Why do they have those scary lights on them? Why do they have those ladders?' 'Tell me what you know about a circus. I have difficulty remembering. Can you (teacher) write down some of the things that they say so I can remember?'

Tell me about it

Pet Puppet did not go on the school trip, or he slept through a special event. He wants the children to tell him all about what they saw and did. The puppet can ask questions to expand the children's answers. 'Did the firemen have any special clothes?'

Supervision of cleaning up time

Have a special puppet whose job it is to supervise cleaning up time. He could start out by going to each area and notifying children that cleaning up time will start in five minutes. (Give the children in the block corner a little extra warning time). Then he could go to each area and help organize the children. 'You put the boxes back on the shelf, and you line up the shoes, and you hang up the dress-up clothes.' Then he could join various groups of children and help them for a time, cheering them on and encouraging them. When the job is done he might admire the appearance of the room and congratulate individual children on a job well done.

Dismiss children

At the end of group time, Pet Puppet could pick one child at a time to come up and tell him a secret, give him a hug and then go on to the next part of the day (for example, wash hands to get ready for lunch).

Puppet has a problem

Pet Puppet can have a problem similar to those of children in the group. For instance, he can afraid of the dark. He might ask, 'Have any of you ever been afraid of the dark when you go to bed at night? What do you do?' Or he might be upset that his friends will not play with him because he is purple. Maybe he is ashamed because he was mean to his friend or little brother and feels bad about it, but does not know what to do now. He needs advice about how to make up. Let the children advise him and assess the merit of various solutions.

Pet Puppet can also talk with one child at a time. Sometimes children will tell a puppet things that they are afraid of or reluctant to tell a person. Using puppets in this way is especially useful when working with children in crisis.

Create a home for Pet Puppet

As a class project, create and decorate a special home for Pet Puppet. The puppet could be there to say what his preferences are, in case there is disagreement. Would he like a square dog house? Would a basket with a lid be better? Does he want it to be soft inside? What should the outside look like? Whenever Pet Puppet is not being used, place this puppet in his home on a high shelf, out of reach of the children, so he can sleep in peace.

All these ideas are just here for suggestions:. If you use your pet puppet with children on a daily basis, he will develop many more games and jobs. You will be amazed at how he comes to life!

Resources

Art

Smith, Charles, *The Peaceful Classroom,* Floris Books, 1998.
Petrash, Carol, *Earthwise: Environmental Crafts and Activities with young Children,* Floris Books, 1992.
Cherry, Clare, *Creative Art for the Developing Child,* (2nd ed.) Lake Publishing Company, 1990.
Hereford, Nancy Jo, *Art: A Practical Guide for Teaching Young Children.* Scholastic Inc., 1992.
Kohl, MaryAnn, *Preschool Art: It's the Process, Not the Product,* Brilliant Publishers, 1999.

Books and storytelling

Raines, Shirley C., and Canady, Robert J., *Story S-t-r-e-t-c-h-e-r-s: Activities to Expand Children's Favorite Books,* Gryphon House, 1989.
Raines, Shirley C., and Canady, Robert J., *MORE Story S-t-r-e-t-c-h-e-r-s: More Activities to Expand Children's Favorite Books,* Gryphon House, 1991.
Raines, Shirley C., and Canady, Robert J., *Story S-t-r-e-t-c-h-e-r-s for the Primary Grades: Activities to Expand Children's Favorite Books,* Gryphon House, 1992.
Raines, Shirley C., *450 More Story S-t-r-e-t-c-h-e-r-s for the Primary Grades: Activities to Expand Children's Favorite Books,* Gryphon House, 1994.

Chapter Twenty-Four

Helping Children to manage their Behaviour

Nobody is surprised when children who are experiencing trauma in their lives act in ways that may be difficult for staff to handle. Their feelings, their frustrations, their fears must be expressed. Very young children are more likely to use actions rather than words to express themselves.

Sensitive and caring guidance from a trusted carer can have a positive impact on how children cope. Giving this guidance may be the most difficult thing you have to do. Since each situation and each child is different, nothing works for every child or situation. This chapter will give you strategies to try, and ideas to think about as you approach each situation.

It is useful to think about what you are trying to accomplish when you help children learn to manage their behaviour. There are really two major goals:

— to maintain a safe setting so that all the children can thrive; and
— to help the individual child express feelings and interact with the other children in positive ways.

Staff constantly work to balance these two goals.

As a professional, you have a responsibility to maximize the experience for all of the children. It is most important that children feel safe and respected. This is the baseline. If they worry about physical or verbal attacks from other children, they cannot relax and benefit from the learning environment and activities you have prepared. Staff and parents can feel very frustrated when one child seems to absorb much more than their fair share of the attention because of difficult behaviour. Staff and parents also express concern that one child can be a bad example to others and that undesirable behaviour can spread to other children if it is not handled quickly and appropriately.

An equally important goal of behaviour management is to build *coping* skills and competence in each individual child. So, while the immediate goal is to stop the offending behaviour, be it hitting, verbal attacks or tantrums, the ultimate, long term goal is to teach the child other, acceptable behaviour for expressing the same emotions.

It is very important to generate a curriculum that is sensitive to the needs of the children. Only then will it be developmentally appropriate. Flexibility is essential. The teacher must see interactions as centrally important. Learning how to get along with others and develop friendships is an important aspect of all the children's education. They must have these skills in order to succeed in school and in life.

The following may help you enjoy the process of teaching children to manage their behaviour.

Create roles for yourself. Think of yourself as a coach working to teach children appropriate strategies for dealing with hurt, anger and frustration.

Think of the classroom as a human interactions laboratory in which children have endless opportunities to learn skills. Each encounter or conflict between children is an opportunity for them to exercise their abilities.

Celebrate successes. Most teachers report that seeing children's progress is the one thing that makes behaviour management activities enjoyable. It is wonderful when you hear a child using a conflict resolution technique you taught them rather than an aggressive action. So watch for these successes. Praise the children. Record the successes in your diary and in the child's file. Share them with parents. Focus on these successful experiences, and be sure to pat yourself on the back!

Do not be discouraged when the child resorts to previous behaviour. They need your support. As with all other types of learning, they will make mistakes along the way. Help them build on their successes.

Show you care. Realize that the children have to like you first before they can care about your reaction to a situation. So work on building friendly, affectionate relationships. Laugh with children. Let them know that they are important to you.

Everyone benefits when children learn how to control their behaviour. When you worry that you are taking time away from other children, remember that they will benefit from watching you help their classmate. From your example they learn kindness, empathy, understanding and a vocabulary about feelings.

Be careful not to blame the victim. When a child repeatedly spoils your plans, tries to hurt other children, embarrasses you in front of colleagues and parents and makes you feel ineffective, it is easy to feel angry at that child. But young children are not calculating. They do not make plans and lay traps. They just act and react. It is tempting to ascribe negative characteristics to the child and make dire predictions for their future, and we correctly fear for the child's future, unless effective intervention is possible. The hopeful part, however, is that in early childhood, there is still time to help. Children are still malleable. We can still make a difference.

Use professional supports

Really difficult behaviour on the part of children can leave staff feeling overwhelmed. It can be a prime burn-out factor. When nothing you try seems to help, you can end up feeling ineffective. Your professional self-esteem suffers. It is extremely important to have the support of other professionals, so take advantage of your team. Let's look at how various team members might help.

Other staff

When several people look at the problem together, they can brainstorm and perhaps come up with more resources and ideas than an individual can by working alone.

If you know of a problem ahead of time, you might do some advance planning together. For instance, a four-year-old boy who bites had been referred to a new centre. The staff brainstormed what to do. Their plan was that:

— They would work hard to teach him how to deal with frustration.
— They would be careful to greet him warmly every day and give him lots of loving, special attention.
— They would give him a special comforter; a stuffed toy to carry around that would be just his.
— They would focus on meeting his emotional needs, reading his moods and supporting him as much as possible.

It was no surprise that, after a few false starts, the plan was successful.

Your fellow workers can be useful in other ways. Ask someone who does not work in your room to come in and observe a child. Sometimes they can notice subtle things that lead to a child's actions.

Discussing a particular child with a group (never in front of the child) allows you to tap into the insights and experiences of other professionals. Some centres do this in a routine, systematic way with very good results. A staff team presents a case study describing the child, the child's background and situation, the behaviour that is causing difficulty, and what has been tried. Then the rest of the staff brainstorms with them. The team goes back and tries the suggestions. They report at the next meeting and either congratulate themselves for their collective success or go back to the drawing board.

The child's parents

Depending on the situation, the parents may be your best resource when working out what is bothering their child. Regard them as expert consultants.

At first, you may have to make special efforts to break down their defensiveness. Often parents know that their child has behavioural problems that need to be worked on. When you phone to discuss them, they might be afraid that you are going to ask them to remove their child from your centre, and they probably fear that their child's behaviour reflects on their skills as parents, and that you will be critical of them.

Consider the following when working with parents.

THEY ARE PART OF THE TEAM. Help them understand that you see them as vital members of the team.

ASK FOR THEIR INSIGHTS. Why do they think their child is acting a particular way? What light can they shed on the subject?

PARENTS KNOW THEIR CHILD BETTER THAN ANYONE ELSE; they are the experts on that particular child. You know about child development, positive discipline and various strategies that could be tried. With the help of all involved, a complete plan is possible.

REGULAR COMMUNICATION. After you decide how to handle a situation, make a date to meet again and evaluate progress. This helps everyone feel included and successful. The child benefits, and you and the parents have formed a collaborative bond.

The other children

Do not forget about the other children who know the situation very well. Staff are often surprised at the positive effect of group problem solving.

Staff have also reported success with younger children, even when the situation required dealing with the behaviour of a particular child. A group of three-year-olds sat down to talk about a child who bites other children. With the biter present, they discussed ways to deal with the situation. In a very supportive and respectful way, the carer told the children, 'Sean has a problem. He gets angry sometimes when he wants something and before he knows it, he ends up biting someone!' (Everyone, including Sean, nods in recognition of the situation.) 'What can we do to help Sean remember not to bite?' The children decided that whenever it seemed that Sean was getting angry and might bite them, they would say, 'No biting!' They even practised saying it forcefully a few times. Success! This peer support helped the child stop biting. The children became aware of Sean's moods and *invested* themselves in the problem.

Other professionals

Whenever necessary, your manager may consider inviting other professionals such as a child psychologist to observe the child in the environment of your classroom.

You are not alone

Your Health Visitor and in some cases social worker may have suggestions.

How to identify and analyse behaviour problems

When you have a specific method for identifying and analysing a problem behaviour and work systematically to resolve it, you will feel less overwhelmed. In essence, you are saying to yourself and others, 'This is my best effort,' and you know that you are making a sincere attempt to help the child.

Observe and get the facts

Write down a description of the problem behaviour. Be specific and narrow it down. Focus on the specific behaviour you want to modify. Observe the child for a couple of days. When does the behaviour occur? What leads up to it? Who is the child interacting with at the time? Is it the same indoors and outdoors?

Be a detective. While exercising good professional ethics, find out as much as you can about the child's situation. Is the child going through a crisis or trauma? What are the family dynamics? Look for insights to help explain the child's behaviour. In some cases this may influence how you handle it.

Take another look at the environment, routines and planning to make sure they are not causing or worsening some problems. Is there too much waiting time? Does the child have to sit still too long? Does the child feel crowded and need to protect their personal space?

Record what happens

Keep a diary. You can add this information to the regular observation files you keep on each child or, even better, create a separate notebook. The first entry could be the description of the problem and the background information described above.

Write down the plan of action you will try when the behaviour occurs.

Record incidents as they occur. Include time of day, location, other children involved, possible events that precipitated it, how you responded, what the child did and the aftermath. Do this consistently so that you notice any patterns that might emerge. You could even develop a frequency graph. This will help you notice small decreases in the behaviour that you might otherwise miss.

Record preventative activities. In addition to writing about how you reacted to an incident, record other preventative activities you try with the child that might reduce the behaviour; offering more sensory play to relax the child, reading a book on a particular topic, or playing near the child when the behaviour is most likely to happen.

Use this diary when you involve other adults

Everyone benefits from clear notes. Another staff member, parent or outside professional will benefit from a clear picture of what has gone on before.

Continue adding to the diary, including involvement and interaction with any other person. That person could add to it by noting thoughts and observations.

Brainstorm with others

Work with the other person to generate possible strategies and then narrow them down, deciding what you will do first.

Record successes or failures. Analyse. Decide what to try next.

Celebrate successes

See the results of your efforts. This recording process allows you to look back and see real progress with the child. It helps you see the results of your efforts. Pat yourself on the back.

Quietly, and respectfully help the child to feel the satisfaction of mastering a behaviour.

And if the interventions are not successful:
Recognize your best efforts. No matter what happens, you will know that you gave it your best professional effort.

You will have valuable background information for other professionals who will work with the child.

Child development factors that influence behaviour

There are child development factors to keep in mind when working out how to approach behaviour problems of young children.

Egocentricity

Young children are egocentric. The term *egocentricity* does not have the same negative connotation that it has when applied to adults, meaning that the person is selfish and inconsiderate. With young children, egocentricity is natural and understandable. They come into this world knowing only their own body sensations. Their world gradually expands to include those who care for them. Young children have not had enough time on the planet to consider that other people have feelings independent of their own feelings. In fact, they assume that everyone else has the same perceptions and feelings that they do. That is why they are so impatient when another child does not hand a toy over immediately, and why they work so hard to be the centre of attention. Helping them to grow out of their egocentricity and to consider other people's points of view is one of the major social tasks of the early childhood years. Even when the young child does learn to share and engage in social situations, they may still act according to egocentric reasons believing that 'then he will be my friend,' or 'she will invite me to her birthday party.'

Another aspect of egocentric thinking is the child's perception that all events happen for or because of them. We are amused when a child tells their father that he can turn the ocean waves off now because they want to go home. But when a child thinks they are the cause of their father's drinking, or parents' fighting, or grandmother's death, difficulties occur. Even though adults say over and over again, 'It's not your fault. You had nothing to do with what happened,' the child does not quite believe it.

All or nothing

It is difficult for young children to consider that someone or something can be both good and bad at the same time. Someone is all good or all bad. Johnny who hits is a bad boy. The teenage brother who plays ball with the child cannot possibly be bad because he stops out late. A child cannot look at both sides of a question or easily consider a situation from a different point of view.

Anchored in the present

The young child considers a situation only from their immediate perspective. They have difficulty thinking about events that led up to something, or what might happen in the future because of it. Understanding cause and effect requires abstract thinking, and the young child is still in a very concrete mode.

Focus on the physical

The young child has to be able to perceive something with their senses to understand it. Responses to behaviour have to be immediate. Waiting until the end of the day to discuss a problem with a child is much less effective. The child is not skilled at hypothetical thinking. The following response to a child's aggression, 'How would you like it if someone did that to you?' is usually completely ineffective. The child does not understand. In fact, the child may even perceive such a comment as a threat that someone will do the same thing to them.

Magical thinking

The young child has a difficult time sorting out fantasy and reality. Images on television, even cartoons, seem real to the child. Bodies spring back to life. Punches do not hurt. The child may also believe that wishing for something makes it come true. This does not usually cause problems until the child wishes for something negative, such as wanting a bad thing to happen to a sibling. If a real tragedy does occur, then the child can be overwhelmed by guilt.

Vulnerability

Young children are vulnerable and dependent. They learn to depend on the adults around them. In early years, they focus on ways to get the adults to attend to their needs. Infants learn to cry when they are uncomfortable, hungry or bored, and, like magic, someone appears. Toddlers learn to whine. Two-year-olds learn how to throw tantrums. Three-year-olds learn how to manipulate. This is why the issue of trust is such a major one. If a child's needs are met with relative consistency, the child can relax and enjoy the world. If they are not, the child will become tense. When children have not been able to trust the important adults in their lives, or when they feel betrayed, they become more fearful and clinging. Children need ways to feel more powerful to counteract feelings of helplessness. Children who feel helpless may become bossy, belligerent and aggressive, and may challenge rules and limits.

Different temperaments

The basic temperament a child is born with will also influence how they adjust to circumstances and what kinds of interventions work best. Although there are different labels, three basic personality types have been identified:

— easy or flexible
— feisty or difficult
— fearful or sensitive

Every staff member knows that some children enter the classroom eager to learn and make friends, while others hang on to the teacher's leg and only gradually venture out. Some children can take a lot of abuse from other children and roll with the punches, while others blow up at the least provocation.

It is useful to consider the child's temperament when you think of different possible intervention strategies. Adjust your responses to the personality. Some sensitive children are very cautious about trying anything new. Letting the child approach new material on their own terms works better than sitting the child down and insisting that they try something. A flexible child can be paired with a feisty child to help the feisty child learn give-and-take. But one needs to avoid ignoring *easy* children because they do not make waves. A feisty child needs advance warning of transitions in your daily schedule. A fearful child needs reassurances and contact with a safe adult when there is a special visitor.

Remember that difficult behaviour is a sign that a child needs something. Try to work out what that need is — attention, security, control, feeling valued — and try to fill the need so that the child will not continue to act in undesirable ways.

Building self-esteem

Children's self-esteem often suffers at times of crisis. They may think that they have caused the bad things that have happened to them, be it their parents' divorce, or the death of their baby brother. When parents' patience wears thin and they lash out at the child because of their own stress, the child may become even more convinced that they are bad. In addition, when adults are consumed by a particular crisis, they may not have much emotional energy left over for the child. As a result, the child may feel worthless and abandoned. Children also feel powerless and helpless in many crisis situations, further eroding their self-esteem. When children have low self-esteem, they tend to act in ways that reinforce this image, often alienating people who might be their friends and supporters. It is important to try to break this negative cycle.

You can tell a child's self-esteem is low when:
— They have problems interacting with peers and have no friends.
— They whine or throw tantrums to demand their way.
— They have low tolerance for frustration.
— They misbehave to gain attention.
— They are overly fearful.
— They are bossy and bully other children.

When children have high self-esteem, they are generally more flexible and willing to take risks. Children who feel confident and capable of handling themselves in various situations are less aggressive than children who feel helpless. The bully in your classroom often turns out to be the child who has the weakest self-image.

Much of a child's self-esteem is built on successful interactions with adults and other children. Self-esteem can be eroded when adults make the child feel bad about himself. So, while you want to stop or change behaviour, it is important to figure out how to do that and still leave the child feeling valued or respected. Besides being careful with the words you use, try to establish a caring, friendly relationship with the child.

Although a child's self-esteem is most strongly influenced by their parents and family, there is much that a carer can do to make them feel like a worthy, capable person.

Feeling valued and having friends

The most important way to build a child's self esteem is to be kind, gentle, supportive, available, and responsive.

Pay attention to the child. Give them a warm greeting when they arrive. Take time to listen when they want to tell you something.

Talk with the child rather than just telling him what to do or offering simple praise.

Avoid judgmental statements. The child needs to feel that you are on his side.

Help children play together. One of the most important ways children develop self-esteem is by having good relationships with their peers. All children want to have friends, but sometimes young children are quite clumsy in their efforts. By helping children learn how to play, solve problems, work together, and negotiate conflicts with other children, you can enhance their ability to make friends and keep them.

Create a *Who's Here Today?* board. Take a photo of each child. Punch a hole in the top and write the child's name on a label at the bottom. Put pockets, hooks or Velcro on the board so the child can find their picture and attach it to the board at arrival time. This board gives the child a feeling that they are an important member of the group.

Look at this chart, or some variation of it, every morning with the children. Talk about who is here and who is missing. When a child returns after an absence, make sure the group welcomes them back.

Use a puppet to greet each child in the group. The puppet should use the child's name and say something pleasant to them.

Feeling useful and capable

Children love to help, especially if this gives them one-on-one time with a significant adult. Create jobs that a child can help you with, such as setting the table, cleaning up after lunch, feeding classroom pets, watering plants, or folding notes to parents. After the child has helped you, be sure to express your appreciation and compliment them on a job well done. This will make them feel special.

Encourage children to help each other. When possible, ask a child to help a classmate with such tasks as zipping up a jacket, tying shoelaces, carrying something or opening a door. Children feel good about themselves when they help others.

Involve children in arranging the environment. When you feel a need to rearrange furniture, solicit suggestions from the children. Then let them help you push the furniture around. They also love to decorate. Let them help put up seasonal decorations or artwork.

Support the child's ideas. 'I noticed you arranged the shapes in an interesting pattern.'

Recognize efforts. Even when children try something and do not succeed, comment on their willingness to make an effort.

Teach children how to act in different social settings. Children also gain self-esteem by knowing how to act in different situations. For example, they may need to know how to behave in a restaurant, or when visiting someone who is ill. They may also need to learn how to call for help when there is an emergency. In some cases, rehearsing these scenes ahead of time can help.

Feeling powerful

Give children many opportunities to make choices and direct their own activities during the day.

A sign-up system for popular activities can help children to be self-regulating. A child can then relax and enjoy the activity rather than worrying about defending their right to be there.

Let children help to decide what activities will be available. How long shall we stay outside? Shall we put out clay or water?

Ask and heed their opinion. Where do you think I should hang this picture?

The role of language development

It is hard to over-emphasize the role of language development in learning to manage emotions and behaviour. Just look at the difference between two- and three-year-olds. In general, two-year-olds are more likely to hit, pull another child's hair and scream when they do not get their way. Three-year-olds tend to use verbal weapons: 'I won't be your friend.' 'I won't invite you to my birthday party.'

Children who are frustrated because they cannot communicate their needs and wishes may act aggressively. This is true for older children who for one reason or another are behind in their language development. Neglected and abused children who have not been talked to and encouraged to express themselves fall into this group, as well as children with developmental delays, hearing impairments or other communication difficulties.

All of the activities that encourage language development also relate to behaviour management. Children must understand language in order to understand the messages others are trying to communicate. And they need productive vocabulary to express their opinions and wishes.

Consider non-verbal communication first

With non-verbal children, demonstrate what you want them to do while saying the words you want them to use in the future. If you see a two-year-old reaching for the hair of a playmate, for instance, stop them. Say, 'Touch gently.' Then demonstrate by touching the other child's hair gently. Let the more aggressive child touch your hair and the other child's hair gently (if the other child is willing).

A non-English-speaking child or a toddler can learn vocabulary on the spot, connecting words to your actions. You can stop a child's hitting motion and say firmly, 'No hitting.' The child will see by your facial expression, body language and action that hitting is not allowed.

Simplify your language

Although most parents and experienced staff do this without thinking, it may take some practice for new staff to simplify language and use words that children understand. Give one instruction at a time rather than stringing them together. For instance, 'Push in your chair, carry your plate to the table and go sit in the story area until I call you to come to the bathroom to brush your teeth,' is too complicated for young children. Adults must also learn to speak at a slower pace than they normally would.

No is a word that enters a child's usable vocabulary very early on, but sometimes it triggers an emotional response and causes the child to assert their autonomy. You might find that the word, *Wait!* works better to stop an action, allowing you time to move in close.

Give appropriate responses

Even children who have productive language may not know how to string the words together to say what they want, especially if they do not have experience playing co-operatively with others. Give them words to repeat.

'Susan, when that happens again you can say, "Stop. I don't like that!" Let me hear you say that.'

When you hear a scream of protest say, 'Mark, tell Jason, "I'm playing with this now."'

Help a non-verbal or timid child to be understood

— 'Cathy, you didn't hear Katie. She said that she doesn't want to wear that hat.'

— 'Daniel, Kevin is screaming. That means he doesn't want you to push his chair.'

Help children talk it over

Once children have a reasonable facility with language, you can help them learn to communicate effectively. Children who do have language may still need help expressing themselves. When an altercation between two children occurs, you can ask them to explain the situation to you. Rather than trying to fix it for them, see if they can come up with the solution themselves. Sometimes your presence will help them remember what they have heard many times before, and you can help each child hear the other's point of view.

— 'But Danielle said she didn't want to build a road. She needed the long blocks for the side of her house.'

— 'Danielle, Jonathan said only the long blocks would go over his bridge.'

— 'Can you two think of any way to solve this problem?'

You are not taking sides. You are demonstrating your support to help them solve their problem in a way they both think is fair.

Rules and routines

All children thrive in environments with consistent rules and routines, but children in crisis especially need them. They find comfort in having one place where they can count on having limits. Ways to develop predictable routines are discussed in Chapter 22. Solid rules for good behaviour also help create a safe environment.

The younger the children are in your group, the simpler the rules should be. You might have just two: *Do not hurt people,* and *Do not break things.* With older children you can be more specific. Rules generally fall into three categories: treatment of others, safety issues and classroom policies. How to treat people includes not hurting people either physically or through verbal taunting, and sharing and taking turns. The safety rules include no running in the hall, no playing right in front of the door and other things specific to the environment. The classroom rules concern handling of toys and materials, helping at cleaning up time and taking turns at the activities. You can have rules for certain types of materials or activities as well. For example: 'No splashing at the water table,' or 'Wear an apron when you paint.'

Try to involve the children in creating the rules. 'We had a problem at the water table today. Jennifer got wet, the floor was slippery because there was water all over it and Joseph fell over. What do you think we should do?' As children generate ideas, write them down. You might decide to give several of the suggestions a try during the next play period and then decide what the final rules will be.

Rules are worth repeating. Do not assume that all the children know or remember the rules. It does help if they are involved in making rules. However, rules are worth repeating on a regular basis. As a pre-reading exercise, you and the children could read some of the rules when you gather for your group time.

Review rules. When you bring out special materials or equipment that are not used on a regular basis, review with the children how to handle the materials and how to clean up when they have finished.

Children are often quick to recite a rule when another child disregards it. If you must intervene, try to stay neutral. 'This is our rule. I expect you to do your best to remember it. I think you can do this.'

Consistency is important. Because of children's *all or nothing* thinking, they are more comfortable when the rule is enforced all the time.

Do not bend the rules because you feel sorry for a child. Sometimes when a child is going through a traumatic situation, adults feel sorry for them and bend the rules. This teaches the child how to be manipulative and may actually make them feel less secure.

Change rules when it makes sense. Involve the children in the discussion and perhaps take a vote. All this makes them feel secure, respected and powerful.

The territorial imperative

Children's squabbling in early childhood classrooms often involves the territorial imperative; defending space or materials. The younger the children, the more this is the case. Young children are more egocentric and may simply not see the other child's point of view. Fighting over possessions can also be a way of asserting power.

When a child in a stressful situation has low self-esteem, sharing can be a more difficult issue than it would otherwise be When a child's life is in turmoil, they may have little generosity of spirit left over, and children should not always be required to share or take turns. Sometimes they have a strong need to possess something, even if it is just in the classroom.

A starting point is to have plenty of equipment so that there is enough for everyone and waiting is minimized.

Some children are inexperienced in play. Younger children (infants through to three-year-olds) and children who are not accustomed to playing with other children may be impulsive. If they see another child playing with something that looks like fun, they may try to take it away so they can have fun, too.

Some children are surprised when others protest, because they think that everyone sees the world the way they do, and are sometimes genuinely surprised when there is a protest at the other end of the object they are grabbing.

Provide duplicates of the same toy. The teacher can redirect the child by showing him the duplicate toy. This might lead to productive parallel play.

Note issues of dominance and power. However, sometimes children want what the other child has, even if there is an identical one close at hand. Then you know you are dealing with issues of dominance and power, not just impulsiveness.

Learning to take turns is important. Even if a centre can afford to have an identical tricycle for each child, this would probably be unwise. Children benefit from your guidance as they learn to negotiate, consider other children's desires and practise taking turns.

Sharing

Heather Wenig, a staff member working with toddlers, shares the following scenario, which illustrates children's thinking about sharing.

Josh is playing with the school bus (a favourite toy in the toddler room). Lisa decides that she would enjoy playing with the bus as well and tries to take it away from Josh. (Enter the cries: 'Mine! Mine!') The staff member tells Josh, 'You need to share,' and allows Lisa to have the bus.

What have Josh and Lisa learned? Josh loses his possession and learns to aggressively protect his playthings, while Lisa learns that she may take whatever she wants from others, and sharing has become a negative concept. What do you suppose the staff member really expected? It is my opinion that many adults, quite inadvertently, expect sacrifice when they use the word *share.* Therefore, children experience loss rather than mutual gain. In situations like this, when children are struggling over a toy, I have found it best to ask the original possessor, 'Could Lisa play with your toy when you have finished?' This question will quite often satisfy Lisa and prompt Josh to be generous. This simple method assures Josh that his rights will be protected and allows him to be in control of the decision. In addition, both children have a positive experience taking turns.

What does *sharing* mean? Heather's scenario points out that children may not even know what sharing means (and in this case, the staff member does not seem to know, either). To share really means that two or more children use the same materials at the same time. Taking turns means alternating the use of a toy. We have to make sure that sharing does not translate into *giving up* in the mind of the child.

Use *share* in context. Notice when children do share. 'Marcus and Sarah are sharing the playdough.'

Be a good role model. 'I brought some stickers to share with you today. We can all have some.'

Set up situations where children share naturally and then comment. For instance, put a bowl of crayons between two children who are colouring and say, 'You two can share these crayons.'

Point out the reaction of the other child when sharing happens. 'You made Lisa happy when you shared your biscuit with her.'

Issues of space

For some children, especially those who are tense or very active, space issues can be a problem. One child might crowd another child or accidentally knock down a block construction. Children often do not realize that a bump is an accident, and they react with distress and aggressiveness. You can try helping the two children work it out together, with one understanding that the incident was unintentional, and the other working to repair the damage. However, some children need a clearer definition of their space. Try these ideas.

Give children hula hoops or small rugs to define their space. Tell the child that the materials are to stay within that defined space. This will make it easier for other children to recognize the boundaries.

Put lines of masking tape on a table top or in the block area to define a child's work space.

At times, give children individual basins of water, sand or other sensory materials to play with. These can be placed inside the larger water tray, in a plastic wading pool or on a table top. Children benefit from parallel play without having to share the materials directly.

Taking turns

Taking turns is not exactly the same thing as sharing, although some of the same issues are involved. When children share crayons, each child gets some, but when children share a tricycle, only one child can ride it at a time. Taking turns can build social skills as children learn to give and take. The following suggestions show how to facilitate turn taking, in this case with a tricycle:

Teach children how to ask for a turn. With younger or less experienced children, you might even have to give them the words. 'Say "Tiffany, I want to have a turn on the tricycle when you are finished."'

Help the asker be heard. Repeat the child's request clearly to the rider. 'Stuart would like a turn on the tricycle. Will you give him this tricycle in a few minutes when you have finished your turn?'

If possible, let the rider give up the tricycle on their own terms. This sometimes happens very quickly. If you force it you are more likely to encounter resistance, or even a tantrum.

Have alternative activities for both children. 'Stuart, while you're waiting to ride the tricycle you can work the petrol pump here at the petrol station.'

When the rider gives up the toy, express appreciation if the other child does not do it themselves. 'You made Stuart happy when you let him have a turn on the tricycle. Would you like to use the petrol pump now?'

You can also help children work out other ways to take turns, such as using a timer or signing up for something ahead of time. All of this gives them valuable experience with social give-and-take.

Teaching children conflict resolution skills

Teaching children to resolve conflicts peacefully is challenging under any circumstances, but teaching these skills to children in stressful life situations is extra challenging because they may have difficulty focusing on the needs and wishes of others. Consider also that some children, especially those from violent homes, may never have seen people working their problems out peacefully.

Bear in mind that you cannot get children to talk through a problem and come to a co-operative agreement in a highly charged emotional situation. If one child is frightened or extremely angry, let them calm down first. Perhaps you will need to separate the children or encourage them to sit down quietly for a few minutes before they can think.

Staff often ask how much they should intervene when they see two children struggling. There are a number of different options, each appropriate in different situations.

You direct the behaviour. With this option, the adult is acknowledged as the most powerful person. This is probably the most common response of adults. 'Lisa, give Jason the lorry back.' It can solve the problem of the moment, but probably is not teaching the children very much, except that they can trust you when they need help. You are not teaching them any skills. If you do not have time to sit down and talk to the children, you might resort to this approach. Maybe you can bring them back together to talk about it later, when you have more time. However, children learn best when the situation is immediate.

You are a trainer, a facilitator. Help children to clarify their meanings and wishes. Point them in the right direction to come to a mutually satisfactory solution. 'There seems to be a problem here. What are some of the solutions you can think of? Let me help you think about what to do.' You might have to help them understand how the other person feels, and to express themselves clearly. When they come to a satisfactory conclusion, help them notice how good it feels. 'I'm glad you worked how you can both play with the lorry. Now you're both having fun.' You do this when you think the children might not come up with a non-aggressive solution on their own.

You are there. Just move closer and say nothing. The children are aware of your presence. They have heard your advice and guidance before. Your physical presence reminds them of what they already know, that they should work it out and come to a solution without your active intervention. You can either move away and say nothing, or praise them once they have worked out the problem. Obviously, this approach works only when children already have been exposed to the skills.

Ignore the children and keep your distance, keeping an ear open. You might do this when you think your presence could undermine the resolution process. The children might expect you to solve the conflict for them, or they might seek your support or sympathy for one side or the other.

Feelings

Weave the discussion of feelings into group activities. Rather than doing a theme unit on feelings, bring up the subject frequently when doing all kinds of things with the children. Young children need to learn about feelings. They need to recognize the different emotions that they have and understand also that everyone has and is entitled to a whole range of feelings.

First, acknowledge that children have a right to their emotions. Sometimes adults have an idealized vision of childhood, or think childhood should be a time of blissful happiness and innocence. Of course, this has never been the case, but children who are experiencing stress in their lives need to have their emotions defined for them and acknowledged. They must know that it is not bad to feel angry, jealous, sad or frustrated.

As we help children identify and acknowledge their feelings, we also need to help children learn what to do with them. Staff can help children to see many different ways to respond to certain situations or to control their impulses.

This is not to say that we should pry or try to force children to talk about stressful situations in their lives. Teachers often wonder, 'Should I bring up the topic if the child doesn't?' You can let the child know that you are aware of a particular situation and are there to talk about it if they want to. Some children will be relieved to know that they can share a problem with someone they trust. Other children will prefer to keep their thoughts to themselves, and we must respect that. In either case you can talk about emotions in more neutral ways by including general activities and discussions about feelings in your curriculum.

Knowing about the range of emotions people can have helps children talk about how they are feeling. Be aware of how you enable children to express their feelings and thoughts. Develop a wide repertoire of options.

Here are a few ideas:

Teach children a vocabulary about feelings. Use words about feelings in context. Talk about your own feelings. 'I'm feeling sad today because I really miss my Dad, who's in hospital.' 'I was very annoyed this morning when I missed the bus.' Also describe children's emotions as you see them happening. 'Margaret is sad. She's crying because she misses her mummy. Did you ever feel like that?'

Sing children's songs about feelings. *If You're Happy And You Know It Clap Your Hands,* is a familiar example. You are at least naming various emotions and making children familiar with the concept. You can precede or follow the song with a group discussion of the things that make them feel happy, sad, angry etc.

Use a puppet to express emotions. A classroom Pet Puppet can talk to the children about his feelings. 'My name's Sam and I have a problem. My mum just had a new baby and now she doesn't pay any attention to me anymore. Everyone thinks my new brother is so nice, but I think he's ugly and all he does is cry. My mum doesn't love me anymore.' Ask the children, 'Have you ever felt that way? What do you think Sam can do? What might help him?' Then talk to the puppet. 'You see, Sam, everyone feels that way sometimes. But Kathy found out that her mum really does love her very much, but she was just very tired and busy. Your mum loves you, too.'

Create a picture file of feelings. Find magazine pictures of faces that exemplify different emotions, or of situations that elicit emotions. Mount the pictures on construction paper or cardboard and cover with clear self-adhesive paper, or laminate them for durability. Then you can ask children, 'What's going on here? Why do you think the little boy has that expression on his face? Do you think he's scared?' This activity helps children identify various emotions and talk about when they have felt them, too. They learn that they are not the only ones who have ever felt a certain way.

Collect pictures of people expressing a range of different emotions. Mount them on individual cards and let children sort them according to the feelings represented. Then ask the child what each pile represents (the emotions the child has identified) and why they sorted the pictures in the way they did.

Mask making can be a wonderful creative experience for older preschoolers and school-aged children. Children can make masks out of many different materials, including paper plates with lollipop stick handles glued on, paper bags, construction paper and papier-mâché. Talk about feelings first, and let the child identify a feeling of which they would like to make a mask. Provide glue, paint and a rich variety of collage materials and scraps for the child to use for features. The child will probably need help in deciding where to put eye holes on the mask and in actually cutting the holes. Older children might enjoy creating plays in which they can use their masks. Younger children might simply hold up their masks and tell friends about the feeling they represent.

Use creative movement. Start with simple walking. Get all the children to walk randomly around in a space, perhaps while you are beating a drum. Then announce, 'Now walk like you are angry.' After a few minutes, change the emotion. 'Now walk like you are happy, afraid' etc. This gives you an opportunity to talk about emotions and how to tell what someone is feeling.

Dance a feeling. Find a variety of music for children to dance to that brings to mind different emotions. Classical music often lends itself to different moods. Do not tell children how to move, or what they should be doing. Just let them express themselves freely. Add large squares of chiffon or scarves for them to wave around for extra expression. After each dance, you might ask the children what the music reminded them of.

Children's books. Collect favourite children's books about feelings and read them to the children. Invite the child to find a book about how they are feeling after they are familiar with your collection and offer to read it to them. Children might even like to act out the story.

Anger

The emotion of anger needs special attention as it is the emotion that is most upsetting to adults when they witness it in children. We want to stop its expression, sometimes at all costs. Anger is frightening, both to the child who is angry and to the people around them, and anger can be dangerous when it leads to destructive behaviour. Yet, children need to know that it is natural for everyone to feel angry from time to time and to have occasional squabbles. We need to find ways to allow children to recognize their anger, express it appropriately and move through their anger to a more productive emotion.

When a conflict arises, and also during neutral times such as circle time, talk to the children about appropriate things to do when they are angry. Work with the children to generate a list of possible actions.

Talk it over. Encourage the child to say out loud, 'I'm angry, or I'm cross.' This should be one of the first things they do when they feel very angry. Children must know that it is okay to use these words.

Lead a discussion about anger with a puppet. A puppet could talk about something that made them angry, and the children could give the puppet suggestions for what he might do. Or a puppet might act as an *anger consultant*. The children tell him why they are angry, and the puppet helps the children think of how to respond.

Offer lots of active play opportunities. Outdoor time is very important and should not be cut short (unless, of course, dictated by the weather). Running, shouting, jumping, climbing, riding wheel toys all expend physical energy and release tension. Make provisions for active physical play inside as well.

It's-okay-to-be-angry area

Create an *angry area*. Since anger is an emotion that causes such physical tension, you might have a special place in the room where children can go to express anger appropriately. You might decide not to call it an *angry area* though, because you do not want children to think that they must be angry to use the materials in this place. Maybe call it the *express yourself area*. In it could be such things as:

— Things to punch such as large pillows, punch balls or punching clowns so children can release their physical tension.
— Tactile play materials that tend to be soothing and comforting such as water; cool, moist potters clay; fine, smooth sand; and shaving cream to smear around.
— If supervised adequately, a woodworking bench is a great addition. Banging golf tees into a block of styrofoam with a wooden mallet also has great appeal.
— Aggression bags. Help children squirt shaving cream into zip-lock freezer bags. Then let them choose two bottles of food colouring and put a squirt of each into the bag. Zip the bag closed. Now let the children squeeze the bag to their heart's delight to mix the colours. This is a good tension reliever.
— An easel with bright, bold colours (including black and red) of creamy paint to encourage the children's creative expression. Especially with a child in crisis, let them make painting after painting rather than stopping them after one painting so that others get a turn.
— Other expressive art materials. Bright marker pens, crayons, coloured pencils, a rich collection of collage materials, glue and paper invite children to make marks that express how they feel.
— Newspapers and old magazines to cut or tear up, fabric to rip and other collected junk for children to take apart.
— An unbreakable mirror for making angry faces.
— Soft balls to squeeze.
— Noise makers: shakers, baking trays to bang wooden spoons against.
— Put a target on the wall and let children throw beanbags against it as hard as they can.
— Teddy bears to hug or tell their problems to.

Work with the children to paint the outside of a large cardboard box and decorate it on the inside. Cut a door in one side. Invite children to go inside the box, close the door and yell or roar like a lion when they need to let off steam.

Books

Have children's books on hand that talk about anger, such as *Alexander and the terrible, horrible, no good, very bad Day,* by Judith Viorst, Caedman, 1984.

Bear in mind that all of these activities are not intended to get rid of the feeling of anger, or other emotions, but to acknowledge it, express it and learn to deal with it in a healthy and constructive way. These are all therapeutic activities. They are beneficial in and of themselves and do not need adult interpretation or mediation to make them effective.

Understanding and dealing with aggression

Aggression is defined as any act that causes physical or psychological harm to someone else. Aggression is frightening for everyone involved, including the aggressor. Since most aggression in early childhood classrooms comes from frustration, it makes sense to try to reduce some of the frustration children might feel in the environment. If you can reduce the amount of direct competition among children in your room, you may have fewer situations where children feel the need to be aggressive.

A common type of aggression is when a child uses **PHYSICAL FORCE** to obtain an object or keep the object they currently possess. For young children it seems often to be the quickest means to an end.

Another type of aggression is **HOSTILE AGGRESSION**. This is when a child purposely says or does something to hurt another individual. Retaliation and jealousy are often the cause. This type of aggression can take the form of hitting, tripping someone, scratching or hair pulling. Name calling and humiliating another child is more common with older children.

As children see aggressive examples of problem solving around them, both in life and on television, we should not be surprised when they imitate negative behaviour that seems to work well for others. Sometimes children are even taught to be aggressive. This is especially true of boys. 'Stand up for yourself.' 'Hit them back!' One staff member reported an incident in which two children got into a fight while the class was on a field trip. When the parents were told about the child's fight, their first question was, 'Did he win?'

Do not ignore **PHYSICAL OR VERBAL AGGRESSION**, as doing so actually increases aggression in young children. Remember that young children think everyone sees the situation in the same way they do. If the teacher ignores it, the child actually comes to think that the adult approves of, or even expects, the behaviour. You have the formidable task of showing them a different way. If children could think of a better way of dealing with their frustration, they would use it. They want to be successful. Grabbing someone's toy or kicking someone to get them out of the way may seem to work. If they discover another way that works even better, they will use it.

Strategies to try

ESTABLISH EYE CONTACT. Make sure you have the child's attention when you are trying to get them to respond.

CATCH AGGRESSION AS IT IS BUILDING. Once you know the children well, you can read their moods. As frustration builds, approach the child. Divert their attention if possible. Of course, aggressive behaviour can happen very fast. *Wait!* is a good word to use.

Try to dissipate some of the child's tensions in sensory play or other **CALMING, SOOTHING ACTIVITIES.** Use the calming effects of water, clay or playdough.

DEAL WITH THE UNDERLYING TENSION. Although dissipating the child's tension is useful, do not forget to deal with the underlying emotion. Help the child figure out what to do with the angry feelings they have.

EMPATHIZE WITH THE CHILD'S FEELINGS. Validate the feelings. 'You're cross. It's okay to be cross. Sarah hurt your feelings and that's not okay. You really want to let her know you're angry, but I can't let you hurt her. I will help you think of another way to tell her you are angry. People need to feel safe here. I won't let anyone hurt you, or let you hurt anyone.'

Teach children to use words instead of actions. Then, keeping both children together, teach them the words to use to express their feelings. If they are fighting over a toy, help them learn the words they need to negotiate a turn or a trade.

Be consistent in your interventions. If you stop a child the first time he pokes someone, then let them get away with it later, you are actually increasing the likelihood that the child will poke or hurt other children more often.

Praise children when they try non-aggressive solutions. Although children's non-violent attempts at negotiation may not always be successful, aggressive children should not always get the most attention. If children are successful at attracting your attention and approval by trying conciliatory modes, they are more likely to try again.

You may have to **teach children how to be kind and empathetic** to each other. If a child is crying, of course, you show kindness and try to comfort the child. But you could also involve the other children. 'What do you think we could do to make Matthew feel better?'

Victim child

We all know the victim child. This is the child who everybody else bullies, the child who crumbles easily under aggression and is constantly on the losing end of the stick. Victims feel they have two choices: either to yield to the aggressor, which reinforces the behaviour of the aggressor, or to counterattack. You can teach the victim to use words. 'Tell him you don't like it when he takes things from you.' Teach the child how to get angry at other children acceptably. 'Susie, say,"Stop hitting me! I don't like it!"' You can also teach the child how to ignore aggressive children and walk away from them or come to an adult for help. When children learn effective ways of dealing with other aggressive children, they are less likely to become frustrated and aggressive themselves. You are building their own sense of self-esteem and control.

When a child hurts a member of staff

The child must learn that it is not okay to hurt you in any way. A child who is allowed to hurt an adult will ultimately feel unsafe and guilty. Other children in the room will not feel safe either, if they think the adult is not in control. Staff are also included in the rule, 'Everyone needs to feel safe here.'

Dealing with swearing

Foul language is everywhere in our culture. Children hear it on prime time television, in films, from older children and sometimes from their parents. Since young children imitate others, we should not be surprised when they use expletives. Staff wonder what to do about it, and what parents will think of them if they do not stop it.

The key to dealing with young children who use foul language is to focus on the intent, not the content. Is the child using the language out of frustration or to hurt someone? When a child drops their lunch on the floor or accidentally knocks over a block structure and then uses an expletive, do not immediately lecture the child about the appropriate use of language. Instead, simply address the situation. 'You were really hungry and now your lunch is on the floor. I can see you're upset. Let me help you clean this up and then we can get you more food to eat.' If the child consistently uses swear words, wait until the child is calm to talk about it. Coach the child, 'I understand you were really frustrated when your building fell over before, but using that word (say the word here) can really upset other people around you. Let's think of another word you can say when you feel like that.'

When a child uses bad language to hurt someone's feelings, the situation should be dealt with the same way you deal with other types of aggression. It is important not to ignore verbal aggression. 'In this classroom it is not okay to hurt people's feelings by calling them names.'

When a child is angry enough to swear at you, this is not the time to lecture them. Later, when their temper has subsided, you can address the situation. 'I understand you were really angry at me, but it is not okay to use (say the word).' Another response for the moment is, 'You're calling me ______ but my name is Sandra.'

Even if a child is attempting to curse at you or another child and it comes across as funny, or is a word that does not offend adults, do not smile or ignore it if it was meant to be hurtful. *Stupid* and *baby* are aggressive swear words for young children. When a child screams, 'You doo-doo head!' the intent is still there. Treat the child's anger seriously. Find out why the child is angry, and help them deal with it.

Often children who frequently use swear words have a limited facility with language. We want to help children become adept at using language to communicate. You might ask the child, 'What were you trying to say? Let me help you find some better words that say what you mean.' You can also have an intellectual discussion about swear words with children at some neutral moment, such as circle time. 'Isn't it interesting that just saying certain words, making certain sounds come out of your mouth, can make people so upset?'

Some staff worry that correcting a child's language, when the child probably learned the language at home, is the same as criticizing the family. This can be a sensitive issue. It is a lie, of course, to tell them that 'nice people don't swear.' Yet, you do not want other children to pick up the swear word. One solution is to simply explain in a non-judgmental way that in school those words are not used.

When a child comes to you and tattles about another child who has used a swear word, teach the child to be proactive. 'Tell Michael you don't like it when he says that, or calls you that.'

Temper outbursts

Some children, especially those in crisis, have real *trouble putting on the brakes.* When frustrated, they quickly turn to temper tantrums or uncontrolled behaviour as a way of expressing the feeling. This may be a difficult situation for the staff to handle and can be frightening for both the out of control child and the other children.

Catch it before the child is out of control. Intervene as early as you can. This means that the adults in charge must be very aware of this child's problem. One strategy is to assign one adult on the team to stay close to the child without being too obvious.

Diffuse and redirect the child's frustration when you see it building. Enter the play yourself. Add a little lightness and humour (not sarcasm or teasing). Invite the child to join you in an activity that offers a physical release of tension, such as dancing or running around outside. It might be best to get the child away from the stimulation of other children for a little while. Offer quiet solitary activities such as looking at books with or without you, listening to music on headphones or doing simple puzzles. Sometimes offering a small snack can help.

See if you can find special training on techniques for handling children who are truly out of control.

When dealing with temper tantrums, try to distinguish between a tantrum to manipulate adults and a tantrum that occurs purely out of frustration. Treat these differently. Sometimes it is hard to distinguish between the two, especially if you are dealing with a combination of reasons. If you are sure the child is throwing the tantrum just to get their own way, you can tell them when they have calmed down that they will never get their way with you by throwing a tantrum. If the child has a tantrum because they could not handle their frustration, you can be empathetic but firm. 'I know it is hard for you to change activities, but it'll be alright.' Later you can work with the child to deal with the stressful situation. In both cases, see that the child doesn't hurt themself or others.

Encouraging positive social skills

Learning to control behaviour and respond to social stresses in acceptable ways is hard work for children. Their progress will not be continuous. They will occasionally revert to earlier forms of expression. You can help them with positive words to give them encouragement.

When the child does achieve some success, it is important to **ACKNOWLEDGE THEIR EFFORTS,** not by raving ecstatically about every minor accomplishment, but by letting them know in a loving way that you have noticed that they are trying harder.

MEANINGFUL PRAISE. Children catch on quickly to empty praise. For example, when a staff member says, 'Oh, how wonderful!' to everything, even if it is not wonderful, praise loses its meaning. Instead, ask them how they feel about their work. 'Are you pleased with the way your painting turned out?' 'I bet you feel proud of that big building you made with the blocks.' Some children are so hungry for compliments or praise that they create a quick scribble and bring it over to you to hear what you think about it. This is another situation where asking them how they feel about their work has more meaning.

Rather than praising a child for appearance or possessions, **PRAISE THE CHILD FOR HARD WORK OR IDEAS.**

PRAISE CHILDREN FOR SUCCESSFUL PROBLEM SOLVING.

BE GENUINE WITH YOUR PRAISE. Try not to manipulate children through praise.

Observe children doing something correctly, such as sharing with another child or cleaning up in a co-operative way. Instead of praising, notice. Smile. Mention it privately to the child.

HELP CHILDREN DEVELOP INTERNAL CONTROLS and a sense of responsibility. You want a child to feel that they can handle things on their own.

Conclusion

Everyone wants a *recipe book* for handling behavioural problems with young children. You look up the problem in the index, turn to page 47 and there is the recipe for how to handle it! Of course there is no such *behavioural cook book* because we have no standard *ingredients*. Each child is different, and the elements of the situation always vary according to how many people are involved, the time of day, what the child's morning was like and so on. The most we can do is to try to understand the variables and their impact on children's behaviour. What works with one child or situation may not work with another. Our goal is not necessarily to solve the immediate problem, but rather to determine what will help the child become a competent, caring and successful human being.

Above all, do not forget your importance as a role model. For some children, you may be the only positive adult role model in their lives. Helping children learn to control their behaviour is an art. Develop pride and mastery in the art. You have much to draw on, much to try. Even the most experienced teachers are constantly rethinking what they do, looking for better ways. Read what others have done, talk to colleagues, go to workshops, build support groups. It is always worth the effort.

Resources

Books for children

Simon, N. and Leder, D., *I was so mad,* Albert Whitman and Co., 1991.
Anholt, C. and L., *What makes me happy,* Walker Books, 1998.
Vipont, E. And Briggs, R., *The Elephant and the bad Baby,* Puffin Books, 1971.
Murphy, J.B., *Feelings,* Bungalo Books, 1985.
Sendak, Maurice, *Where the Wild Things are,* Picture Lions, 1992.
Kerr, Judith, *Mog in the Dark,* Picture Lions, 1986.
Zion, G., *Harry the dirty Dog,* Bodley Head Children's Books, 1999.
Burningham, J., *Come away from the Water, Shirley,* Red Fox, 1992.
Edwards, Dorothy, *My naughty little Sister,* Mammoth, 1989.

Hoban, Russell, *Bedtime for Frances,* Red Fox, 1999.
Viorst, Judith, *Alexander and the terrible, horrible, no good, very bad Day,* Caedman, 1984.
Conlin, S. and Levine, S., *All My Feelings at Preschool: Nathan's Day,* Parenting Press, 1990.

Books for adults

Smith, Charles, *The Peaceful Classroom,* Floris Books, 1998.
Lindon, J., *Working with young Children,* Hodder and Stoughton, 1997.
Miller, Judy, *Never too young: Booklet,* National Early Years Network, 1997.
Miller, Judy, *Never too young* (spiral-bound), Save the Children Fund, 1996.
Lear, Roma, *Play helps,* Butterworth-Heinemann, 1996.
Grimshaw, R. and Berridge D., *Educating disruptive Children,* National Children's Bureau, 1994.
Mitchell, Grace and Dewsnap, Lois, *Common Sense Discipline: Building Self-Esteem in Young Children, Stories from Life.* Telshare Publishing Company Inc., 1995.
Mitchell, Grace and Dewsnap, Lois, *HELP! What Do I Do About...? — Biting, Tantrums, and 47 other everyday Problems.* Scholastic Inc., 1994.
Prutzman, P., Stern, L., Burger, M.L., and Bodenhamer, G., *The Friendly Classroom for a Small Planet: A Handbook on Creative Approaches to Living and Problem Solving for Children,* New Society Publishers, 1988.
Turecki, Stanley K., and Tanner, Leslie, *The Difficult Child,* Piatkus Books, 1995.

Appendix

Useful contact details

British Association for Early Childhood Education (BACE)
136 Cavell Street, London, E1 2JA.
Tel. 020-7539 5400

The Pre-School Learning Alliance
61 Kings Cross Road, London,
WC1X 9LL.
Tel. 020-833 0991

National Children's Bureau (NCB)
8 Wakley Street, London, EC1V 7QE.
Tel. 020-843 6000

Children in Scotland (Scottish partner of the NCB)
Princes House, 5 Shandwick Place,
Edinburgh, EH2 4RG.
Tel. 0131-228 8484

The National Early Years Network
77 Holloway Road, London, N7 8JZ.
Tel. 020-607 9573

Kidscape
152 Buckingham Palace Road, London,
SW1W 9TR.
Tel. 020-730 330

Equal Opportunities Commission.
Overseas House, Quay Street,
Manchester, M3 3HN.
Tel. 0161-833 9244

Commission for Racial Equality
Elliott House, 10-12 Allington Road,
London, SW1E 5EH.
Tel. 020-828 7022

Magazines and newsletters

Nursery World and *Nursery World Scotland*, Scholastic Publications.
Child Education Nursery, Scholastic Publications.
Early Years (Quarterly magazine). Trentham Books.
Bereavement Care. Published by Cruse Bereavement Care.
Children and Violence Newsletter. Published twice a year this booklet is available from The Forum on Children & Violence

Organizations and helplines

Please note that there will be other organizations in your local area which will also be able to assist you. Check your local telephone directories, or contact your local library and Social Services for further details.

General

The Samaritans, Tel. 0345-909 090

For children

NSPCC. Tel. 0800-800 500
ChildLine. Tel. 0800-1111
Barnardo's. See your local *Yellow Pages*.
Save the Children. See your local *Yellow Pages*.
Kidscape. Tel. 020-730 330
CareLine. Tel. 020-514 1177

Family issues

ParentLine. Tel 01702-559 900
The National Council for One Parent Families. Tel. 020-267 1361
Gingerbread. Provides lone parents with support and advice. Tel. 020-336 8184
Parent Network. Tel. 020-735 1214
Family Mediation Service. See your local *Yellow Pages*.
Relate. Tel. 01788-573 241

Illnesses, disabilities and other health issues

Carers National Association. CarersLine. Tel. 0345-573 369
DIAL. UK network of disability information and advice services. Tel. 01302-310 123
Disabled Living Foundation. Tel. 020-289 6111
RADAR. The Royal Association for Disability and Rehabilitation. Tel. 020-250 3222
Royal National Institute for Deaf People. Tel. 020-296 8000
Guide Dogs for the Blind Association. Tel. 0118-983 5555
Royal National Institute for the Blind. Tel. 020-388 1266
Asthma Helpline. Tel. 0845-300 0336
British Stammering Association. Tel. 0845-603 2001
SCOPE (Cerebral Palsy) Tel. 0800-626 216
Epilepsy. Tel. 0800-309 030
British Diabetic Association. Tel. 0800-834 247
Disability Benefit. Enquiry Helpline. Tel. 0800-882 200
NHS Direct (NHS 24 hour helpline) Tel. 0845-4647
CancerLink. Cancer Information Service. Tel. 0800-132905
Macmillan Cancer Relief. Information Line. Tel. 0845-601 6161
Cancer BACUP. Tel. 0808-800 1234
British Diabetic Association. Tel. 020-323 1531
AIDs Helpline. Tel 0800-567 123
Alzheimer's Helpline. Tel 0845-300 0336
Asthma Helpline. Tel. 0345-010 203
National Association for Mental Health (MIND). Tel. 0345-660163
Terrence Higgins Trust Helpline. Tel. 020-242 1010
SANELINE Tel. 0345-678 0000
Health Information Service. Tel. 0800-665 5 44

Bereavement and death

Cruse Bereavement Line. Helpline for bereaved people and those caring for bereaved people. Tel. 0345-585 565.
Child Death Helpline. Helpline for anyone affected by the death of a child. Tel. 0800-282 986
Cot Death Helpline. Tel. 020-235 1721.
The Compassionate Friends. Support for bereaved parents by bereaved parents. Tel. 0117-953 9639

Violence, bullying and refuges

Rape Crisis Centre. Tel. 020-446 441

Refuge. 24 hour crisis line providing advice and support for women experiencing domestic violence. Tel. 020-995 4430

Shelter. Tel. 0800-446 441

Women's Aid National Helpline. Tel. 0131-221 0401

Zero Tolerance Charitable Trust runs campaigns which are excellent for staff training and parent evenings. They also have a wide range of publications and information. Tel. 0131-221 9505

The Forum on Children and Violence. Tel. 020-843 6309

Victim Support. See your local *Yellow Pages.*

Alcohol and drug issues

Alcoholics Anonymous Helpline. Tel. 020-352 3001

National Association for the Children of Alcoholics. Tel. 0800-289061

DrinkLine. Offers advice, information and support to anyone concerned about their own or someone else's drinking. Tel. 0345-320 202.

National Drugs Helpline. Helpline for drug users, their families, friends and carers. Tel. 0800-776 600.

Release. Advice on health and welfare aspects of drug use and the legal consequences. Tel. 020-603 8654.

Turning Point. Helpline for drug users. Tel. 020-702 2300.

Acknowledgments

A book like this would be impossible to write without the collaboration of many respected professionals. It is a true example of synergism with many minds contributing experiences and viewpoints to create something useful and practical. First of all, I'd like to thank the many people I met at early childhood conferences, who in casual conversations about this project encouraged me and said, 'Go for it!' Many of their stories are woven into this text.

Nancy Alexander, Executive Director of Childcare Services of Northwest Louisiana, Shreveport, LA
Joyce Allan, family therapist, Charlottesville, VA
Doretta Allison, teacher, Prince George's County Public Schools, MD
Jane Bingham, my neighbour and friend, psychotherapist and authority on child sexual abuse
Donna Bloomer, Early Childhood Specialist and Training Director, Bryan Centre, Hagerstown, MD
Carolyn Brooks and Betsy McAllister Groves, Directors of Boston City Hospital Women's and Infant's Programme and Child Witness to Violence Programme
Vicki Carrington, family childcare provider, Steamboat Springs, CO
Tammy Chatterton, parent, Moses Lake, WA
Louise Derman-Sparks, Director of the Culturally Relevant Anti-Bias Education Leadership Project
Jane Erckenbrack, social worker, Washington, DC
Mattie and Dick Feldman, Bank Street College, NY
Polly Ferraro, Director of Child Development Services, Port Hueneme Naval Base in California
Bev Fuqua, teacher, North Park Elementary School,
Walden, CO
Bobbie Grantham, Director of Educational Services, Children's Home-Chambliss Shelter, Chattanooga, TN
Sharon Greenlee, grief counsellor and author of When Somebody Dies, Centennial, WY
Mary Gregory, family childcare provider, Canyon Country, CA
Mary Hammond, The Heart Centre, Salem, OR
Patty Hishke, Director of Bright Start Children's Centres, Inc.

Susan Huffman, teacher, Montgomery County Public Schools, MD
Cindi Hunt, Activities Co-ordinator for First Start/Parents as Teachers family support programme, Canon City, CO
Sue Johnson Jacka, Vice President of Bright Start Children's Centres, Inc.
Betty Jones, mentor to everyone who passes through Pacific Oaks College
Barbara Kilkka, parent, Orchard Lake, MI
Carol Krysko, owner of Early Explorations, Encinitas, CA
Maureen Moreland, Executive Director of Parent and Child Services, Inc., Portland, OR
Mary Rivkin, Assistant Professor, Early Childhood Education, University of Maryland Baltimore County, Catonsville, MD
Hedda Sharapan, Associate Producer of Mister Rogers' Neighbourhood, produced by Family Communications, Inc., Pittsburgh, PA
Hanne Sonquist, NAEYC Governing Board member and family therapist
Muffy Stright, owner of Aspen Child Development Centres, Denver, CO
Jacqueline Wallen, Associate Professor, Family Studies, University of Maryland, College Park, MD
Francis Wardle, Executive Director of The Centre for the Study of Biracial Children, Denver, CO
Heather Wenig, teacher of toddlers in Kearney, NE
Karen Williams, University of Wyoming

The publishers would like to thank Nancy Taylor, retired Nursery Advisor for Fife, for her valuable contributions in adapting this book for Great Britain.

The Peaceful Classroom

Compassion and Co-operation: Activities for three to five-year-olds

Charles A. Smith

An essential guide for teachers, *The Peaceful Classroom* combines useful life skills with easy, enjoyable activities. It introduces over 160 activities for three to five-year-old children which promote skills such as friendship, compassion, co-operation and kindness. Activities are organized by age and skill, preparing children for the themes that follow.

The book contains step-by-step guides for teachers of young children, together with suggestions for parental involvement.

Activities emphasize how children's beliefs about themselves and others influence their relationships. Teachers may choose and introduce skills in an appropriate, developmental sequence, or activities may be chosen for a specific quality such as gentleness.

Dr Charles A. Smith is Professor of Human Development and Family Studies. He has considerable experience of teaching young children, and is much sought after to speak on issues of self-esteem and social development.

Floris Books

Earthwise

Environmental Crafts and Activities with Young Children

Carol Petrash

Earthwise offers a year-round programme of practical ideas for encouraging young children to be aware of their environment. Written from the author's personal experience with kindergarten groups, *Earthwise* presents a rich and varied selection of nature crafts and seasonal activities for children from the age of three upwards.

The fully illustrated activities are carefully graded by difficulty. Through them, children learn to play safely with the elements of earth, air fire and water, thus developing knowledge and respect for Nature, the living Earth and its creatures.

There are suggestions for growing an indoor 'seasonal' garden, and advice on making your home or classroom more Earth-friendly. The book includes a comprehensive list of resources and suppliers.

Carol Petrash has over fifteen years experience of teaching pre-school children. She has been active in local environmental projects for many years, including organic gardening and waste-recycling.

Floris Books